# TO WAR WITH GOD

# TO WAR WITH GOD

## The Army Chaplain Who Lost His Faith

PETER FIENNES

MAINSTREAM
PUBLISHING

EDINBURGH AND LONDON

First published in Great Britain in 2011 by
MAINSTREAM PUBLISHING COMPANY
(EDINBURGH) LTD
7 Albany Street
Edinburgh EH1 3UG

ISBN 9781845966522

Extracts from Alan Wilkinson, *The Church of England and the First World War*
(London, SPCK, 1978) used by kind permission of SPCK.
Extracts from Siegfried Sassoon © Siegfried Sassoon by kind permission of the Estate
of George Sassoon.
Extracts from Michael Snape, *The Royal Army Chaplains' Department: Clergy Under
Fire* (Boydell & Brewer Ltd, 2008) reprinted by permission.

A catalogue record for this book is available
from the British Library

Printed in Great Britain by
Clays Ltd, St Ives plc

1 3 5 7 9 10 8 6 4 2

# Contents

For Anna

# Introduction

My grandfather didn't talk about the war. In common with most men of his generation – and the next – he wouldn't say very much about what he had seen and done when he had served with the British Army in the cataclysm that engulfed their world. If he talked about it at all, it must have been to the other survivors from his regiment. They would meet occasionally at the reunions that happened with less frequency as the years went by, until, as he put it, anyone he wanted to see was dead. He may have talked to them, but he never talked to us.

Over the years we gathered together a few little scraps, and hoarded them. We knew my grandfather had served as an Army Chaplain with the 52nd Oxford and Buckinghamshire Light Infantry and that he had been sent to France in September 1916. He had stayed at the Western Front until the end, when he marched with the Army of Occupation into Germany, and had finally made his way back home in April 1919. At some point my grandfather had won the Military Cross (although he always said he didn't deserve it). After the war, his colonel had given him his horse to look after – my mother remembers longing to ride the huge military charger. We also knew he once sat up all night with a man who was going to be shot at dawn for desertion – he had told his seven-year-old grandson, my brother, about that. We even knew, although no one seems to remember how, that at some point during those long two years my grandfather, the Army Chaplain, had lost his faith in God.

He stayed, though, and did his duty. After the war, he worked at St Martin-in-the-Fields with Dick Sheppard, the charismatic pacifist preacher who helped him back to his faith and became his great friend.

My grandfather's name was Edward Montmorency Guilford. Everyone knew him as 'Monty'. He had married my grandmother, Kathleen, in 1913 and they had three daughters. Their first, my aunt Ruthie, was born in 1914, just one month before war broke out; the next two, my mother and my aunt Biddy, arrived after Monty got back from France.

Monty died in 1971. In the emotional turmoil that followed, his daughters didn't pay much attention to a battered brown suitcase he'd left behind. They looked inside, saw it contained some old letters and photos, and shoved it in my mother's attic until they would have time to go through it properly. When my mother died in 2002, it was my turn to move the suitcase to another attic for a later date. And there it might have stayed, except that in 2008 my 13-year-old son began studying the First World War. I told him that his great-grandfather had kept a few interesting bits and pieces that might be helpful and together we dragged the disintegrating case out of the attic, popped open the lid and watched as the story of my grandfather's life poured onto the kitchen table.

There were trench maps and medals, letters and newspaper cuttings. There were photos: murky snapshots of tanks and trenches, and startlingly clear ones of soldiers smiling or sprawling in muddy fields. We discovered his diary (although his handwriting is diabolical) and found dozens of letters and postcards home, most of them in Monty's scrawl and posted to Kathleen and Ruthie from France. There were wild and wonderful letters addressed to 'Dear Hedge Priest' from someone calling himself 'Pullthrough'. There were pamphlets telling the victorious Army how to comport itself in Germany, and a tattered mock newspaper from the Somme, its editorial politely suggesting that if H.G. Wells was so keen on the next offensive, he might take up 'the opportunity of doing 48 hours in a frontline trench in the chalk country, when the weather is "soft" and "engaging the enemy" more closely'. We even found his sermons.

Some of what we found was chilling. Two sheets of paper were the official orders telling my grandfather to be present at the execution of Private J. Bateman at 'about 6.30 a.m.' on 3 December 1917. A note on the back showed that this was the condemned man who had meant so much to Monty.

We dug deeper and found photo albums from before the war, wedding menus and wafer-thin, hand-drawn invitations to the 'Annual Children's Concert held at Aberfoyle on Xmas Day, 1901'.

In short, we found what we thought had been missing all along: the story of what my grandfather did during the war. Of course, no suitcase can contain *that* much. There were plenty of gaps. His diary ends, frustratingly, in January 1917. Many of the photos are bleached by age. Pages of letters are lost or remain tantalisingly unanswered. We wanted to find something about his faith and why he lost it. In fact, we now wanted to know *everything*: when did he first go up to the trenches? Did he ever have to flee a German attack? What did he think of the Germans? Was he scared? Would he rather have been fighting? What happened to the young chaplain who waved goodbye to his wife and young daughter early one September morning in 1916 and set off with such earnest good faith for the blood-soaked fields of France?

Soon I found myself wondering what it must have been like to serve as a Chaplain to the Forces in a war that is remembered as a murderous farce. How can a man be a priest and preach God's love and yet lead the prayers calling for total victory and the machine-gunning of the enemy? Is that what Monty preached? I wanted to know, but I was nervous about what I might find. My ignorance – about Monty, about almost every aspect of the war – fed my anxiety.

When I first started thinking about these things, my grandfather had been dead almost 40 years, but every memory I had of him was a good one. I remembered a man of warmth and energy, of jokes and chats and games of cricket in the garden. For my seventh birthday, when he was over eighty, he refereed the football match I had insisted on holding on a rain-lashed day in January – and he galloped from end to end, blasting on his whistle and exhorting the frozen teams to run faster and harder. My brother and I adored him and not just because he kept a genuine magic cupboard in his house, which was always, miraculously, filled with sweets whenever we visited.

My knowledge of the First World War was sketchy when I began digging into my grandfather's life. I did know – or thought I knew – that the war Monty found himself swept up into was 'The Bad One', the one in which innocence was slaughtered by a bunch of braying nincompoops. But the war I found, and the part Monty played in it, was much more complex than that. It wasn't *just* hell on earth. At times Monty's diary reads like he's gadding about at some kind of holiday camp. I was amazed to discover – after a diet of Sassoon and Owen and A.J.P. Taylor – that there was laughter at the Front, even if for much of the time the laughter sounds like it has been cut loose from its moorings.

No one really survived the Western Front, though – not entirely. After the war, and after Dick Sheppard had helped him find his bearings, Monty chose to live his life as a country parson in Rutland. He brought up his family. He sat on committees, held church fetes and played for the local cricket team. He preached his sermons of love and wonder but was no doubt distressed to find that in the Second World War his parish of Cottesmore was on the edge of an RAF aerodrome and, once again, he found himself burying countless young servicemen. After many years, he and Kathleen retired to a small village in Dorset, where he continued to preach, and then to Sussex. Wherever he went, he built the most beautiful gardens.

We knew all that. But there had always been a blank space in the story of his life – right up to the moment when we pulled back the lid of that dusty brown suitcase – and now the blank has been filled, at least as much as it ever can be. I do hope he will understand. He must have kept all of these things for a reason. Many of them are funny or uplifting, as well as distressing, and he would almost certainly have enjoyed the idea of his grandson trying to make sense of it all. Years ago I was told that my grandfather went to war and lost his faith, but I was also told that he was a brave man, so he stayed and endured and did what he could to help others.

It is almost 100 years since Monty stepped onto the train that took him to France, and it is, I think, about time that his war emerged from the shadows.

# Preface

Letter from James Neville, Lieutenant in the Oxford and Buckinghamshire Light Infantry 1916–19, to Reverend E.M. Guilford, dated 4 January 1966:

Dear Godalming,

Yours was a really beautiful card and I am very grateful for it and your additions within.

We are never going to send any more cards. They have become a commercial racket and the postage is such as to bring consolation truly to the PMG (rot his guts) alone. Instead I shall try to write a line to my old friends who only matter. And if I forget you can still know that I am thinking of that dwindling band who learnt the value of life and friendship in a dangerous school. I know I was a fiendish tease to you, but I have certain memories that will never die and the most vivid a communion service in the open at Rochincourt before that cruel Oppy party. I can see you now bareheaded in the wind, ruffling your hair and billowing your surplice. That is still more vivid than the hell which followed. And now, would you believe it? I am the Rector's warden. We have completely restored the village church for the few who attend regularly and the greater number who make use of it for what? Form? Status? I wish I knew.

Blessings and my gratitude

James

# ONE

# 'Slept fairly well, with intermittent attacks of sneezing'

It didn't take long for Monty, my grandfather, to be moved to the Western Front. On Tuesday, 26 September 1916 he was at 'The Croft', his in-laws' house on the edge of Mitcham Common in Surrey, with his wife Kathleen and their baby daughter Ruth, and the next day he was in France. We have to assume the call-up did not come as a complete surprise. He had volunteered as an Army Chaplain the previous year but was ill when the summons arrived. We ought not to read anything into that – my grandfather had a knack for falling ill, just as he did for getting lost, handing over money and setting himself on fire. But an air of drama clings to the first, torn page of his diary, with its hurried note:

> On Tuesday Sept 26 receive orders from War Office, Albermarle to catch 8.30 a.m. to Folkestone on following morning at Charing Cross.

Above it sits:

> Diary, Strictly Private and Personal.

And on the other side of the page he has written:

> Vestment being a stole, and the only incense, the smoke of battle.

I like that quote. I suspect there's nothing 'strictly personal' about it – I'm sure it was the kind of thing doing the rounds among the Church of England chaplains as they were shepherded into France, bewildered, eager, anxious and almost certainly unclear about what they were meant to be doing or how they could possibly deliver Christ's message to an Army currently unleashing seven shades of hell onto its enemy and – in one way or another – its own men. But it does show that my grandfather was as ready as any eager young subaltern to wrap himself in a juicy bit of high Victoriana and do his bit in the battle to save civilisation from the ravening Hun. It just wasn't the way he felt by the time the war was over.

Monty was a couple of weeks past his 28th birthday on the day he headed for the Front. He had been married for three years, his daughter Ruth (my aunt) had been born in 1914, and he'd been a Church of England priest since 1912. So he wasn't one of the young ones – the eighteen year olds signing up en masse, or the even younger ones who were lying to join their mates – but he was, it seems, ill prepared for what was to follow. And if his later years are anything to go by, he was also deeply impractical. My grandfather once slunk back from a canal holiday a week early because he'd filled the barge's fuel tanks with water. If he wasn't directly responsible, then maybe it was one of the ex-Army chums he'd gone with. They were all equally hopeless, it appears, although at some point they'd been part of the most efficient killing machine the world had known.

In 1916, Monty also *looked* young. Not just young but achingly handsome. Have a look at the photos. These things are indeed a matter of taste, but my grandmother used to relate proudly how when their marriage banns were read out in church, no fewer than three women shrieked and fainted clean away. He was also a Cambridge Hockey Blue, a dilatory scholar and, even when I knew him in his 70s, a snappy dresser. So I can quite clearly see him and Kathleen stepping out in the dark, early on Wednesday morning, polished and brushed and loved, weighed down with superfluous equipment and the worst kind of anxiety. This is how he puts it:

Wednesday, 27 September 1916

Left 'The Croft' with K at 6.50 for Victoria. Breakfasted together at Charing Cross Hotel. Caught 8.30 a.m. train to Folkestone after meeting W.D. Geare, Queens Court friend on the platform, he also going out for first time.* Reached Folkestone 10.30 – embarked 'SS Victoria' and left for Boulogne at 11 a.m.. Lifebelts and escort of two TPBs. Deck chair with Geare on deck. Disembarked Boulogne at 1 p.m. Reported AMLO and then RTO. Informed train on to St Omer at 7.30 p.m. Put Baggage in Consigne, lunched together at Officers Club at 2 p.m. Wandered around Boulogne and took tram along front till 4.30. Tea in Hotel Folkestone. Returned to Club. Wrote to K. Took our seats and left about 8.15 p.m. Arrived at St Omer at 11.30 p.m. Conducted by Browne, CF [Chaplain to the Forces] to YMCA Officers Mess. Given rooms.

* Here, at some later point, Monty has added with another pen: 'Killed in Action'.

The last part of this entry is illegible: my grandfather's handwriting was a beetlish, clerical scrawl at the best of times, but by the time this diary ends in early 1917, it has disintegrated into something a man might produce when drunk and distraught, clinging to a hurricane-torn treetop.

The tone, however, of these early entries, reads like he's on a school day trip to France. There's nothing here of how he felt to be leaving Kathleen behind in England – although that breakfast in the Charing Cross Hotel must have tested them – and the only sign that this is not just another jolly to the Continent are the lifebelts and escort of torpedo boats as he and Geare lounge in their deckchairs in the autumn sunshine. But it's clearly an efficient organisation that brings these thousands of men and dozens of priests across from England, meets them, gives them rooms and eases their way smoothly onwards to the killing fields.

The next day, one of Monty's preoccupations surfaces. He slept 'only fairly'. Two lines later, there's another of his concerns:

the timing of his breakfast. When I first deciphered his diary, I used to cringe at this and picture Monty as just another clichéd Church of England vicar bumbling and breakfasting his way through the carnage – 'doesn't he even know there's a war on?' But these incongruous statements are anchors, or lifelines, thrown out in an attempt to keep some kind of connection with a normal life; they're there to keep Monty in touch with his home.

> Thursday, 27 September 1916
> Slept only fairly. YMCA four sides of a square – courtyard in middle, long old and rambling (St Omer old General Headquarters).
>    Breakfast at 9.15 a.m. – Geare, Wright, Gravell and Leaky and self. Reported to Deputy Chaplain General, Bishop Gwynne at 10.30. Pleasant interview. All five told to return at 12.15 for Orders. In meantime went to Army Ordnance Stores and Jewellers for Identity discs. Returned to DCG and informed by Drury that we were all for the 'Front'. Received orders. Discussed and asked questions. Geare, Leaky and self for 4th Army on Somme – self to 5th Infantry Brigade 2nd Division – Geare to 165th Infantry Brigade, 55th Div. Lunch at Hotel de Commerce. Reported RTO 2.45. Instructed train to Abbeville at 9.50 a.m. next morning. Returned Hotel. Slept till 4.30. 5 p.m at DCG with O'Rourke and Shepton. Went over Cathedral. Returned Hotel. Wrote K. Service at Military Church 6.30–7 p.m. Dinner at Club. Billiards Geare till 9.45. Bed.

The holiday atmosphere lingers. Monty manages to fit in some sightseeing, a hotel lunch, a quick snooze, dinner at the club, and some billiards with Geare, but there's no avoiding the demands of military life. Except, of course, this is not (and nor will it be) military life as it is experienced by the vast bulk of men in the Army. Monty and Geare and the rest are Army Chaplains receiving their orders from the Deputy Chaplain General, Bishop Gwynne. They (like all chaplains) are ranked as officers, with the lowliest being the equivalent of captains (and Monty is just that, a Chaplain to the Forces, 4<sup>th</sup> Class, Temporary), and the highest, like Gwynne, taking the rank of general. They are part of the Army structure, but separate from it, with their own organisation, their own reporting lines, and indeed a direct line to the Highest Authority of them all – although they're generally too polite to mention it.

Monty's arrival in France coincided with a great recruiting drive to bring more chaplains to France. In the previous year, Sir Douglas Haig had collared Bishop Gwynne and told him that 'A good chaplain is as valuable as a good general'. Haig's view was that a well-judged sermon, the right soft or stirring words, would keep his army's morale high, and he was calling for more chaplains to keep his men at a fever pitch of righteous bellicosity. A strange role for a clergyman, you might think, but Haig's call went out just as the Church hierarchy at home was deciding that the First World War was probably the best chance they'd had for decades to reignite interest in their evangelical mission. The apocalypse at the Front would draw the British soldier closer to God – or at least that was the theory.

So chaplains were pouring into France (89 Church of England chaplains in 1914 soared to nearly 2,000 in the year 1918) and were heading for the Western Front, even though no one seemed particularly clear about what they'd do when they got there. Well, it might be more true to say that a lot of people were very clear about what they expected from the chaplains – it's just that they didn't seem to be able to agree. Some thought they should be in the trenches, sharing the misery and dangers of the front line. Unarmed, of course. Others thought they should be at the dressing stations, not falling over the troops at the Front but helping with the wounded. There was a theory that it would be terrible for the morale of the men to see their padre down, dead or wounded. Others wanted them on burial duty (and God knows by this stage of the Somme there was plenty of work to be done); others thought they should be handing out cigarettes, cheery words and organising football matches and knees-ups as near to the base as possible. Many thought they should perform a bracing sermon on Sunday and then keep out the bloody way. Some (chaplains among them) thought they should be taking up arms and fighting the Good Fight against the forces of the Antichrist. Others couldn't care less what they did. But many wondered, as this industrialised war grew ever more savage, what had happened to Christ's message of peace. Shouldn't the churches be doing something to try and stop this horror?

At this stage, there's not much to show my grandfather's attitude. His approving nod towards Bishop Gwynne was probably only relief. There were some pretty terrifying bishops at large in the Church of England in the early years of the twentieth century and interviews could be fraught affairs, but the 50-year-old Gwynne was, by all accounts, a saintly figure. Before being put in charge of the chaplains in France in 1915, he'd been the Bishop of Khartoum – and that's where he returned as soon as the war was over, despite offers of high office in Britain.

Gwynne has this ringing endorsement from F.R. Barry, one of the chaplains who served under him. I think Monty might have agreed:

> *Many of us, I think, would have gone under or have suffered shipwreck of their faith had it not been for the pastoral care and guidance of the great and saintly Bishop Gwynne, Father in God to a whole generation of young men . . . I have used the word 'saintly' deliberately. For he made it easier to believe in God . . .* [1]

Until Gwynne's arrival, things had been pretty chaotic and confusing for the Church of England chaplains. They were posted to their units and ordered not to go anywhere near the front line, with the vague suggestion that they should know what to do with themselves. So they conducted burial parties, held services on Sundays, censored the letters and dispensed consolation and cigarettes safely out of harm's way. And because, in the main, they were from the officers' class that's who they tended to fraternise with. It's no wonder there was such a jaded view of the Church of England chaplain at the Front, ranging from indifference, through amusement, to contempt. Certainly, it's one that has lingered. Robert Graves's sneering verdict is typical, that if the Anglican chaplains had only:

> Shown one-tenth of the courage, endurance and the other human qualities that regimental doctors showed . . . the British Expeditionary Force might well have started a religious revival. But they had not, being under orders to avoid the fighting and to stay behind with the transport. Soldiers could hardly respect a chaplain who obeyed these orders, and yet not one in fifty seemed sorry to obey them. Occasionally, on a quiet day in a quiet sector, the chaplain would make a daring afternoon visit to the support line and distribute a few cigarettes before hurrying back.[2]

That was written after the war, in a weeping rage, as was Siegfried Sassoon's commentary on his 1916 poem 'Christ and the Soldier', which he dubbed 'an ambitious failure':

> Like Wilfred Owen, I was anti-clerical, and the Churches seemed to offer no solution to the demented doings on the Western Front . . . Could anyone – from a fully informed religious understanding – have made a success of the subject?
>
> As far as I can remember, no one at the Front ever talked to me about religion at all. And the padres never came near us – except to bury someone.[3]

Sassoon's poem 'They' was written while the war was still raging, on 31 October 1916; it must have been brewing in his mind just as Monty took his first anxious steps in France.

> The Bishop tells us: 'When the boys come back
> They will not be the same: for they'll have fought
> In a just cause: they lead the last attack
> On Anti-Christ; their comrades' blood has bought
> New right to breed an honourable race,
> They have challenged Death and dared him face to face,'

'We're none of us the same!' the boys reply.
'For George has lost both legs; and Bill's stone blind;
Poor Jim's shot through the lungs and like to die;
And Bert's gone syphilitic: you'll not find
A chap who's served that hasn't found some change.'
And the Bishop said: 'The ways of God are strange!'[4]

It wasn't just the poets, atheists and anti-establishment intellectuals who held these views. I found the letter I quoted from earlier, from Monty's friend James Neville, slipped into Monty's copy of Neville's book, *The War Letters of a Light Infantryman*, a collection of letters and diary extracts from the Western Front, written by the very young ex-Etonian to his family back home in Norfolk. A letter to his father written on 16 November 1917 ends with this:

> We have just had a great discussion on Christianity, and no one has come to a very sound conclusion. It strikes me that our religion, as we have been taught it in the past, has failed rather badly in this war. Why, for one thing, should the parsons be exempted from sharing the dangers of their flocks, and bigger flocks than they generally have at home in their churches?[5]

Neville, bear in mind, was Monty's friend – or he certainly was 50 years later when they exchanged their non-cards at Christmas. He was also in Monty's regiment, the 52nd Oxford and Buckinghamshire Light Infantry. *He* was one of Monty's flock. But there is no mention of Monty or of anything he might have done to promote his religion, just the usual complaint about padres skulking out of harm's way. In the letter written to Monty in 1966, he claims that the sight of Monty preaching in the open air at Rochincourt was still more vivid to him than the hell that followed. Those words seem meaningless in the context of the earlier wartime letter.

I can't help wondering if Monty was part of the 'great discussion on Christianity' in which no one came to a 'very sound conclusion'. The family myth has it that my grandfather lost his faith in God in the gore and mud of France, that it was blasted out of him by the relentless, unending slaughter. Many chaplains did. They arrived at the Front, fresh and eager from the villages of Buckinghamshire, Ayrshire and Kent, woefully under-prepared and with almost no training (at least not until 1917), to be thrown into unspeakable deprivations and horrors. Only the most uncompromisingly faithful could accept that this mechanised apocalypse had some meaning. They couldn't even pick up a gun to give at least the illusion of self-protection.

Was Monty at the discussion, but was he too disillusioned to defend his faith? Did words fail him? Was he just too friendly or unassuming? Was he simply one of the boys whose opinion, even on this subject, held no more sway than anyone else's? Why doesn't Neville even mention his padre, my grandfather? He was there, wasn't he?

It was clearly upsetting for Monty to read his friend's contemptuous thoughts on the clergy and their church – and Monty has scrawled in the book:

> X. The proportion of Padres killed during the War was a higher percentage than of any other branch of the Army. C of E: 97 killed or died of wounds. 69 as result of War service.

He also added: 'Number of chaplains in France: 50 per cent C of E; 25 per cent RC [Roman Catholic]; 25 per cent other.'

Until I found my grandfather's diary, I had never given much thought to the First World War. I'd certainly not made any kind of connection between it and my grandfather. But when I told my aunt Biddy what I was writing about, she said, 'Yes, you know, my father always said that, relatively speaking, more clergy were killed in the war than any other part of the army.'

This may not have been true, but it mattered to Monty, and it must have mattered to all the Church, this slur on their courage, their religion – their *purpose*. And it must have burned Monty to read his friend's comments. But it's not clear-cut. My grandfather won the Military Cross in 1918 – and he won it for 'continuous gallantry, self-sacrifice, and devotion to duty'. Not only that, the official document states that 'he shares, to the utmost of his power, in all the conditions of their life'. Colonel Richard Crosse, his Commanding Officer, goes on: 'His presence has been and is of the very greatest value to officers and other ranks alike. He comes up always to the trenches. He magnificently fulfils the duties of his calling.'

It goes on to state that he has done 'especially fine work between 22 September 1917 and 24 February 1918'. The dates given for this especially fine, trench-dwelling, MC-winning heroism exactly coincide with Neville's offhand remarks about the Church and its skiving padres. When I started digging into my grandfather's war years, I didn't have much idea of what I was going to unearth, but I probably didn't want to hear that he'd lost his nerve and spent his days cowering at the base. It's not what any of us would hope to find. Up to the age of seven, I suppose I knew my grandfather as well as I could expect – he was warm and exciting and funny – and I certainly knew how loved and cherished he was by so many people. But even so I had no idea what kind of war he'd had.

Then again – so what if Monty had not had a 'good' war? Who am I – who are any of us – to judge those who found themselves facing the Western Front? The First World War hoovered up almost 5.4 million British men (about 12 per cent of the total population) and put them in uniform. The way they reacted is as varied as you'd expect. So for now I'm going to assume that Neville's off-the-cuff strictures on religion and the padres are a young man's remarks, a thoughtless repetition of the reassuring clichés of the Front, that the general staff are all incompetent cowards and the priests a bunch of pusillanimous skivers, and leave it at that. We need to get back to Monty in St Omer.

Friday, 29 Sept 1916
Breakfast at 8.15am. Cab to station at 9.15. Orders from RTO. Entrained – the 5 of us – at 9.50. Arrived Calais at 11.15am. Wandered around chasing baggage on platform. Discovered Senior Chaplains' House (Rev Williams).

Lunched with Geare, Leaky and Gravell at Hotel Continentale. Lots of Belgian and English Officers. Cinema in Rue Royale at 3 p.m. – 5 p.m. Tea at Senior Chaplain's. Wrote K. Walked to Army Post Office on Quai with Leth. Returned to Senior Chaplains' House. All proceeded to station. Informed train possibly about 9 p.m. Went to the Hotel Metropole for dinner. Returned to station 9 p.m. Told Train at 11.06 p.m. Got carriages and waited in train. Carriage filled with Belgian and French Officers. Amusing effort at conversation. Geare distinguishes himself at the lingo.

We're still in holiday mode, aren't we, really? Rattling from Boulogne to Calais, chasing baggage along the platforms, hanging around in the Senior Chaplain's House (there's always a club in those days, if you know where to look – and if you *belong*), tea, more trains, and Geare, poor doomed Geare, chattering away amusingly in a foreign tongue. There's even a trip to the cinema. I wonder what they saw . . .

Saturday, 30 September 1916
Night in train. Fitful sleep. Passed St Omer at 2am. Arrived Abbeville at 9.30am. Received orders RTO to entrain at 4.40 a.m. next morning. Others by different trains. Put baggage in Consigne and walked to YMCA Officers' Rest Room, 22 Rue Ledieu. Wash shave breakfast. Read and slept till 2.30. Strolled in town. Tea at Cafe – excellent. Looked over Cathedral. Read papers. Recreation grounds. Wrote to K. Dinner at Hotel France at 6.45. Saw Geare to station to catch 8 p.m. train. Left him at 8.20 to return to YMCA with Gravall. Evensong together in our bedroom. Bed at 9.15.

Monty's progress up to the Front seems fairly relaxed, but it is relentless. He has time to read the papers, sleep fitfully, sleep some more, investigate the cathedral and take Geare to the station. He and another padre, Gravall, hold evensong in their bedroom and pray together. There could be no self-consciousness in this. Religion and the rituals of the Church of England are central to Monty's life, just as they still played a part in the lives of large numbers of his fellow countrymen. Even with church attendances falling (and they had been for decades, especially in the cities), the Anglican faith remains a potent force. After nearly 100 years of external attack and infighting, when the established Church has been savaged, satirised and ridiculed, before drifting into near-irrelevance, it's hard for us to remember that in the early twentieth century the Church of England had genuine power and influence. In 1916, the Archbishop of Canterbury, Randall Davidson, was a power in the land with a direct line to the prime minister, the cabinet and the King – and most people were still ready to listen to him.

The Anglican Church *mattered* in 1916, and its bishops and vicars were treated with respect, but that had started to change even before the war accelerated a loss of faith in all the old institutions. The Church establishment knew it and was shovelling its men forward not just to help Haig's war effort but because here was a chance to build a new, modern church. There was a genuine sense among the Army Chaplains that if the world was going to be blown to smithereens, then a new church could emerge from the devastation. As the war went on, that feeling only intensified among most chaplains at the Front. Quite what this new church was going to be was not entirely clear, but they knew they didn't like their old one.

I don't believe Monty was thinking this way in 1916. He was probably concentrating on getting to the right place at the right time without accidentally mistaking a colonel for a quarter-master. Nor did he probably realise that where he was heading was the one place where indifference to his religion, not to mention a gathering rage against it, was at its strongest. Then again, it wouldn't be long before his own faith would be tested to breaking point.

A few short hours after evensong, Monty is back on the train. And then, quite suddenly, he is within earshot of the guns.

Sunday, 1 October 1916

Rise at 3 a.m. (Summer Time) to catch 4.40. Breakfast in Recreation Room. Reach station at 4.10 to find it 3.10 Winter Time. Withdraw baggage from Consigne. Chat with our MD. Embark on train at 4 a.m. with Peters, Caius Cambridge man and MO of 1st KRR 99th Infantry Brigade. Leave about 7.30. Three in our carriage. Sleep and read. Reach Belle Eglise at 1.30. Find I am contracting bad cold in the head. Pick up our RC Padre bound for 6th Infantry Brigade by name Collingwood. Walk over to Louvencourt together. Get tea there at Church Army Hut. Get first glimpse of our 'Planes being shelled. Hear big guns. Can see lines of Observation balloons. Return to Belle Eglise at 4.15 p.m. Leave in Motor Lorry with reinforcements at 5 p.m. Reach Divisional Headquarters at Couin at 6 p.m. Divisional Headquarters in jolly Chateau. Very pretty wooded country. Report to Q branch. Told to go on to 5th Infantry Brigade at Sarton 9 kilometres away.

The country is pretty and wooded, the Chateau is jolly, and Monty has a head cold coming.

Lorry in ditch – given car at 7.15 which takes Collingwood to Congrulet 6th Field Ambulance, me to Sarton. Reach Sarton at 8 p.m. Find Staff Captain Wild on sofa with arm in sling. Farquharson comes in. After chat takes me round to Field Ambulance Dep. Introduces me to Medical Officer Lieutenant Stevenson. Have supper in Marquee. Chat. Bed at 9.30 on stretcher. Sneeze a good deal but have fairly comfy night. Five or six miles behind firing line but can hear guns.

Monday, 2 October 1916

Slept fairly well with intermittent attacks of sneezing. Breakfast at 9. Wrote letters and diary. Lunch at 1. Raining hard all the time. Left in F.A. car at 3.30. Arrived Coigneux at 6th F.A. at 4 p.m. Introduced to Mess. Share Bell tent with

Stevenson. Tea. Go in F.A. car to Couin. Report to Major Bate, Senior Chaplain to the Forces, at Divisional Headquarters. Chat. Find that am attached to 52$^{nd}$ Light Infantry 2$^{nd}$ Oxfordshire and Buckinghamshire (Colonel Crosse) in place of Dallas (52$^{nd}$ Foot). Introduced to Col . . . QMG and General Walker VC, GOC Div. Return to Coigneux in Car 6.45. Read paper till 8 p.m. in Mess. Dinner at 8.15. Bed 9.30. Fairly good night. Heavy batteries firing a mile away.

Five days after waving goodbye to his wife on the platform of Charing Cross station, Monty has arrived at the Western Front. He finds he is attached to the 52$^{nd}$ Light Infantry, 2$^{nd}$ Oxfordshire and Buckinghamshire. What a strange thing – to arrive at the front line and only at the last minute be told the name of your regiment! His Commanding Officer is someone called Colonel Crosse, and he exchanges a few words of welcome with the Divisional Commander, General Walker, VC. The Army's maw is tightening round its latest recruit, but it doesn't seem to be a wholly unpleasant experience.

Nearly a hundred years on, I find I can see Monty quite vividly, sitting in the Mess beset by the anxieties of the new boy, hiding behind his paper, one nervously joggling leg crossed over the other, sharing a stilted first dinner with some nameless old hand and, just one mile away, the heavy guns firing through the night. He is at war.

# TWO

# Pullthrough

The village of Coigneux sits about ten miles north of the town of Albert and twenty miles south west of Arras. The line of the River Somme meanders from east to west a little under 20 miles to the south of the village, as the crow flies. Monty is joining the 2nd Oxford and Buckinghamshire Light Infantry, which is part of the 5th Infantry Brigade, which in turn makes up part of the 2nd Division of the 4th Army. On the day Monty turns up, the entire 2nd Division is in the process of moving back into the front line after ten days of 'resting and training'.

There is no mention in Monty's diary of 'the Battle of the Somme'. I'm not sure there would have been, as for the vast majority of fighting men on the front line there simply was no such thing. To them it was a series of local assaults, a relentless sleep-starved struggle against the constant bombardment of shells, shrapnel and gas amongst wire and machine guns, bombs and mortars. In that squalor of mud and rain, they met dread and terror, and found themselves capable of unimaginable heroism. It was only those in charge who saw the larger picture – and the full enormity of what they had unleashed on 1 July, three long months before Monty arrived, ready to lend spiritual succour.

To this day, historians debate the Battle of the Somme. Strangely enough, the latest view (the backlash to the backlash to the backlash) is that it wasn't necessarily the bloodiest cock-up in the entire history of the British Army. It's difficult for any of us brought up on the War Poets and *Blackadder* to take this view seriously. There were 60,000 British casualties on the first day of The Somme, most of them killed as they stepped out of their trenches, weighed down with equipment they didn't need, following an artillery barrage of unparalleled ferocity and length that had, in large part, failed to do its job of pulverising the German lines. Those that weren't mown down in the first few yards were machine gunned on the German wire, which remained for the most part intact. From 1 July to mid-August, the British casualties were about 5,500 officers and almost 140,000 'other ranks'; by the time the 'Battle' drifted to its ghastly, inconclusive end in mid-November the British had lost 400,000 and the French 200,000 men. German losses were probably about 600,000.

The big picture in October 1916 – the generals' picture – was that The Somme had to continue in order to relieve the French at Verdun and ease the German pressure on our allies on the Eastern Front. The phrase 'bite and hold' had currency. The men would advance under cover of a barrage, secure a limited part of the German front line, and then hold it against the inevitable German counterattack. The other idea that held sway by this stage was that the British were going to grind down the enemy more effectively than he ground us down. We might lose men and equipment, but he would lose more. And anyway, we could *afford* to lose more. We had the wealth and manpower of the Empire – and the French – and our naval blockade was choking the main German supply lines. We would out-endure the enemy.

These ideas weren't necessarily crazy, especially 'bite and hold'. The war of attrition seems unacceptable today – as it did to many people at the time. I believe it's also fair to say that when Haig launched his attacks on 1 July he was hoping for a big breakthrough that would punch a hole through the German lines. He was looking for victory, not a blood-soaked holding pattern. He wanted to unleash his cavalry through the gap made by his artillery and infantry and charge on to Berlin. The scale of the operation – a million shells were launched at the German lines *every week* of the battle – is unimaginable; to a newcomer, the organisational skills and care of preparation shown by the despised generals and their staff is often hugely impressive. It was only later, as he contemplated the men who had floundered and died in the mud, that Haig had this to say in his self-serving dispatches of 23 December 1916:

> *The three main objects of our offensive in July had already been achieved at the date when this account closes; in spite of the fact that the heavy autumn rains had prevented full advantage being taken of the favourable situation by our advance, at a time when we had good grounds for hoping to achieve yet more important successes. Verdun had been relieved; the main German forces had been held on the Western Front; and the enemy's strength had already been very considerably worn down. Any one of these results is in itself sufficient to justify the Somme battles.*[6]

Today, it's hard to read Haig's complacent prose without a feeling of revulsion. No wonder the veterans, or more accurately the survivors, of The Somme, who had experienced the stupefying chaos of the endless days and nights of attack, counterattack, raid and bombing party, of freezing fog and howling shrapnel, could never forgive the man. And as they found themselves ignored and sidelined in post-war Britain, while Haig and his supporters tried to justify the slaughter in newsprint and memoirs, it's no wonder that their pride turned to rage – so that everything we now think we know about The Somme is coloured by their feelings of betrayal. To most Britons, Haig will always be a byword for high-ranking, unfeeling stupidity.

All that said, by early October 1916 there was in some quarters the dawning of a feeling that the British Army had the measure of the Germans. There probably wasn't going to be a big breakthrough or a triumphant folding up of the German trenches, but there was a sense that they could be beaten. The Allies were launching more raids, hurling more shells in their direction and were, however slowly and bloodily, inching forwards – which was at least the right direction to be heading . . . The British had even used tanks for the first time on 15 September, spreading mayhem in the German lines before they sank in the mud.

However, as Richard Holmes points out in *Tommy*, we must also guard against thinking that everything was just bloody awful all the time. Certainly we shouldn't assume that everyone on the British side of the Western Front wanted to pack up and go home. British morale never really came close to collapsing (unlike, say, the Austrian, German or French); it was one of Monty's responsibilities to help make sure that it didn't. The howls of pain and rage have drowned out the possibility of any other message, but Holmes quotes Cyril Falls, 'a veteran turned Oxford don', who saw how his more nuanced experiences of the war were changed by other people's hindsight:

> *Every sector became a bad one, every working party is shot to pieces; if a man is killed or wounded his entrails always seem to protrude from his body; no one ever seems to have a rest . . . Attacks succeed one another with lightning rapidity. The soldier is represented as a depressed and mournful spectre helplessly wandering about until death brought his miseries to an end.*[7]

It's a useful reminder. We may imagine that when my grandfather first poked his head round the Mess door of the 52nd Ox and Bucks he'd find a haggard, grim-faced lot. *The History of the Second Division* seems very clear that he would have done: 'The wholesale slaughter of men, the almost continuous roar of the guns, left their mark on the faces of those who carried on in the battle area.' But that's not the whole story. An undated letter (but hand-delivered to Monty some time after mid-1917), written by his friend, Fullbrook-Leggatt (signing himself 'Pullthrough') includes some first impressions of the new padre:

To:
    Senior Chaplain, 2nd Division
    Commanding Officer, 52nd Light Infantry
    Archbishop of Canterbury for Information

Mrs Guilford for Information

Rev EM Guildford [sic], CF

The Senior Chaplain of the 2nd Division, taking advantage of the Course for Junior Aspirants of the Church Militant under the Acting Brigade Major, 5th Infantry Brigade, sent the above, as a 'plaguey priest' for a period of attachment.

The Rev EM Guildford has so far failed to show any appreciation of or aptitude for the path in life which he has chosen to adopt.

An absolute failure to look at things in their true perspective, his blind obstinate persistence in preaching his own distorted opinions have not failed to create a very unfavourable impression.

This fair, fluffy-haired, blue eyed fledgling arrived with all the baggage and impedimenta of an effete civilian, even including pyjamas in his trousseau for the battle zone.

He arrived among men who are deeply engaged in a life and death struggle on which they are told depends the preservation or destruction of civilisation.

In a cock a hoop manner he declared that he was waging a war of his own against something he called Cynicism.

He has no respect for his superior officers.

He is a slumber hog, never rising before 8.45am.

A General has had occasion to complain of his wastefulness at meals.

He dines out frequently, invariably losing his way back, also his collar, tie and studs.

On one occasion when informed that he was to be reported, he ran five miles on a hot day to prejudice the ears of him to whom he was to be reported before any formal accusation could arrive.

Simulating a Christian humility, he has with clumsy guile endeavoured to create strife and disregard of all authority and discipline.

I consider this pampered pet of a country parish so impossible a learner that I am retaining him at present not for instruction but as a warning to others.

He appears to rely for success on a gushing volubility and a theatrical smile.

He is wholly wanting in judgement having delivered a tactless tirade against the ascetic celibacy of the Acting Brigade Major.

He is an incongruous medley of antediluvian superstitions, heresies and doctrines shabbily camouflaged beneath a tired smattering of present day conditions.

I regret that it has more than once been necessary to humiliate this blond braggart by physical force. Under the treatment his baneful blatancy swiftly subsides, bleatings and bellowings following the punctuations on his squirming torso.

It was explained to him the other day that owing to the stress of war, dates, seasons, and festivals were often forgotten and that it would help the memories of those more busy than himself if he were to vary the colour of his tie in accordance with the colours laid down in the rubric of Sarum. In view of his present taste in collars it was felt that he would have no objection to colour if even a brighter shade. He callously declined – partly from spite, partly in dudgeon because he was ignorant of the Rubric of Sarum.

As a last piece of evidence to prove how pitiably unsatisfactory is the Rev EM Guildford I would state that WHEN ASKED THE DATE OF WHITSUNDAY HE DID NOT KNOW.

It is deplorable that while the morale of the Division is so good, that of a padre should be so low.

Pullthrough

I love this letter. It lifts us straight into the real war, fought by people who were every bit as individual as you'd expect in a conscript army drawn from the whole population. It tells us (and after a century stretching from Sassoon to *Birdsong*, I think we all need telling) that Monty's new home was not just a place of gas attacks and eviscerations but also one of teasing and practical jokes, of lost collars, of padres galloping across fields in the hot sun to avert a telling-off, of grumbling generals and celibate acting majors, of a war for the preservation of civilisation that is more than a little tongue-in-cheek.

It's great to get that first glimpse of the fluffy-haired Monty, turning up at base with a trousseau filled with pyjamas, ready for his War on Cynicism. There's plenty here on attitudes towards chaplains and the Church, if we want to draw conclusions from the particular to the general.

But never mind that. Because most of all I love this letter for its sign-off – 'Pullthrough', a command as well as a name. I have no doubt that the letter was written at a moment when Monty's faith was crumbling: 'While the morale of the Division is so good, that of a padre should be so low' . . . and the letter radiates warmth and love and *encouragement* for my grandfather. Just pull through. You may have seen your friends and family killed; the war may never end; you may be losing faith in your God; but just pull through. We can make it.

# THREE

# 'Rather disturbed night, what with rats and tummy ache'

In early October 1916, 'the slumberhog' is up at 8 a.m.

> Tuesday, 3 October 1916
> Rise at 8. Breakfast 9. Walk to Couin to see Bate. Picked up
> by FA car. Meet Bate on horse outside Couin. Instructed to
> wait at 6<sup>th</sup> FA till sent for by 52<sup>nd</sup>. Walk back to Coigneux.
> Still raining. Mud on roads and in camp terrible. Write
> letters. Lunch. Walk. Tea. Write and censor letters. Dinner.

That is a fairly typical day for Monty and many other chaplains.
There is plenty of waiting around, on this occasion because he
has to meet Bate (who is in charge of organising the chaplains
of the Division) to find out when he'll be sent for by the 52<sup>nd</sup>.
He censors the letters, one of the main duties of the chaplains,
which probably gives him a better insight than most into the
mood of the men. It is raining and the mud is everywhere.

> Wednesday, 4 October 1916
> Breakfast 8.45. Drive in car with Sarday (Wesleyan Padre) to
> Bertrancourt. Pass heaps of troops on road. Pick up Murray
> (CF C/E 6<sup>th</sup> Infantry Brigade). See Bate (SCF). Long chat.
> Walk over together to 5<sup>th</sup> FA to see Major Robinson CO and
> fix for me to come to them on the morrow. Back to lunch at
> Division Headquarters . . . Walk over to Mailly wood. Meet

Crosse Commanding Officer of 2nd Oxf and Bucks 52nd Light Infantry on road. Bate tells me that latter is trying to avoid having me attached to his Battalion. [added later: Because of his objection of the way my predecessor, Dallas, was sent to another Division . . . nothing personal] Call on HLI mess. Tea with 2nd Oxf and Bucks Mess. Nice set, especially Major Barnes, 2nd in Command . . . Walk back to Bertrancourt and on to Coigneux except for one short lift. Write to K. Dinner. Bed. Cold better.

There's a lot of walking in Monty's diary. He often doesn't say why, but he's tramping around, meeting and talking with people. Monty loved to talk and he grew to be good friends with Colonel Richard Crosse, the Commanding Officer of his new regiment. But their first meeting sounds distinctly chilly, as Monty was replacing the previous padre, the Rev. Dallas (who was later killed in action) and Crosse could not bear people leaving his regiment. Indeed, Crosse was obsessed with the 52nd Light Infantry. His father and uncles had served with the regiment and his family had been part of it since its inception. In 1823, his ancestor John Cross had written 'A System of Drill and Manoeuvres as Practised in the 52nd Light Infantry Regiment', dedicated to the Duke of York, which explained how to train recruits; and Richard Crosse had crossed to France with the regiment on 13 August 1914 as a lieutenant and the Regimental Adjutant. Indeed, it would have taken an armed battalion to have kept him away. He has cold words in his memoirs for those who are 'extra-regimental', those who took up jobs away from the action.

Of the twenty-seven officers who crossed to France that day with Richard Crosse, eleven were killed, one died of pneumonia in 1918 and one was invalided out. Every officer who survived was wounded at some point, except for a man called Lieutenant (later Lieutenant-Colonel) Southey.

Colonel Crosse (as he was by the time Monty met him on the road to Mailly Wood) loved his regiment, hated change and didn't much care for Monty (the fact of him, not the person,

Monty stresses). He was a rigid man who, in an age of hierarchies, stood out as being on the far side of inflexible. But he was very clear about where he thought his duty lay: with his men at the Front, and for that he had their total respect. He was famous among them for never taking a day's leave from the moment he stepped off the boat onto French soil to the day when a shell exploded next to him and he was invalided home. Most admired him for this tireless devotion to duty, among them Fullbrook-Leggatt, who in a letter written almost 60 years later in 1970, has this to say:

> I have read your tribute to R.B.C. very carefully and I have made no attempt to re-write it [Crosse had died not long before and they were both sending in pieces for a book of tributes] . . . I have wondered about your second paragraph in which you relate how Crosse refused to take leave due to him. There were some of the more senior officers in the Regiment who spoke of him as a crank for doing this, but they were of the breed that always puts self first and they made their remarks from the comfort of armchairs at the Reserve Battalion in England. Of course, there were others who considered that home leave was essential for the mental and physical well-being of all ranks. I think all those in the first category must now be in their graves. (I also forewent leave when I was with the Regiment.)

The quixotic 'Pullthrough' was always ready with an opinion, but it is abundantly clear that Richard Crosse loved his regiment more than anything and that most of his men loved him for it. The bond between the men at the Front was often stronger than anything that home could offer – or at least that was what they found themselves thinking. We know that even though he believed the war was being run for profit and needlessly prolonged Siegfried Sassoon was drawn back into the Army because he could not abandon his brothers at the Front. Many demobilised men felt grief and guilt, not relief. And I suspect that Monty felt a guilty lurch, even 60 years on when he read

Fullbrook-Leggatt's fulminations on leave-takers. Monty was always quite keen on taking his leave, if he could.

Mind you, it's probable that Crosse would not have cared what any of them thought. As he puts it in his very brief, privately circulated memoirs, at the moment when he was placed in temporary command of the regiment in July 1916:

> *I had achieved my ambition. After more than one hundred years my family had at last provided the 52nd with a commanding officer, if only an acting one temporarily promoted for the job in the field because senior men were scarce; and I was content.*[8]

He was only 28 years old, the same age as Monty. The war was bringing opportunity for promotion, if nothing else.

Speaking of Sassoon, Monty had kept a poem by one of the officers of the 52nd, C.M. Chevallier. Entitled 'To the Colonel of the Fifty Second', it is dated Christmas 1916, so it's worth reproducing it here. But maybe not all of it . . .

To the Colonel of the FIFTY SECOND

You've asked me for a poem, Colonel Crosse
And be assured it gives me much remorse
I cannot write a line
Worthy to offer you at your behest
Though I would fain fall in with your request
As oft you do with mine.

There is one theme alone that can be reckoned
Next to your heart, and that the Fifty-Second
And when I strive to write
As best a special reservist can
Of all its gallant deeds in rear or van
My spirit leaves me quite

For half its fortune in this German war,
The days when most it showed its ancient core,

I've not been there to see:
Its prowess on the Marne, the Aisne, at Ypres
Or where the Ancre by Beaumont Hamel creeps
Is but a tale to me

But though I've never shared in your success
Yet have I known you in some hours of stress
Grim Richebourg's lines you'd left
When first I joined you: on Givenchy edge
I was with you; and when your luckless wedge
Its path to Guillemont cleft.

And in the prosier paths of trench routine
Tis my good fortune to have mostly been
Where e'er you were
At Cuinchy, Vermelles quarry, Hulloch road
On Souchez ridge, or in some swamped abode
Of Festubert.

But when I try to write of all these things
My all-unworthiness back to me brings
Thoughts of the Brave,
Owen and Jacob, 'Carey' Hunt and Kite
All partners with me in Givenchy fight
All in their grave.

And when I think on these and such as these
At once the streams of song within me freeze,
For who am I
Too small for such in life, in time of death
To sing the Regiment, their very breath
When dead they lie?

Yet from the dead, when I turn to the living
And see the mountains moved by one man giving
His whole self, I believe
The regiment could beat the powers infernal

That marches into action with a Colonel
Who's never been on leave.

In fact, that is the whole poem – never before published, I presume. What bit could I leave out? The poem tells us, more powerfully than I ever could, just how strong a bond there was between his officers and the Colonel. Not only that, it shows how vital the unit of the regiment was in keeping the British Army fighting keen and in the field. Although it has been said many times, these men were fighting and dying for their friends and for their pride, as much as they were for their country and its ideals. As I typed the poem onto the page, I could see C.M. Chevallier standing and reciting his poem, on Christmas Day in a crowded and fuggy Mess, to his glowing Colonel and dozens of appreciative fellow officers and men. The Front is never quiet, they are far from home, but they know what they are fighting for.

Thursday, 5 October 1916
Breakfast. Cold much better. FA car to Bertrancourt. Dump kit in billet. Same farmhouse as M. Dupont (interpreter) and Boyd (HLI Presbyterian Padre). Pretty bare room but large. Walk over to SCF for Chaplain's weekly meeting at 10am. Meet Morgan and Murray (2 Emmanuel men), St John (99th Brigade), Browne (5th Brigade) and Hornby (6th Brigade). At 12.15 walk with Browne to Brigade Headquarters at Beausart. See Capt Farquharson. Arrange if possible to live with Brigade MG section. Walk on. Distribute Daily Papers to HLI. Lunch with Browne at 24th RF mess . . . Walk over to MG section. See Major Todd (CO) and arrange to go to them next day. Mailly Maillet pretty badly shelled at one time. Go over Roman Catholic Civil church. Large shell hole through sanctuary roof. Walk back – picked up by Medical Officer of 24th RF and motor to Acheux. Find Harland's room (CF of Corps troops). Leave card. Walk back to Bertrancourt. Lift. Tea in 5th FA Mess. Go round to billet. Return to Mess. Censor letters and write to K. Dinner. Capt

Roberts (RAMC) I find is a Sydney man and knows the Hutchinsons especially Lloyd quite well. Write up diary. Go back to billet 9.30 p.m.

Monty is meeting up with Cambridge University contacts but he's also keen to be living with the Brigade Machine Gun section. In other words – and I hope Robert Graves is listening – he is trying to avoid the soft option of staying at the base.

Friday, 6 October 1916
Rather disturbed night, what with rats and tummy ache. Tummy upset all day. Evidently eaten something which has disagreed. So determine to take a quiet day and not to go up to Mailly Maillet until tomorrow. Lie down till tea. Cup of tea. Short walk with Boyd. Lie down and go to bed at 8 p.m. Jolly good night.

The mud and the rats would keep intruding. But I'm struck, again, by the extent chaplains were left in charge of their own time. He has a tummy ache – so he decides to spend a 'quiet day' – when just a mile or so away the Battle of the Somme is raging.

Saturday, 7 October 1916
Feel much better. Breakfast 9.10. Pack kit. Wait in Mess for car to Mailly Maillet at 1 p.m. Lunch at Machine Gun Company's Mess in Brasserie. Have room upstairs with spring mattress. Look about for Brown, who is with Trench Mortar Company. Tea in Mess. Stroll with Kinsey towards Beaussart. Rain. Find Brown in Mess on return. Also chit to bury two men at Euston Cemetery at 9.30. Go with Brown to Brigade Headquarters and see Capt Farquharson. Return. Another chit about a burial at 9.30 next morning up trenches at White City Cemetery. Have dinner. Leave at 8.30 with Brown for Euston. Go past the Sugar Refinery where Battery is firing. Have to go along an 'unhealthy' bit but quite quiet at present. Have difficulty in finding cemetery. When found

no one there. Go back and enquire at the Advanced Dressing Station Dugout. Finally walk home. Star shells frequent. Sudden short burst of rifle and machine gun firing. Go to bed at 10.45. Mailly must be a nice country town in peace time but is badly spoilt by shelling.

It's interesting how quickly Monty has adapted to his new world. He talks of walking 'home' after a day spent trying to find someone to bury, of 'star shells', machine gun fire and batteries. He 'strolls'. The homely names of the overflowing cemeteries add a note of unreality: 'Euston' and 'White City'.

The next day, Monty wakes early to the sound of shellfire. Imagine being killed in your bed because you'd decided everything must be OK, just because someone else was snoring through the barrage. Maybe he was too shy to be the only one scampering down to the shelter of the cellar.

Sunday, 8 October 1916

Woke up at 4 a.m. to hear the whistling and exploding of shells. Not knowing whether they are far or near feel rather 'windy' and think of descending to cellar, but the snoring of someone next room reassures me and I turn over. Rise at 7.15. Breakfast at 7.55. See Brown at 8.15. He tells me that guide will meet me at entrance of 6th Avenue at 8.45. Set off and go wrong way for 10 minutes. Retrace my steps and arrive at 6th Avenue at 8.50. See no guide so proceed up 6th Avenue (Communication trench). I finally reach 'White City' about 9.30. Find them digging grave still. Talk to Sergeant Hurst, Pioneer Sergeant of HLI and C of E. Things pretty quiet. Occasional burst of our MG fire and continuous RFA firing at batteries on both sides. Cemetery pretty healthy in depression. Take funeral of Canadian (Trench Mortar Batt) by name Reade (Tall fine man). Proceed with an HLI Padre with cross for grave at Euston Cemetery. Get to Euston but find no one. See someone hurrying after me from 'Sugaries' Cemetery to tell me that the bodies were taken there on previous night and half covered in. Proceed across fields with him to Cemetery – a very unhealthy spot, because of close proximity of our batteries shelled all day before. Graves continually blown up. Not supposed to be used any more. Read service over bodies. Can get no particulars. Not place to tarry in so hurry away back to Mailly. Great activity along road. Many batteries taking up positions along road. Reach Mess at about 11.30 without mishap. Feel hot and dirty after tramp in muddy trenches. Sit in mess and read till lunch at 1 p.m. See Brown. No services possible for me as Brigade is moving out of trenches in afternoon. Hang about all afternoon and finally leave with 2nd Lieuts Grey and Galway at 4.30. Ride a spare mare for about 1 1/2 miles. We take long way round to Lealvillers through Hedauville, Forceville – Acheux – about 8 miles walk. Arrive in dark feeling pretty tired. Lounge in Mess which is in Farm House and quite good. Turn in soon after dinner. Billet in sort of long oblong canvas hut. Sleep on floor but jolly well. Well out of shell fire.

This is Monty's first trip towards the front line. It is also his first funeral – for a Canadian called Reade who was a 'tall fine man'. Burials were popular with the men, in the sense that they liked to respectfully mark the passing of friends and comrades, no matter what their religion, and at least it was a clear-cut duty that the chaplains could perform.

Monty, characteristically, gets lost. There is no great shame in that; everyone did, although he'd still be getting lost in the same spot many months later. More disturbing, though, is the image of that second, hurried burial service: the nameless bodies, the hastily spoken words, the graves continually blown up, the endlessly mashed, mixed and re-churned contents. For the first time, Monty is facing sights for which there is no preparation. Not only sights, but smells. Private Frank Hawkings wrote of the 'penetrating and filthy stench which assailed our noses and filled the atmosphere – a combination of mildew, rotting vegetation and the stink which rises from the decomposing corpses of men and animals'. And then there was the noise – of shells, barrages, machine gun fire and the sound of hundreds of thousands of men, wedged up against one another, wallowing in the toxic mud.

Father Benedict Williamson wrote of his first trip up the road to the front line in his memoirs 'Happy Days'; it would have been familiar to Monty:

> *We passed on up the road, with its press of moving limbers, guns, pack animals, and men all pressing relentlessly forward like a great machine. Piled up on either side of the road or trampled underfoot were the carcasses of decaying mules and horses, streaking the mud with red, the bodies of men, slain as they went up, smashed and overturned limbers, and all the wreckage that marked the roads of the Ypres sector, shells occasionally bursting in the desolate, war-torn country on either side, the unceasing song of shells passing overhead; by the roadside at one point lay horse and rider, just as they had fallen the night before, half buried in the mud and slime, trampled down by the ceaseless forward movement that never seemed to stay by day or by night.*[9]

With the previous day a Sunday without services, and with still no sermon to deliver Monty slips back into a kind of routine.

Monday, 9 October 1916
Rise at 8.45. Breakfast at 9.30. Browne turns up. Go over to Oxf and Bucks camp with him. Not very comfy camp. Walk with him to Acheux to see Harland. Find Harland with Major Campbell 5th Corps SCF. Chat for an hour. Return for lunch to Lealvillers. After lunch chat about Religion with Lieutenant Stevens (MGC) and Lieutenant Kinsey (MGC) in Billet. Stroll over and watch footer match between Oxf and Bucks and 24 RF. Score 1–1. Look in at Oxf and Bucks Mess. Talk to Lyle. Return to Mess to tea and stroll with Kinsey. Interesting talk about man's moral responsibility. Write this up. Rejoice in bulky mail from K and 2 parcels. Dinner. Censor letters and write 2. Bed 10 p.m.

Monty is having chats about religion and 'interesting' talks about man's moral responsibility. Of course, if you're with the chaplain, religion is one of the things you will probably end up talking about. Monty was someone who loved to talk, though, on any subject. He was full of stories and he knew how to connect with people. He would find out what interested them, or what was on their mind, and it would feel like he had all the time in the world for you and your preoccupations. Certainly that's how it felt to me as an averagely bloodthirsty seven year old, when he told me, thrillingly, that he'd killed his great aunt when he was my age. We were standing in our dining room when he told me how he'd demanded that she chase him round and round the dining room table until she could run no further. She died in her sleep that very night, he told me with considerable relish. And then, with an almighty roar, he started chasing *me* round the table, and I was laughing and shrieking at him to stop, terrified that he'd drop dead any minute. He must have been at least 80 years old and the survivor of two heart attacks – although he was down for breakfast the next morning, late as usual, but much to my relief.

# FOUR

# 'God shall wipe away all tears . . .'

Whether they murdered their great aunts or not, we like to imagine that our forebears knew much more about death than we do today. There was more of it about, for one thing. Children died young. Horses dropped dead in the street. Old people breathed their last in parlours and bedrooms, not hidden away in hospices. The Christian religion also kept thoughts of death at the forefront of life and encouraged people to believe that the moment of death was just a passing over from this world to the next. Spiritualism thrived in the early twentieth century and was given a tremendous boost by the grieving families of the First World War. And, in Monty's case, his mother died when she was forty-nine years old, and he was just six.

Monty was miserably young when this happened, but he was already away at school in Ramsgate, Kent, and the first he heard was when he received a letter from his aunt, Eliza Chase, his mother's sister. His father was in India, converting souls.

> 35 Wellington Square
> Hastings
> 22 May [1895]
> My precious Monty
> Who do you think came here to see dearest Mother yesterday, you will think that it was dear Father. No! it was not Father, but good, kind Mr Greatheart, come with a message from his Master the King that He wanted Mother soon to come

into his presence in the Celestial City. Mr Greatheart asked Mother if she was ready and willing to go through the river up to the City of God and she replied Oh yes, Oh yes!! She is longing for the angels to come and fetch her to her Heavenly Home. She often says 'I'm going Home, don't try to keep me from going Home'. She says she shall be waiting for us all, so we must all get ready when the King sends for any of us.

Mr Greatheart has been again today to bring Mother food from the King's own table to strengthen her for the journey through the river, and she ate and drank the food sent by the King and she is refreshed.

I hope I shall be with her when the angels come to take her across the river, and if I get a peep inside the golden gates or see the shining angels or hear the heavenly music I will tell you all about it.

God bless you my darling

Yr loving Auntie

Two days later, young Monty receives another letter from his aunt:

35 Wellington Square
Hastings
24 May [1895]
My precious Monty
I told you in my last letter that Mr Greatheart had been to tell dearest Mother that the King of the Celestial City wanted her to come, and she was so pleased to go. She told everyone 'I'm going Home'. One morning she said 'I wish the angels would come for me'! and yesterday the angels did come to take her through the dark river. I watched her going through, she heard sweet words of God whispered to her as she passed through. One word I heard was 'I will never leave thee nor forsake thee.' And just before she reached the furthest shore she looked up with such a happy, earnest, wondering gaze, we all longed to see what she saw. No

doubt she saw 'Jesus Himself' standing to receive her and perhaps dear Grandmama too, and others who have 'gone before', with the holy angels. She entered into the Golden gate of the City and we saw her no more. She left word with me that she should be waiting for you all so you must get ready for when the King shall send for you.

　　With best love from your loving Auntie
　　Eliza C. Chase

I don't know if Monty was consoled by some kind Matron when he opened these Dickensian letters or if he was alone at the school breakfast table while the other boys stopped what they were doing and stared. He must have gone home, to be with his aunt, I suppose. He would have found out later that his mother died of double pneumonia. I presume that he met up with his sisters Lilian, Edith and Evelyn and they grieved together. His aunt's faith is palpable and strong, even if her sentiments seem alien to us now. And surely, even with her exhortations for Monty to get ready for 'the King' to send for him, it must have been comforting to the bereft little boy – this heavy dose of Bunyan.

　　Monty's mother was Louisa Chase, the third child of Samuel Compigne Chase, a solicitor from Reading, who with his wife claimed Huguenot descent (hence the Compigne in the name, which crops up again when Monty names his first daughter Ruth Compigne). They were all rather proud of their exotic Huguenot heritage. Her father, Samuel emigrated to New Zealand in the 1850s, taking his wife, seven-year-old Louisa and her two older siblings with him, as well as a small mountain of furniture and a wooden house broken down into sections, to be hammered together when they got to Wellington. Six months in that windy city persuaded him that it was no place for a professional man with a young family (although they'd managed to add another baby by then) so he sold everything, both the clip-together house and its contents, chartered a schooner and headed home. I have a portrait of this restless young man in my attic, looking debonair but slightly fuddled, as well as a lengthy 65-stanza poem which he wrote off Plymouth Sound in 1854, after a particularly tiresome journey home. Here is the briefest of extracts:

> Fair breezes blow, away we go,
> Swift bounding o'er the billow;
> Night long advanced, we go below,
> Take grog, then jog to the pillow.

The quick précis of 'Home Voyage Stanzas' is that the sea can be pretty blustery, but sometimes calm, and it is nice to be home. And if you *are* going to take a long sea journey, make sure you're well stocked up with champagne. I'm proud to claim the man as my great-great-grandfather.

Perhaps a sliver of wanderlust lingered in his daughter Louisa because in 1883 she was in Bombay, India, marrying Edward Guilford, Monty's father. I don't know how long she had been in the country, but she was almost certainly practising as a nurse. She was a relatively elderly 37 years old – getting on a bit for those days to become a first-time bride – but still youthful looking. Her new husband was a vigorous 29-year-old Christian missionary who was making a name for himself in the Punjab, running both the Christian Missionary Society mission to the Sikhs in Tarn Taran as well as the local Leper Asylum which he ran with 'sympathetic but firm control', according to his *Times* obituary. He spoke Punjabi fluently and well enough to translate and publish the first book of Psalms to appear in the Punjabi language. He was known, even in those early days, as 'Guilford of Tarn Taran' and a glittering career as a Church Missionary seemed to beckon. And so it did: Monty's father ended his days as an eminent and well-respected man, as an OBE, as recipient of the Kaisar-i-Hind Medal 1st Class (for quelling a riot, it is said), as head of Army recruitment and propaganda in India, and as author of the definitive Victorian work on Sikhism.

But much of that was ahead of him. When Edward married Louisa, I would guess the match was considered a good one for him, in those class-crippled days. Only about six years earlier,

Edward had been an apprentice blacksmith on the railways, along with his brothers, working on the London and Brighton Railway; his father had been a guard on the same line but had died of TB in 1863. His grandfather (and many Guilford fathers before him) had been a Brighton fisherman. So Edward really had taken the Biblical route and become a fisher of men. I've no idea how he did it – in the mid-1870s he was an apprentice on the railways, the next thing we know he's fluent in Punjabi, training at the Church Missionary Society in Islington, and then being ordained in St Paul's Cathedral in 1881. Two years later he's marrying Louisa in Bombay. He may have found a patron who spotted his potential; he may have been extraordinarily driven; most likely both. We do know that he was charismatic, highly ambitious, entertaining and perhaps rather happier in India than in England.

After Louisa had churned out four children in metronomic succession (Lilian Compigne in 1884; Edith Louise in 1886; Edward Montmorency in 1888, and Evelyn Helen in 1890), Edward took her back to her home town of Reading and then headed off alone for the hills of the Punjab. That is not to suggest anything reprehensible; his career and his prospects lay in India and there may have been some discussion that England would be healthier for Louisa and their children. Well, if that was the case, then all four children did survive but, disastrously, Louisa did not. She was struck down by double pneumonia, leaving her motherless children to the care of her older sister, the unmarried Eliza Compigne Chase. Edward came back for a few months that summer to comfort his children and to make the arrangements, but then he was off again to Tarn Taran, leaving his children alone with their 'loving Auntie'.

It sounds like she did a wonderful job in bringing up her sister's children. When she was on her deathbed 20 years later, Monty wrote this to his father:

> The Bishop of Ely spoke in such high terms of his respect for Auntie. He said that there were few women whom he respected more, or thought more highly of than Auntie. He

felt she is such a simple good woman and he always feels that her life work in bringing us children up is a singular illustration of the working of God's grace. There she was middle aged and already tired out through nursing others, and in many ways apparently little aptitude for the task and yet God gave her the strength as she bravely took us under her wing – and now here we are all of us launched out into the world.

It must indeed have been quite a shock for dear old Auntie. She was fifty-two years old, tired and living alone (I'm sure quite happily) when she suddenly found herself looking after four bewildered young children with apparently 'little aptitude for the task'. There wasn't going to be much help from the father. Not only was he back in India but the next year he married again, to a woman called Elizabeth Rose Grimwood. The attractions of this woman are uncertain, but her maiden name seems ominously appropriate. On being told of the engagement, the Bishop of Lahore remarked, 'I knew you were meant to love your enemy, but I didn't know you had to marry them.'

Monty and his sisters grew up bathed in the love and support of their remarkable aunt, who was thrown into surrogate single motherhood late in life and seems to have poured everything into it. She looks quite Wodehousian in the photos – somewhat stern and chunkily formidable – but that just goes to show how those formal, late-Victorian photographs can deceive us into thinking that it was a grim, straitjacketed, static and humourless world. 'Auntie' wasn't like that at all: she was self-effacing, kind and desperate to do the right thing for her new brood. She seems to have been keenly aware that the children were her temporary charges, which may have given them, and especially the young man of the house, more leeway than was usual. Her deeply held Christianity is evident from every word she wrote and everything written about her. She had memorised numberless passages of the Bible and other religious works, and was ever ready with the appropriate quote. Here's Monty, writing to his father in 1915 just after his aunt's death:

One little memory I must tell you – when Auntie fully realised that we should have many days of watching by her bedside – and then the end, she said in her dear thoughtful way 'I am afraid it will be a great strain for you all, dears, but it will be an education too, won't it?' Never a thought of her own pain, but as always for the added experience it would be for us in our equipment for the battle of life. You remember how apt Auntie used to be in quoting from the Bible, and how well stored her mind was with 'precious' passages. Well! I of course always misquote and know very very few passages by heart and those very inaccurately. So Auntie used to help by suggesting her favourite pieces, and we used to say passages together. She loved Rev: vii 9–17 and quite near the end when I was saying this in a very stumbling way – she was quite unable to speak them poor darling – I could swear I saw a flicker of a smile on her dear face at her 'dear boy's' blundering effort to be a 'comfort' to her.

So, with Edward Snr away (although Monty writes with such warmth and ease to his father that it would be wrong to assume that their relationship was necessarily as remote as the thousands of miles that separated them would imply), Eliza Chase set about bringing up his children as best she could. They lived in Hastings, and when they were home Monty and his sisters tended the small garden (sparking a life-long interest in grand gardening schemes), went for long walks along the front, visited the neighbours, attended church and sang their favourite hymns in the drawing-room. It was a deeply Christian upbringing, and a joyful one. On her deathbed Eliza Chase regretted not 'speaking more for Jesus', but at least she spared her charges too much fire and brimstone. They were happy when they were home, even if, at their father's behest, most of the year was spent away at boarding schools.

Monty attended St Lawrence College in Ramsgate, a red-brick Victorian boys' school just up the coast. He remained there until he turned 18 in 1907. He seems to have thrived academically (except at maths) and in particular at sport: cricket, football and most especially hockey, at which he excelled. The headmaster, Mr Morris, wrote this startling testimonial to Monty's school years in 1911:

> *During the whole of the time he was with me his conduct and bearing were irreproachable. His life was ruled on the highest principles and he had the strongest sense of duty and honour and was in an eminent degree conscientious and straightforward as well as diligent and thorough.*

It goes on (Head of House, the cricket team for three years, the 'happy blend of manliness and gentleness . . .') and of course it's absurd. What 14 year old lives his life on the 'highest principles'? But people do seem to have loved Monty and wished him well.

I have dozens of black-and-white photographs of 'E.M. Guilford' in sports teams from this period and later from Cambridge. He sits, sometimes cross-legged on the ground at the front, sometimes at the heart of the team with a cup or a shield. In the very early ones, he is standing diffidently at the back. He holds footballs, hockey sticks, cricket bats and occasionally a tennis racquet. He can look whimsical, dreamy or debonair. Is it my imagination, though, or does he also, on almost every occasion, look as though he would rather be somewhere else? In many of the photos he's gazing off to his left, caught at the moment when someone has called out or beckoned him. In some, he has folded his arms, hugging himself. In one of them (The Kangaroo Club, 1911), he is the only one wearing a bow tie – although in this particular case he looks mildly amused. I have probably stared at them for too long, but is there an atmosphere of absence hovering over Monty in many of these photos? It can seem that way. More than that though, looking at these pre-war photos of dandies and sportsmen, who connect with the camera with such unfiltered confidence, it's impossible not to wonder how many of them, these wholesome young Englishmen, are about to be ploughed under by the coming apocalypse.

One of Monty's great friends at St Lawrence's was Walter Bigger, who lived in a house called Aberfoyle in Streatham, south-west London, with his parents (an Irish doctor and his wife), three brothers (Bill, Jack and Edgar) and an older sister, Kathleen. At some point during their schooldays, Walter must have invited Monty to stay with his family, and by mid-1907 Monty was clearly feeling sufficiently confident – or smitten – to be writing this postcard to Kathleen. The front shows a group of young men in blazers and is captioned: 'St. Lawrence College Monitors' Concert, May 25, 1907'. Monty is gazing distractedly off to the left. He's 18 – and looks oh so young.

> Please do me a great favour and don't look at my face. Am longing to hear whether you have decided to take up that new work or not. Hope you won't very much object to a short note from me in the next letter I send to Mrs Bigger?? I shall never forget the ripping time I had on Monday. Do you remember the monkey nut sweets you were so greedy about? Everything going on beautifully here. The VIII went off this morning. Heaps of etceteras. Monty.

Monty left St Lawrence's with an all-consuming love of sport, a deeply Christian education and a place to study theology at Queens' College, Cambridge. I have no idea if Monty was driven to follow a life in the Church, or as a missionary, or if he was just drifting that way. We have heard of his faultless character, but there's no indication that he saw life as a priest as his vocation. Nor is there any evidence of contact with his father, although I suspect there was plenty by post. His father, that profoundly ambitious man, was clearly set on Monty following his path – quite possibly to India and the leper asylums. But what Monty thought, with a home life that was quietly religious and overwhelmingly female, and whose schooldays were filled with boxing and hockey, is unclear. He enjoyed himself, is my guess, in between bouts of illness and put off thoughts of the future while his energetic father bounced around India, conversing in Punjabi and quelling riots.

Monty loved Cambridge. He could play all the sport he wanted, he made good friends (Walter Bigger continued to be one of them), and he seems to have taken the opportunity to read a lot and sleep even more. He and his friends had a five-seat 'tandem' on which they sped around the streets. The Lent Term issue of the Queens' College magazine, *The Dial*, had a feature called 'Men of Mark', and this is an extract of what it had to say about Monty when he was preparing to leave:

> *Our geographical knowledge of India is but slight, and our readers must be content with the information that Edward Montmorency Guilford first saw the light of day at Dharmsala 'up in the hills', on September 2nd, 1888. The house has since been destroyed by earthquake – we draw no conclusions, except that happily his birth-place will thus be saved from the intruding gaze and tread of unborn generations of American tourists. Of the earliest days of his life little is known. His christening cake was not adorned with sugar hockey sticks, we think that more probably its device was that of a sleeping child with the motto 'dormi puer'; at any rate he is said to have slept soundly for the first six months of his existence, while his subconscious mind was imbued with something of the magic mysticism of the East.*
>
> *At the age of 'a half' he made his first long journey, but as his personal diary does not go back so far we cannot record the impression made on his infant mind by the wonders of nature, and later by the wonders of English suburban architecture in Reading, where he next took up his abode. He has no recollections of these early days, he must have been a pensive, dreamy boy. After six years in the 'Biscuit City' it was decided that the sunny South coast would provide a more nutritious environment for a growing youth and another move was made. From this date Ramsgate became his home and it is an open secret that a well-known Railway Company has offered a fabulous sum for his photograph as an advertisement of that secluded watering hole.*
> . . .
> *Of scholastic attainments the records at our disposal give but scanty information, but his unhappy habit of catching every*

*infectious disease that attacked the school – we believe he ran up a record in measles – must have interfered greatly with his chances of academic distinctions.*

. . .

*In October 1907 a new world opened to him. He arrived at Queens' to all appearances a timid, unassuming 'fresher', but many of the escapades of his first year are better left unpublished. In the Athletic world his varied powers soon won him distinction. In his first year he represented the College at Soccer, Hockey and Tennis, and took part in the historic match against Caius for the Soccer League Championship, which was only lost (1–0) after two-and-a-half-hours play . . . Meanwhile his hockey was winning him wider fame . . . His Blue was fittingly celebrated by a select and quiet dinner followed by a variety entertainment in the Walnut Tree Court. He has figured in the College Sports at Fenner's, and if his time had not already been so much occupied, he might have taken up putting the weight or even running. This term he is adding a course of gymnastics to his other activities, after that he must try rowing to complete his education.*

*We must not, however, let our readers think that athletics and the more frivolous things of life have bounded his horizon. With characteristic vigour he attacked the Theological Tripos, and his success in this direction may be estimated from the fact that the College awarded him a prize on his first year Mays. But, as at school, his work was interrupted by unfortunate attacks of influenza and at the end of his second year he was prevented from sitting for his examinations . . . His plans for the future are still uncertain, but eventually he hopes to return as a missionary to India.*

. . .

*Of his personal appearance we need say little, appreciative crowds at Soccer matches have been known to call him 'snowball' – his portrait speaks for itself. He is not yet in love. It is impossible to give an adequate impression of his varied tastes and fancies. He does not smoke or dance, but has been known to taste wine. A fondness for reading, he would say, is his hobby, and certainly we might admit that a comfortable arm-chair with a book within reach seems to constitute his ideal of happiness. Never has he shown any sign of being afflicted with that unpardonable weakness of early rising. He has slept through the small hours of the afternoon and we are afraid that were it not for the gnawing pangs of hunger he would seldom be visible before 10am. An alarm clock is always a useful though unwelcome present – he can now sleep through three. By nature he is reserved, and with strangers shy. His philosophy of life, based on Browning, Stevenson, Chesterton and the Hebrew Prophets, is eclectic but eminently sane. In conversation he is ever ready to uphold his opinions and as he knows his own mind, is tolerant of other points of view. He keeps his choicest wares for his best customers. We shall never expect him 'to set the Thames on fire,' but we may confidently prophesy that the same success that has attended him so far, will crown his future, and we take this opportunity of wishing him all joy and happiness in his life's work.*

My grandfather kept this magazine, although I've no idea if he'd have wanted to see it reprinted 100 years later. He'd have been amazed, I guess – in his shy way. But I'm thrilled to have found another insight into the undergraduate Monty, and even if it is tinged with a Best Man's jollity, it confirms much of what I thought I knew about my grandfather. For one thing, I've known from the earliest age that he liked to sleep, even without the three alarm clock revelation. My father called the family he'd married into 'The Bedridden Guilfords' and loved to scorn the late-rising slumberhogs who drifted blearily down to the breakfast he'd cooked three hours earlier. Then again, the Fiennes family could just as well be accused of being a touch frenetic.

That Monty loved to read is another thing I knew for certain. Many of his books from this period line my shelves: gnarled and battered copies of the great Victorian novelists and poets: Robert Louis Stevenson, Anthony Trollope, Sir Walter Scott, Charles Dickens – above all, Dickens. There seems to have been very little religion in his reading. Presumably that felt too much like work. 'Barkis is Willing'; 'I'm an 'umble man'; 'Something will turn up', these are sayings I somehow knew long before I read them. I think it was my grandfather, chuckling to himself and relishing the words, even after half a century of repetition.

My grandfather's repeated illnesses are puzzling. It is mentioned time and again. When he left Cambridge there was some thought that he might become a private tutor, so the Dean wrote a short testimonial. The matter of his illness surfaces immediately:

> Queens' College, Cambridge, 10 April 1911
> <u>EM Guilford</u> came up to this College in October 1907. He read for Honours in Theology; and took a second Class last year, in spite of the fact that he was never well in Cambridge [the 'never well' is then crossed out and replaced with 'often unwell'] and that his reading was much interrupted.
>
> Of his character and ideals I can speak in the highest possible terms. He was always a force on the side of good, and took a prominent part in the religious life of the College. He also had no small share in its social life, and was a general favourite. He is a very good athlete, having got his hockey 'blue' and very nearly his 'blue' for Association Football, while at tennis he represented the College.
>
> I can recommend him unreservedly. Anyone who secures him as a private tutor, will be fortunate.
>
> CT Wood
> Dean of Queens' College.

We are used to the idea of Monty being 'on the side of good' by now, although they certainly gave a forceful testimonial in those days, but the 'often unwell'? Monty was one of the leading sportsmen at his university, but it seems like he was hardly ever out of his sickbed. Did he just want to be looked after? Was he missing his auntie, his sisters or his mother? Was there some psychological need that kept him in bed and therefore no closer to the leper asylums of the Punjab? Or was he just rather frail? He certainly doesn't look it. In the photos, he seems to get more vibrant and more handsome by the year.

My grandfather was shy, of course. It suggests a reluctance to get involved, although he clearly had strong friendships, and there are hints at escapades, dinners and entertainments that show he was fond of a good time. It's clear that, despite his reticence, my grandfather was as fond of long, free-wheeling conversations at Cambridge as he would be for the rest of his life. Underneath the fluffy-haired reserve, though, lurked something stronger; not necessarily a sense of purpose, or ambition (he would not be setting 'the Thames on fire'), but there's a resolve there and an inner belief – perhaps we should call it faith. He would need every scrap of it soon enough.

# FIVE

# 'The meaning of the shadows'

One thing we do know about Monty, despite what they said about him in that Queens' College article, is that by the time the war ended he was smoking like a trooper. Chaplains famously used to distribute cigarettes at the Front – it was one of the things they did: solicit fags from home, then pass them on to the troops in the trenches. The best known exponent of this nicotine peddling was the Rev. Geoffrey Studdert Kennedy, otherwise known as 'Woodbine Willie'; but there were many others, including the Rev. Leighton Green, who in almost every letter from France to his home flock in Norfolk, either started or ended with a desperate plea, of which this (sent 7 May 1916) is typical:

> Dear People
> Since I last wrote another consignment of cigarettes and magazines has arrived from St Barnabas', and that consignment has also vanished. We now want some more cigarettes, please.[10]

It's no wonder, then, that Monty chose to dig into his own wares. In any case, no one thought there was much wrong with tobacco in those days – and if they had, what the hell was there to worry about when at any minute you might be atomised by the next shell? Smoking, for Monty as well as for most priests, must have allowed a chance to chat to the men: to share their experiences as best they could; to get and spread the news; and maybe, just occasionally, to share a thoughtful (and, who knows, possibly a spiritual) moment. For a shy man like Monty cigarettes were probably a godsend. He earnestly wanted to help and liked nothing better than to draw someone out with one of his 'chats'. Smoking also gave him something to do while engaged in interminable bouts of letter censoring, form filling and heel kicking.

In early October, the 2nd Division was out of the front line and in training. Monty, still very much the new boy, is 'wandering around' getting his bearings.

Tuesday, 10 October 1916
Fair night. Breakfast 9 a.m. Write to K and other letters till 12 p.m. Wander around. Lunch. Write Indian mail in Ox and Bucks Mess Club. Walk to Acheux. Tea with Harland and Verity in Church of England Supply Mess. Chat with SCF of Corps (Campbell). Walk back with Verity to Lealvillers. Stroll with Rowley. (Brigade has been out rehearsing Push.) Dinner. Smoke and censor letters. Bed 10 p.m.

Wednesday, 11 October 1916
Fair night. Breakfast 8 a.m. Ride out with Machine Gun Company to Divisional rehearsal. Stay with Galloway and watch proceedings. Fine sight. Walk back with Boyd (Presbyterian Chaplain of the Forces). Back 2.30. Walk to Acheux with Galloway. See 8 'Tanks'. Shop. Walk back after looking at Artillery Battery in Factory. Chat about Fate. He reads some of his poems to me. Good stuff. Distribute daily papers to Oxf & Bucks and chat. Dinner.

There's a rather weird sense that Monty is doing nothing more than sightseeing. The Division is practising for 'the Push' – the latest attempt to move the Germans a few sodden yards back towards the French frontier – but Monty is drifting about with a succession of fellow padres and officers (mainly), poking about in the Artillery Battery and peering at the newfangled tanks. This is not fair, I'm sure. And maybe soldiers like to see their padre there, looking on encouragingly.

Alarmingly, Monty is hanging about with yet another poet, Galloway – was every man on the Western Front engaged in churning out the stuff? – but we have no record of why his verse was so 'good'. To the modern reader, the idea that men within shell's reach of the front line might have been able to 'shop' is also bizarre, but there's Monty, wandering round Acheux and dropping into the boutiques. My grandfather loved spending money and was never trusted with it by his wife or family. When, after this war (and throughout the next one) they lived in Cottesmore, a tiny village in Rutland, they'd make occasional shopping trips to Leicester and Kathleen would have to count out an allowance before letting him loose. Whatever he had, he spent – or gave away.

> Thursday, 12 October 1916
> Breakfast at 8. Brigade Field Day. Walk over with Bourne (Chaplain of the Forces) to Chaplains' Meeting at Divisional Headquarters at Hédauville. Assigned our positions for coming Push. Mine at Beaussart at Walking Wounded Dressing Station. Bate orders horse and tells me to get a servant from 52$^{nd}$. Walk back. Lunch at 1.15. Watch Rugger with Moore (Senior Chaplain Forces) of Royal March Division. Tea with Dr McKenzie in 52$^{nd}$ Mess. Doctor is Anglo Indian (IMS) and knows the Singhs. Chat with Oxf and Bucks men in Bivouac. Cinema with Galloway (now changing his name to Oxenden). Jolly good show. Dinner at 8.15. Bed and read at 9 p.m.

Monty doesn't explain why Galloway, the poet, is changing his name to 'Oxenden'. It seems a strange thing to be doing in the middle of a war, but perhaps it was something that had always mattered to him and he wanted to get it done now, before the Push, just in case. He had probably only had his new name for about five minutes before someone came up with the nickname 'Oxo', which is what he was stuck with for the rest of his war. The officers all had nicknames: there was a Major 'Bingo'

Baines; Chevallier (the poet – or one of them) was 'Shoveller'; Fullbrook-Leggatt was 'Pullthrough'; and Monty, as we have seen, was 'Hedge Priest' and 'Godalming', not to mention 'Snowball'.

It can distance us from these brave men, can't it? The nicknames; the film at the cinema that was a 'jolly good show'; the public school romping and rugger. But they fought and struggled, were wounded and died all the same, and they faced horrifying things with a seriousness and humour that should wipe the smirk from our faces. Here, for one, is what happened to 'Bingo', who dedicated himself to getting as many people safely through the war as he could, who survived The Somme, Cambrai, Ancre and Ypres. He had stayed with the regiment after the war and in 1919 they were sent to Russia, to fight the Bolsheviks. James Neville went with him, and this is his letter home on 27 June:

> *At 3.30 the Regiment retired according to plan, and I found the rearguard with my platoon. The retirement was quiet uneventful, and we reached Canadian Village at 5.30am, where we found the wounded lying on stretchers. 'Bingo' was in frightful pain, because his wound was swelling and he could hardly bear the sway of the stretcher. Yet never did a word of complaint pass his lips. He bore it very bravely. He was wounded right up in front while explaining the situation to Northcote of 'C' Company. He set a wonderful example to us all in calmness under fire and patience in extreme pain. Try and imagine a journey of five miles over a rough road in an old drosky cart!*[11]

On 6 August, there is news of 'Bingo'.

> *We have just heard that 'Bingo' B has had to lose his leg. The doctors apparently, had to operate and sew up his arteries. They hoped the veins would keep the leg alive, which they failed to do. It's too sad for words. I can't bear to think of him maimed for life, for the sake of a bloody Bolo.*[12]

Back to The Somme, and the 'Push' seems to have become the 'Great Push'. Rehearsals continue. Or, as the official history puts it:

> *A short, strenuous period of training was before the Division, for it had been drawn out of the line in order to practise the attack, soon to be launched against the enemy's line north of Thiepval. There were, apparently, delays owing to the bad weather, but the 'attack north of the river Ancre could not be delayed much longer.*[13]

Friday, 13 October 1916
Rise at 7.20am. Breakfast 8.15am. March with Machine Gun Corps (with Sergeant Major Yeoman) to Divisional Scheme (Dress Rehearsal for Great Push). Sit with Oxenden and after with Stevens and Wharry and watch proceedings. March back at 3 p.m. Lunch. Read for half hour (Stevenson's Island Voyage). See Adjutant 52nd about a servant. Promises to get one. Discuss ownership of [of what?! Monty's infuriating handwriting is impenetrable, but at least he's now talking with Colonel Crosse] with Commanding Officer. Go round to see Staff Capt. See Brigade Major. Letter from K. Chat with Corporal Ward of Oxf & Bucks (from Acton, West London. Church of England Communicant. Came out beginning of August. Was at Potsdam, Willy Fort). Write in Hut.

One of the many slurs aimed at the Church of England padres by Graves and others is that they almost always came from the 'officer' class (indeed they were classed as officers and made good use of the Mess) and so they could never communicate happily with the vast bulk of the Army. This may have been true in some instances just as it must have been true that some Church of England chaplains arrived at the Front, twittering and bleating only to swoon and be sent home at their first sight of blood. But Michael Snape, who has written the definitive account of Military Chaplaincy, *The Royal Army Chaplains' Department: Clergy Under Fire*, is adamant that this is not the case:

*What is also implicit in . . . portrayals of Anglican chaplains is the suggestion that their social background proved a major handicap in relating to their men. While this argument was first developed by Alan Wilkinson in his book* The Church of England and the First World War *and has been duly echoed by Michael Moynihan and Richard Holmes, there is in fact little evidence to support it.*[14]

Of course, as Snape says, the bulk of the First World War chaplains were drawn from the middle and upper classes – it was no different from back home – but what made a successful padre was force of personality not working-class roots. And presumably a strong stomach.

Monty chatted with everyone. He wasn't fussed, he just embraced people's stories and looked for ways to join in. Luckily, there was always sport.

Saturday, 14 October 1916
Breakfast at 9 a.m. Spent morning in preparing for Sunday Parades and arranging services. Football for Machine Gun Corps v Company of 52nd in afternoon. Won 2–0. Played a very bad game myself. Met my new groom Finly (52nd) at 6.15 p.m. and went with him and Thompson to 52nd Quartermaster's Stores to take over Altar and Books etc. Went round to Brigade Headquarters re. Services, horse, etc. Bed at 9. Preparation.

It's easy to forget, I find – reading Monty's diary – quite why he is here. I don't mean that we can ever forget the war, for long – but we can forget the *religion*. Sunday arrives, though, and Monty's first service and sermon at the Front. He is up early in the drizzle:

Sunday, 15 October 1916
Got up at 6.40. Celebration in 52nd (Oxf and Bucks) Officers' Mess at 7.20 (7 officers and one private present). Breakfast 8.15. Drizzle. Parade Service for Oxf and Bucks HLI Machine

Gun Corps and TMC (600 men) at 9.45. 2 Hymns rather a failure. Spoke on 'Joy' rather feebly. Wandered round with Browne and Wilkins (CF). Lunch. Listened to Divisional Band in Billet and went round with Oxenden to put up notices of Evening Service and Holy Communion in 70 Billet at 6 p.m. Write to K. Tea in Mess. Moore SCF of RNVR Division dropped in. Went round with him to his Billet and chat. Service = 70. Taken by Browne and Wilkins. Nice address by Wilkins. Back to Mess. Read and dinner. Bed.

The first service of the day is attended by seven officers and one private: not a bad haul for a voluntary service, but perhaps it is telling, despite what Snape says, that the officers outnumber the men so disproportionately. Church Parade Services (unlike Holy Communion, evensong and so on) were compulsory, held on Sundays for every man who was out of the line, and there are 600 men present at this one to grind out a couple of hymns and hear Monty talk about 'Joy'. According to many writers, the Church Parade Services were deeply unpopular – the last thing the men wanted was to be dragged onto another parade, this time to sing hymns they didn't know and listen to a distant churchman they rarely saw hold forth about the love of Jesus. More often it wasn't God's love that was the subject of the address but the need for one last push, the hideousness of the Hun and the righteousness of the British cause.

Generals would often bully the padres into delivering bloodthirsty sermons. Major-General Sir William Thwaites said after the war that he used to get hold of the chaplain before the Sunday sermon and let him know that he 'would not have any texts from the New Testament'. Nothing namby-pamby about 'turning the other cheek' then, and presumably Commandment Number Five from the Old Testament was also banned: 'Thou Shalt not Kill'.

There were many chaplains and bishops who were happy to oblige and one of the most enthusiastic was the Bishop of London, Arthur Foley Winnington-Ingram. Dubbed 'God's Recruitment Officer' by a grateful nation, he was wildly patriotic, a great enthusiast for Empire and British rule, and no fan of the snarling automatons of Prussia. He was also, incidentally, a cockney from the East End. His sermons were insanely popular and while he wasn't always this clear about the need to slaughter Germans, he was never in doubt for long that that was what was needed. Here is what he preached in Westminster Abbey on the first Sunday in Advent, 1915:

> And first we see Belgium stabbed in the back and ravaged, then Poland, and then Serbia, and then the Armenian nation wiped out – five hundred thousand at a moderate estimate being actually killed; and then as a necessary consequence, to save the freedom of the world, to save Liberty's own self, to save the honour of women and the innocence of children, everything that is noblest in Europe, everyone that loves freedom and honour, everyone that puts principle above ease, and life itself beyond mere living, are banded in a great crusade – we cannot deny it – to kill Germans: to kill them, not for the sake of killing, but to save the world; to kill the good as well as the bad, to kill the young men as well as the old, to kill those who have shown kindness to our wounded as well as those fiends who crucified the Canadian sergeant, who superintended the Armenian massacres, who sank the Lusitania, and who turned the machine-guns on the civilians of Aerschott and Louvain – and to kill them lest the civilisation of the world should itself be killed.[15]

This is the kind of noise from home that Monty would have been hearing, and no doubt the kind of thing that many in the Army would have liked him to be trotting out. As far as I can tell (and I have read many of his sermons), my grandfather never felt the need to whip men up into a patriotic frenzy. Instead, he felt compassion and preached on 'Joy'. The complication is this: most writers these days seem to agree that the one place you'd be least likely to find simplistic, anti-German sentiment was the Western Front: the soldiers quite often saw their enemies as fellow sufferers and it was the old men and the women at home who were the baying bigots. Soldiers who went home on leave could be left bewildered by the talk of bayoneted Huns and kill-counts. Then again, many soldiers enjoyed killing Germans. Not just the likes of Julian Grenfell, who 'adored' the war and thought it was all the most 'wonderful fun' but also Monty's friend Neville, who always enjoyed taking a pot at the Boche.

> At 'stand-to' I potted at two Boches and missed them. I had another shot and they ran like hell. Now I have got a rifle grenade emplacement registered on the spot, and we will give them a salvo to-morrow if they show themselves. I think we have got the spot pretty well taped. It's most awfully good fun pooping off these grenades.[16]

I am sure that Neville is tailoring his letter for his (no doubt very anxious) audience, but he sure did love 'pooping off' those grenades, just for the sheer joy of it. But there are many occasions when he makes it clear he actually *likes* the Germans, as well as feeling sorry for them. There was also, we can be sure, a fair quotient of psychopaths in the Army – or those who were now happily in touch with their inner Ripper. Most men killed, of course, because they didn't want to be killed themselves; and because it was part of the plan and their training; and above all else because they didn't want to let down their mates. Many soldiers probably didn't kill anyone – or if they did, it was out of sight, not bayonet-close. Neville keeps loosing off bombs and bullets, although he also knew when to desist:

> I simply longed to have a shot at some of them to pay off a few scores, but it only meant that we should have been sniped or taken prisoner on our lone visits to the posts at night. I believe that if you were lost in this sector the Hun would lead you back to your own line.[17]

To go back to Bishop Winnington-Ingram, though, and his strong desire to see Germans killed, whether young, old or innocent, there were at the same time many other churchmen who did not share those views but who preached for tolerance and restraint and who did not want to see the British enter a spiral of reprisal and counter-reprisal that could only end in a bestial collapse of civilised behaviour. Randall Davidson, the Archbishop of Canterbury, argued incessantly, both privately with the King and the prime minister, but also publicly, against carrying out air raids against Germany, even though British children in British cities were being killed by German bombs. According to Alan Wilkinson (and this is rather surprising given his quoted rhetoric), Bishop Winnington-Ingram agreed with Davidson. Their principled stance was unpopular with their fellow clergy and even more so with the general public, who wanted to see Germany punished for its crimes.

If this sounds familiar from the war that followed so disastrously soon after this one, then we should remember that in the main the Allies did not bother denying themselves the pleasure (or requirement) of reprisals in the Second War. It's a widespread view – indeed, it can sometimes feel that it's the *only* view outside of some history books – that the First World War was a senseless waste of human life, a ghastly slaughter of innocence carried out by the in-bred ruling classes of Europe who should have just got together and sorted out the meaningless and negligible differences between them, whereas the Second World War was a noble fight against Fascism that united Britain and the world against the forces of evil. It wasn't like that at the time; it's not what Monty or the vast majority of the nation or its armed forces would have felt, and it's not even necessarily true. There were real differences between the French and British (and later the Americans), on the one hand, and the Central Powers under Germany, on the other. Ideas of individuality versus an all-powerful state, liberalism versus militarism, were just as deeply felt and hotly contested in 1916 as they were in 1942. Monty was no bloodthirsty warmonger, but he would have *known* that he was on the right side. To imagine that he – and the millions fighting on the same side – were innocent, unthinking lambs being slaughtered by a bunch of royals and arms manufacturers, seems to me to do them a profound disservice. They weren't that naive.

All that said, Winnington-Ingram's use of the word 'crusade' – his call for a Holy War – is something to come back to.

The vast bulk of the British Army was Anglican, either by persuasion or because that was the default option that you selected if you neither knew nor cared. Members of the Church of England accounted for about 70 per cent of the troops on the Western Front. We can assume that many of the men listening to the chaplain on a Church Parade Service would have been indifferent, bored or sometimes hostile, but there would have been many more who were actively engaged or possibly welcoming the diversion and thanking God they weren't up the line.

What particularly riled Siegfried Sassoon, in a description he gives of a Church Parade Service in *Sherston's Progress*, was the unctuous aggression of the Bishop's address. But he also acknowledges that most of the men seemed to enjoy it.

> On 7 July [1918] we were still awaiting the order to move up to the Line. It was a Sunday, and there was a church parade for the whole battalion. This was a special occasion, for we were addressed by a bishop in uniform, a fact which speaks for itself.
>
> In a spare notebook I wrote down the main points of his sermon, so I am able to transcribe what might otherwise appear to be inaccurately remembered.
>
> 'The bishop began by saying how very proud and very pleased he was to have the privilege of welcoming us to the Western Front on behalf of his branch of the service. Every heart, he said, had thrilled with pride when the news came that our Division had captured Jerusalem. The armies in France had been enthusiastic about it. He then gave us the following information, speaking with stimulating heartiness, as one having authority from a Higher Quarter.
>
> '(1) Owing to the Russian Revolution the Germans have got the initiative and are hammering us hard.
>
> '(2) The troops are more enthusiastic about winning the War

*than they were last year. Our lads feel that they'd rather die than see their own land treated like Belgium.*

*'(3) It is religion which keeps the morale of the British Army so high.*

*'(4) (With extreme unction.) Thank God we hold the seas!*

*'(5) The Americans are coming across in large numbers.*

*'(6) A distinguished general told me last week that the Huns are getting weaker every week. Time is on our side!*

*'He then preached a bit about the spiritual aspects and implications of the labours, dangers, and sufferings of which we were about to partake.*

*'Great was the sacrifice, but it was supremely glorious. He compared us to the early Christians who were burnt alive and thrown to the lions. 'You must not forget' he added, 'that Christ is not the effete figure in stained-glass windows but the Warrior Son of God who moves among the troops and urges them to yet further efforts of sacrifice.*

*'He concluded impressively by reciting, with lifted hand, two verses from the American hymn "God goes marching on". Except, perhaps, for the early Christian comparison, the troops rather liked it.'*[18]

Sassoon did not commit his thoughts on Church Parade Services to verse, but it will by now come as no surprise to hear that one of the men of the 52nd Ox and Bucks did – dated 28 May 1918, and written by C.E. Barnes, this could well be about Monty:

> *Tune: Little Brown Jug* [we will have just
> the first two and the last two verses . . .]

1. When I turn out on Church Parade,
My ignorance is soon displayed,
I don't know when to stand at ease,
It makes me shaky at the knees.
    Ha! Ha! Ha! Hee! Hee! Hee!
    We'll all be damned eternally.
2. Our sergeant-major dressed the line,

We got it very straight and fine,
But someone said 'You need not sweat
He hasn't even sized you yet'.
  Ha! Ha! Ha! Hee! Hee! Hee!
  I wish he would not shout at me.
5. They formed us in a hollow square,
To knock old Gerry out with prayer,
The padre fought the hosts of hell,
We thought he did it rather well.
  Ha! Ha! Ha! Hee! Hee! Hee!
  He held his side quite easily.
6. The regimental march was played,
We doubled down a leafy glade,
I never heard who finished first,
I ran until I nearly burst.
  Ha! Ha! Ha! Hee! Hee! Hee!
  A Church Parade's too much for me.

The sermon that Monty gave on Sunday, 15 October 1916, at Coigneux on the fringes of the Battle of the Somme, was on the hidden Glory of God:

The Gospel is 'Good Spell', tidings of great joy. The tidings are from another world, and they are about this world and its significance. The news is so good and reassuring that a new and entirely satisfying perspective is the result. Our eyes are opened to see the meaning of the shadows. The beauty of the picture with its light and shade is such that we can enjoy life. Even the shading has its part in the picture, although we cannot tell the full meaning of its artistry. But we know the 'good news' is precisely this, that the shadows will flee away in the clear shining which shall be in the undimmed light of God's presence. And even here when we are in the shadows of the passing clouds we may know that there, with the glory for a moment hidden from us, is the Son of Righteousness with healing in his wings.

Monty thought he spoke 'rather feebly' but the pressure must have been intense, with 600 men standing to attention in the congregation, all of them wilting (including Monty) under the baleful eyes of the sergeant-majors. He was not going to talk to the men about belting the Boche. He'd only been in France for a couple of weeks and anyway that would never be what he believed. But he does want to make the point that the only possible way to understand what is happening is to acknowledge that we humans cannot understand it. We need to have faith that God knows what he is doing. The clouds will pass and it will be revealed that the slaughter was not senseless.

Truly, it makes me feel sad, thinking of my grandfather giving that first, anxious sermon. Not just because I know how hard he must have found it, facing a large crowd of restless and coerced troops, projecting his voice over the wind and the rain; but more because that wafer-thin message of hope would surely never be enough to sustain him as he travelled ever deeper into the malignant darkness.

* * *

For the next few days of October, Monty gets himself settled, sorts out a servant, does some more shopping and enjoys himself with many more chats. The Push is looming, but it is not often mentioned in his diary . . .

On Monday, 16 October, as well as a brisk march to watch the divisional manoeuvres with Bingo, Monty settles down in a haystack with Oxenden to discuss reincarnation. To his amazement, he discovers that Oxo is a Roman Catholic and they exchange words as to whether it is right for Catholics to hold onto their churches in France and not let them be used by other denominations. This was a hot issue at the time: there were hundreds of thousands of Anglicans, Presbyterians, Methodists and others at large in northern France, but the Catholic hierarchy would not allow use of their (often bombed and shattered) churches by anyone else. There was plenty of resentment about this, and it is one reason why in 1917 Monty found himself digging out and opening a small chapel in the trenches. Also on Monday, Monty has an 'excellent bath' in Acheux. There are two letters from 'K' – but none of her letters has survived.

On Tuesday, Monty gets hold of a Chaplain's cart, which is nicknamed the 'Cathedral'. He is going to use this to trot round to his various congregations and hold services from the back of the cart. 'Quite a useful asset, needs a little patching,' he remarks; and then later: 'Cathedral makes brave show'.

Monty has secured himself a servant and a groom. The former is a man called Allan, aged 20, who lives in Slough. He was a motorbike mechanic before the war and then a servant for Lord Rothschild at Burnham. He lost a finger at Salonika. I suspect that Monty rather likes the idea that Lord Rothschild's servant is now his. The groom's name is Finly, a man with eight children who lives in Highgate. Monty inspects the officers' mess and the men's quarters, and decides he prefers the latter.

There then follow a couple of days of cafes, reading and strolling in the now incessant rain. The Café Continental appears to be his favourite. Monty inspects his 'Battle Post', which is at Beaussart. He is going to be caring for the 'walking wounded', if the Push ever turns to shove, and he makes arrangements for his stay there. In fact, by Friday Monty is feeling pretty saddle-sore (his horse, Mike, is apparently hard as nails), but he cannot spend any time worrying about that because there seems to be a rising certainty that an engagement is coming. At Evening Service in the village schoolroom, there are about 80 or 90 present to hear his address on 'Friendship' and 54 stay on for Holy Communion afterwards; perhaps the enthusiastic attendance (these are voluntary services) is a sign that men want to make their peace, or hedge their bets, before battle. 'Fellowship with others is the proof of fellowship with God,' Monty reminds his congregation. The squash in the Mess that night is immense.

The next day, Saturday, 21 October, is spent preparing for his Sunday parishional services and in posting messages in the billets to let his congregation know. He rides over to meet Kinsey, another padre, to arrange a Holy Communion in

Acheux, but when he gets back he finds out that all services are off, as the 2$^{nd}$ Ox and Bucks will be moving back to the Front at 8.45 a.m. the next day.

Sunday 22 October 1916
Breakfast 7.15am. Move off at 8.45. Walk up with a Corporal. Arrive after being held up on road by great movement of troops transport etc at Mailly Maillet at 12 p.m. Same billets as before. Arrange service at 6 p.m. in a Salle de Reunion. Over 100 present and 35 to Holy Communion. Various units present. Conference after dinner till 11 p.m. to discuss position of the Guns during coming 'push'. Bed. Heavy firing during night from our batteries around.

We are coming to it now – and Monty's service in the Salle de Reunion is packed with various units, just as the roads heading back to the front line are crammed with carts, lorries, men and machinery. The guns are not silenced on Sundays. They are never silent. Monty is doing what he can to make sure he can be with the men during the Push. The 2$^{nd}$ Division is moving forward, and everyone, even the padres, seems to be clogging the roads and crawling up the trenches, inching closer. Monty accompanies Oxenden to Headquarters' dugout. Can there really have been a 'Mount Joy Trench'? Monty would have felt very at home in it.

Monday, 23 October 1916
Breakfast 9.15am. Help tidy up Mess. Walk (part of the way with Marshall) to Beaussart Divisional Casualty Clearing station for walking wounded along track from Red House F.A. Very misty. Chat with R.A.M.C. Sergeant re. my being with them during Push. See several 'Tanks'. After lunch arrange for H.C. next morning at 12.30 with Salle de Reunion. Put up notices. After tea go up trenches with Oxenden. Get into Sixth Avenue via small railway track, stun shells bursting on the Sugaries road a hundred yards to our left. Feel a bit nervous! Go up to White City. A good

many stun shells coming over especially near Mount Joy Trench – some about 20 yards from us. Wait with Oxenden in Headquarters Dug Out for his instructions from CO of 2HLI and 24th RF for the night. Trenches crowded with men. Feel de trop. Eerie feeling creeping up pitch dark narrow trenches with shells screaming overhead and heavy explosions of guns. Go with him to his own Dug Out (20 ft down) where find Blair and 27th Company CO (Green) and one or two others. Have supper (steak cocoa and peaches) and chat. Leave at 8.30 p.m. with Hallows (17th RF). Reach Mailly via 6th Avenue at 10 p.m. A great deal of firing from our batteries. Relieved to get back to Billet. Bed.

It is dark and noisy, the trenches are crowded with men as the shells scream overhead, but there's something almost cosy about the way Monty and his friends tuck into their steak, cocoa and peaches, 20 feet underground and safe, they pray, from the stun shells. Monty, of course, leaves them to it and hurries back to his own billet and bed, leaving his friends to the uncertain night.

The next day, Monty does not go back up to the trenches, but has a Holy Communion to give in the Salle de Reunion (this time there are only nine present) and he has to bury Brigadier Rae (MTMB 11th Division) over at Auchonvillers Cemetery. There are no details of Rae, but Richard Holmes has reminded us that the British Army lost 58 generals in the First World War – a startling number given the popular view that no general ever came closer to danger than a badly aimed champagne cork. The weather, Monty tells us, is 'abominable'. Indeed it was, for this is how the last days of October are described in *The History of the Second Division*:

> *The weather at this period was wet, dull, cold, and misty, and the roads, trenches, and communications were in an appalling state. Day after day the attack [that's Monty's 'Great Push'] was postponed 'forty-eight' hours, until at the end of the month it seemed as if the elements would prevent the projected offensive.*

*Heavy rains caused many dug-outs to fall in, whilst the parapets of the trenches were continually tumbling down. Working parties were everywhere engaged in digging and revetting. To add to these difficulties, heavy hostile bombardments frequently blew in the parapets and smashed up communication trenches. Behind the front-line trenches many gun-pits in the artillery lines were deep in water.*

*In this way October passed.*[19]

Well, that's not quite true: for Monty, October was also passed having lunch with Browne in his hut at Bertrancourt and distributing papers. The end of Monty's Wednesday, 25 October is surreal:

Hot Bath. Dinner. German whist with Heppel. Shells coming over 200 yards away.

It must have been hard to relax in a hot bath with the shells exploding 200 yards away; then again, Monty did love his hot baths. The next day he meets the Assistant Chaplain General, Bishop Neville Talbot.

Thursday, 26 October 1916
Chaplain's meeting at Bertrancourt at 10. Assistant Chaplain General (Talbot) of Reserve Army present. Makes sensible observations. Discussion as to Battle Posts. Return for lunch in side car. Walk and lorry ride with Oxenden to Hédauville, Forceville and Acheux. Arrive back at 5.45. Tea. Write this up. Write K. Dinner. Bed.

Neville Talbot was the son of the Bishop of Winchester and had a brother who was also a chaplain at the Front. His other brother, Gilbert, the only non-clergyman in the family, had been killed in 1915. The most famous religious meeting house of the war, Toc H – or Talbot House – was named after him. Neville believed that the war was the shake-up that the hidebound Church of England needed ('the soldier has got religion, I am not sure that he has got Christianity,' he said) and was convinced that he and his fellow chaplains could galvanise the men at the Front and spark a religious revival. The only problem, he thought, was in all the accompanying baggage and detritus that obscured the true, joyous message:

> Men must dig in that strange field of Christianity through its odd and in part misleading, in part repellent surface: it is a mosaic of kill-joyism and Balaam's ass's ears, and Noah and Mothers' Meetings and Athanasian damns and the Archbishop of Canterbury with £15,000 a year – through to the treasure.[20]

Monty and Neville would have hit it off, I think – they both wanted their religion to galvanise and inspire people to behave in a better way and there is nothing punitive about their message. With the Great Push still pending, Monty has time to get his fluffy locks shorn but also pauses to enjoy the sight of German shells exploding on White City. He is still scuttling about, finding his way, ducking at the gunfire, but he is settling into his new home.

Friday, 27 October 1916
Write. Have my hair cut. Lunch early and go up with working party (MGC), Wharrie in charge, to White City. Have to wait in communications Trench whilst the Hun shells White City. Watch the big shells explode. Fine sight. Chat with the men. Look up 52nd Headquarters. Have tea there . . . Leave about 5.15 with Harley (Lewis Gun officer 52nd) and return via 5th Avenue and along top. They shell the trench soon after we get to the Windmill. Play bridge. Dinner. Bed.

Monty must have been getting very good at bridge, although this news startled his daughter – my aunt Biddy, an inveterate player – who thought he'd never played a hand in his life. I'm tempted to think that there were just too many bad memories, but that may not be so: maybe he simply found the game too damned infuriating. Padres were sometimes warned against hanging around the Mess too much, playing cards and joking with the other officers. They were meant to try and keep some dignity of office. As R.L. Barnes put it in his memoirs *A War-Time Chaplaincy*: 'the Englishman likes his parson to be somewhat of a merryman', but they soon lose their influence if they are too 'hail-fellow-well-met'. 'Little though that padre may know it,' he writes, 'the very men with whom he may seem on such excellent terms are inwardly disappointed with him. To them he is a man who is not truly trying to do his job.'[21] R.L. Barnes, I should point out, does come across as something of a prude.

And yet, as he says, the problem for all padres, and also it seems for Monty, was that they were expected to be on hand to entertain the fighting men: 'How often I have heard the colonel say, "Padre, I shall have finished my work soon; how about a rubber before we go to bed?"' If they weren't making up a four at bridge, then they were supposed to be fixing up the cinema, turning out on the hockey and football fields, handing out the papers, chatting in the Mess and, for all I know, mixing up the drinks. When you have a ready-made Master of Ceremonies on hand, it's easy to forget that their main role is a spiritual one.

Out of the blue, Monty finds himself having a nasty little run-in with an obnoxious sounding Chaplain to the Forces called Browne. This is the same Browne who had met Monty off the boat in Calais, but a much less friendly man this time.

> Saturday, 28 October 1916
> Spend morning going round arranging next day's services with Murray and Browne. The latter having found room in Brasserie (our billets) wants to keep it to himself. Very uncommunicative and difficult. Fix up something. Go round to the 52nd HLI. Spend afternoon putting up notices and chatting in billets. Write in evening. Cards. Bed.

It seems as though Browne has taken a liking to Monty's billet in the Brasserie and wants to appropriate it. Despite Browne being 'very uncommunicative and difficult', Monty somehow manages to fix things up. He was good at that – even if the next day Browne's behaviour is just as tiresome. Monty, a good Christian, lets Browne have his hissy fit and helps him run the service he is so keen to run. It is a Sunday, so the day is awash with services, not all of them well attended.

Sunday, 29 October 1916
Holy Communion at 7.15. One Middlesex man. No one at 8 a.m. About 80 at Morning Prayers (joint service with Murray, Middlesex). Murray speaks. 19 at Holy Communion following. No one at Browne's service at 10.30. Two officers at 11 a.m. Holy Communion. Prepare Collett (52nd Private) for Baptism. Lunch. Go and see Browne re. Baptism. Find he intends to run the 6 p.m. service entirely by himself in spite of fact that he has only half a battalion in place and I have three units. Feel pretty exasperated with him. Stroll up with Oxenden to Mailly Station. Tea 4.30. Baptise Collett at 5.15 in Browne's room. Attend 6 p.m. service and help arrange room and candles. Room crowded . . . Assist Browne in administration after to which 60 stay . . . Dinner. Read. Bed.

Monty had only one person at his 7.15 a.m. service and then no one at 8 a.m. He would have proceeded anyway; God must be served and on the eve of what could turn out to be a major battle, Monty would have wanted to be available. Still, at least there was no one at Browne's service either . . .

Monday, 30 October 1916
Poured all day. Slacked in Mess with Crosse and played Bridge. Went for a stroll after tea with Boyd to Beaussart station. Glorious sunset and evening.

More bridge with the colonel. R.L. Barnes would not have approved.

Tuesday, 31 October 1916
Finley comes over to say that he is sick and for hospital. Go

round to 52$^{nd}$ and arrange for another Groom. Drive back in 'Cathedral' – which sways like nothing on earth – to Bertrancourt and have lunch with 5$^{th}$ FA. Ride over to Louvencourt to BEF Canteen with Blair and Heppel. Arrive back about 6 p.m. via Acheux.

At the beginning of October, Monty heard the guns for the first time; by the end of the same month, the intensifying roar of the artillery has become such a familiar sound that he does not even bother mentioning it. What he does notice, though, is a glorious sunset, heralding better weather. And with that would come the long-delayed Push on Beaumont Hamel and beyond – or at least, that was the theory.

# SIX

## 'O Jesus make it stop!'[22]

November arrives: sick, sodden, beaten and betrayed. The better weather was an illusion. The Push is delayed again and again and again. The 2nd Division has been out of the line for six weeks and the strain is showing. Many of the men would rather be fighting; others pray for the rain to last until there is no longer any chance for the generals to launch one last deranged 'bite and hold'. Except that the rain is hell. Even *The History of the Second Division*, so keen to show that the fighting spirit of the men was high, makes it clear that the 'condition of the trenches was truly appalling' and in the front line:

> *The water in places was waist-deep, the average depth knee-deep. The ground about the trenches was pock-marked with shell-holes full of water and inches deep in mud; the constant traffic up and down the communication trenches had turned the latter into quagmires. Reliefs took hours to accomplish and sometimes had to be completed in daylight, progress to and from the front lines being painfully slow.*[23]

Yes, 'quagmires'. Reliefs had to be carried out by daylight, despite the obvious risk of sniper's bullet and shellfire, because men had an even deeper fear: that of losing their way in the dark, of straying from the duckboards and slipping into the swamp, never to be seen again. We hear of men, gripped and bound by the mud, beyond rescue, begging their mates to shoot them rather than be sucked into an agonising, lung-clogging suffocation. The rain was incessant; the trenches were collapsing; the mud enveloped everything.

There's a game people play, the 'time-machine game', when they have to choose the time in human history when they'd have most liked to have lived. Typical answers include the Golden Age of Athens, pre-Columbian America, Florence in the Renaissance, even the Weimar Berlin of *Cabaret*. Flowerings of innocence and civilisation and fun. Well, if you flipped that game, and had to choose the very worst, the most hellish time in history in which you would be forced to live, then tying for first place, I think, is July to November 1916 in north-western France and Flanders. God knows, there are countless other contenders, but let's not play that game.

Innocence died on The Somme, they say – and this is not just because the sheltered sons of Edwardian Britain were mutilated, gassed and butchered in their hundreds of thousands; it's because whole nations were traumatised by the experience. Not just the British and French soldiers, of course, but the Germans too; and not just them, but the men, women and children at home who were sharing this horror more closely than I had ever realised. Letters may have been censored; most soldiers may not have found themselves able to talk about what they had seen (and done); but the news leaked into the public domain regardless. It didn't *just* leak, though. There were graphic films about The Somme at the time; there were the anti-war poems, of course, although readerships were tiny; but most of all there were the numberless letters and telegrams of condolence and regret being sent out to the devastated families of Britain, France, Germany, Austria and Belgium. And, shuffling behind them, there were the wounded and the maimed, dragging and groping their way home. No one could ever say that they did not know what was going on. The screams of anguish and despair must have been deafening. We can hear them still.

In the face of the delays and the rain, Monty's diary keeping is losing its impetus. Sure, he is still trotting around, chatting with all and sundry. He seems to be becoming friends with Colonel Crosse, after that shaky start. But the entries are getting shorter and his daily activities are becoming repetitive. He, like everyone else on that stretch of the Front, is waiting for something to happen.

Wednesday, 1 November 1916
Am inoculated in morning by Dr McTurk, Medical Officer of 52nd, against 'flu. Interview Willcox my new groom. Distribute papers to 52nd after lunch, having arranged for piano for Thursday and Friday evening concerts in Brewery for 11th Division Trench Mortar Battery. Watch 'C' Company 52nd Sports with Crosse. 'Row' in Officers' Seven in 'boat race'. A good second! Shells come over – one within 80 yards. Tea and chat with Crosse. Dinner with 52nd (with Wharrie) with Captain Hill. Discuss arrangements for Concert.

Like almost every other Church of England chaplain, Monty finds himself organising a concert, horsing around with the officers and watching the sports. They could almost be at some kind of holiday camp, except that the shells continue to tumble around them.

Thursday, 2 November 1916
Ride over in pouring rain to Chaplains' meeting at Division Headqurters at Bertrancourt. Discussion re. admittance of Non Communicants to Holy Communion. Ride back with Holden to Mailly via his Battery. Horse drreadfully [sic] slow. See Crosse who promises to change animal for me. Rain. Walk with Marshall past Mailly wood. See 12 inch shells burst by Beaussart. Concert in Brewery from 6–8. Not bad. Great squash. Dinner. Cards. Bed.

Friday, 3 November 1916
Route march with A section round Englebelmer. Nap in afternoon. Distribute daily papers to HLI. Tea. Cards. Look

in at Concert. Crowded. Go round to chat with Osbourne. Dinner. Cards. Write. Bed.

Saturday, 4 November 1916
Spent morning arranging Sunday services and posting info notices. Distributed papers to Machine Gun Corps and HLI after lunch. Walk with Osbourne past Mailly Wood. Tea. Concert by 52nd in Brewery. Dinner. Preparation. Bed [Monty has crossed this last word out for some reason].

The days are rolling into one another and it is Sunday again. There is just one person attending Monty's Holy Communion (is it the same solitary attendee as last time, I wonder?), but the Morning Prayers has 150 in the room to hear Monty talk on 'Sincerity'.

Sunday, 5 November 1916
Rise 6.40. Holy Communion in Brewery at 7.30 (1). Voluntary Morning Prayers, 10.30 St John reading service. Talk on 'Sincerity' (150). H.C. following (20). (Piano) lunch. Walk with Oxenden past Mailly Wood. Back by Engelbelmer. Service at 6 p.m. St John gives address – about 100. Holy Communion (29). Dinner. Bed.

A lightweight talk on 'Sincerity' would not have pleased either Haig or most of the other generals – and most certainly not the commanding officer of one South African battalion, who Michael Snape quotes one soldier as remembering:

*Today the Padre preached to us on the text Love your enemies, do well to them that do spitefully use you. Afterwards the Colonel gave us a little heart-to-heart talk on the desirability of remembering that we had bayonets on our rifles and using them accordingly. No encouragement to take prisoners unless they can be of value for information. Dead men tell no tales and eat no rations, etc. ad nauseam. The Church cannot be allowed too much rope lest we lose the war![24]*

Monty keeps on walking the area. Now he even seems to be joining in on a route march with the company.

> Monday, 6 November 1916
> Write letters. Route march with Company and walk with Oxenden to Courcelles and Colincamps – home. Parcel of 'goodies' from K. Tea. Bridge. Perform collect for confirmation. Dinner. Bed early.

Every day looks like being the beginning of The Push. On Tuesday, three officers go up the trenches early, with as Monty puts it in his diary, 'five gins' – we should probably assume that this is five 'guns' and that the 2nd Ox and Bucks hasn't hit the bottle. And still it rains.

> Tuesday, 7 November 1916
> Oxenden, Heppell and Blair go up the trenches with five gins [guns?] early. Hot bath at 10.30. Allen ill. Write letters. Lunch. Slack. Go round to billets of 52nd. Chat. Very wet day. Tea. Write. Censor letters. Cards. Dinner. Letters.

The next day, Monty makes a trip up the trenches himself.

> Wednesday, 8 November 1916
> Allen goes sick and is taken to hospital. Take on role. Up trenches with Todd starting at 8 a.m. Go round gun positions and dug outs. Trenches knee deep in liquid and water and sticky clay. Get absolutely wet through up to my waist. Get a good view of German lines – Beaumont Hamel – Thiepval in distance – Serre. Watch bursting shells go into our Front Line. Trenches everywhere breaking down. Main German trenches 150 yards away. Men very cheerful in spite of appalling conditions. Get back at 12.45. Hot bath. Lunch. Rubber. Go round into 'B' Billets and to see Collett. Tea with 52nd. Bridge. Censor letters. Dinner. Write.

As Monty observes, the trenches everywhere are breaking down.

The rain has done its work and the German shells are finishing the job. Men would have been frantically trying to shore them up, but it is cold, wet, desperate work. Remarkably, the German trenches are only 150 yards away; close enough for an easy sniper's bullet but, as Neville pointed out, in this sector you'd be more likely to be led gently back to your own line. This can't have been entirely true – the raiding parties from both sides, intended to bring in prisoners and spread unease, never slacked for long – but it's probable that by this stage there was very little activity other than shelling. More interesting, though, is Monty's comment: 'Men very cheerful in spite of appalling conditions.' Was Monty deluded? Were the men cranking out a smile for the new padre? Is this an example of our assumptions about the war, even about one of its most horrifying periods, being distorted by a later, anti-war culture? Perhaps the presence of the padre made the front-line troops feel better. The fact remains that, despite the rain, mud and constant danger, the men were finding reasons to be cheerful. Or so it seemed to Monty.

The next couple of days are for Monty strangely idyllic – he 'walks home for tea' in glorious weather. German planes are being shelled in the distance. He confirms two new men into the Church of England – and it is only yet another burial and the removal of Allen, a chaplain, with 'partial paralysis' that strikes a note of disquiet. By Saturday, the weather is worsening again, and 'Z' Day (the day of the Push) is up in the air once more. The rumour is that 'Z' Day will be on the nineteenth – but that just goes to show you can't trust an Army rumour, because on Sunday, 12 November the men of the 2nd Ox and Bucks start to move forward in preparation for the long-delayed assault. Relief must have mingled with fear.

The last day before the battle is a Sunday, so there is time for a sermon from Monty at Morning Prayers. His theme, incredibly, is 'He Cometh for You'. Is this really the kind of sinister news that men want to hear before heading up the line towards possible death? Monty struggled with his sermons all his life – they never came easily – so perhaps it just happened to be the one he had prepared. Then again, he would have believed it – it had been ladled into him by his dear auntie from the earliest age and it was core to his Christian belief: get ready for death and make your peace with God, because He will come for you at any time. And if you're about to go over the top in the last days of the Battle of the Somme, then this time it's more likely than most.

Fortified by this news, the men would have headed for the Front; those that didn't may have returned later in the day for Evening Prayers, at which they would have been treated to a sermon from Monty on 'God's Great Love' – more appropriate, for sure, although let's hope there weren't any South African colonels in the congregation. In any case, no one was probably listening too closely because at some point in the service Monty seems to have managed to set himself on fire.

Thursday, 9 November 1916
Chaplains' meeting at Bertrancourt. Watch Hun planes being shelled on my way along Beaussart Road. Senior Chaplain to the Forces Campbell at meeting. Go round after to 6th FA re. Allen, who was removed the day before with partial paralysis. Am inoculated for 'flu [again?!]. Glorious weather. Lunch at 6th FA mess. Walk with Boyd. Bus. Tea at Transport Billet with Brett and Quartermaster. Interview Clarke and Morris for Confirmation. Home. Dinner. Bed.

Friday, 10 November 1916
Arrange about services with Murray. Glorious day. Bury Lieutenant K Parsloe at Commercial City [Cemetery]. Go over to Bertrancourt after lunch and take Morris and Clarke in (first class). Walk home to tea. Bridge. Dinner. Write and Bridge. Bed.

Saturday, 11 November 1916
Get up horribly late. Arrange services with Murray. Everything uncertain because of Z day. Hear Z day is to be on Nov 19th. Walk over after lunch with Boyd and Mole to Beaussart to walking wounded station to make arrangements. Back to

tea. Horrible Scotch mist on. Arrange services with 52nd. Dinner. Bed.

Sunday, 12 November 1916
Holy Communion in loft at Brasserie 8 a.m. Nine present. 11.15 a.m. Morning Prayers, 80 or 90 ('He cometh for you'). Holy Communion 20 present. Spend afternoon writing. Also see Collett before he goes up the line. Evening Prayers 6 p.m. Over 100 present. Very impressive last service before going up to the Attack. My surplice catches alight but is put out by Anderson of the Trench Mortars before any great damage done. Speak on God's great love. Holy Communion about 40 present. Dinner – from officers left (Todd, Bell, Wright and Oxenden). Play Bridge to relieve the strain. Oxenden goes up. Todd goes up. Make up mattresses in front of the fire with Bell and Wright. Doze. Lindsay of 99th MGC looks in at 2 a.m. and stays for a chat before going up. Everything ominously quiet. Leave at 4 a.m. for Beaussart. Get a lift in Motor Lorrie. Heavy mist.

We will come back to the Battle – there is no avoiding it – but it is remarkable how humour and horror intermingled so intimately on the Western Front. Perhaps it's true of every war, but it's not something we've been taught to expect from the First World War. The accepted story is of a war of unrelenting misery and pain, of slaughtered innocence, of zero romance, and it's an easy narrative to fall into if you've soaked up Sassoon and Owen and Paul Nash, all writing and painting from the front line, all of them desperate to convey the truth to a public that needed to be told and to understand that war, and most especially *this* war, is not glamorous, or chivalrous, or even justifiable. Because:

> If in some smothering dreams you too could pace
> Behind the wagon that we flung him in,
> And watch the white eyes writhing in his face,
> His hanging face, like a devil's sick of sin;
> If you could hear, at every jolt, the blood

Come gargling from the froth-corrupted lungs,
Obscene as cancer, bitter as the cud
Of vile, incurable sores on innocent tongues, –
My friend, you would not tell with such high zest
To children ardent for some desperate glory,
The old Lie: Dulce et decorum est
Pro patria mori.[25]

Yes, that is the story that we have learned from the First World War. Or we wish we had. But also, on the eve of battle, we have a padre accidentally setting his surplice on fire and being rescued by 'Anderson of the Trench Mortars'. How the men must have loved that moment. I bet they roared with laughter. Wild practical jokes, rough and tumble, a parson looking ridiculous (even better if it's a senior officer) – these things lit up their days and relieved the tedium and strain. The rougher and wilder the better. Here's James Neville writing to his father in early 1917, at a time when the British Army was readying itself for another year of push and struggle.

> I have very little news for you. We are having great fun here. A chap called Horley re-joined on the 5th, whose brother was at Norfolk House with me, and is now in the Navy. He is a great lad, full of 'quips and cranks and wanton wiles' as Milton has it. One of his tricks is to crawl under the table and light the bottom of the newspaper when Shoveller is reading it!
>
> Yesterday we played a trick on the Doctor, McTurk, who was standing in front of the fire holding forth at great length. 'Shiny' Horley got hold of a Verey light cartridge which we cut open outside the mess. We then extracted the magnesium and powder, and I put the empty cartridge in my pocket. Unaware of a plot, the Doctor was still gassing when we returned. 'Shiny' took cover behind the folding doors which divide the long mess room and which were half open, while I walked up to the fire which was practically out and, quite nonchalantly, dropped the cartridge into it and made for safety behind the doors!
>
> There was a loud explosion and clouds of embers and the grate

*were blown into the room and McTurk was enveloped in dust. For*
*a second he was almost invisible. Then, roaring like a bull and*
*spitting fury, he took up a book and hurled it at me just before I*
*could reach cover. It was a good shot and caught me on the left*
*ear with the point of the cover!*

*Meanwhile, 'Shiny's' face was just visible round the corner of*
*the folding doors, wreathed in smiles. It was damned funny to see*
*the Doctor. He took it jolly well, and it also had the desired effect*
*of stopping him gassing! But though 'Shiny' was the instigator*
*and I merely the perpetrator, the Doctor went for me and left*
*'Shiny' alone, and the latter did not even come to my help in the*
*ensuing rough house!*

*I had no idea there was such force in the ordinary cap of a*
*Verey light. The grate was not irreparably damaged. It was*
*already broken before we blew it out, and it functioned all right*
*afterwards.*[26]

They loved a 'rough house'. On Christmas Day 1917, they even
planned one in the Officers' Mess: after plum pudding and rum
punch, not to mention chicken pulled from its carcass by
Colonel Crosse (he used no knife because he was 'not a married
man'), they pushed back the trestles and tables, blew out the
few remaining candles and wrestled and romped with each
other. They were young men, even their colonel, and Monty
too. There are many references in Pullthrough's letters to my
grandfather of 'buttings' and 'chastisements', and there's James
Neville's apology to Monty for being 'a fiendish tease', so I think
Monty must have been on the receiving end of many of the
jokes and probably much of the teasing and wrestling. In a letter
to the 'Hedge Priest' written in 1970, 'Pullthrough' says:

As this letter has struck a reminiscent note, I am enclosing
a copy of some lines I wrote in 1917. You may never have
seen them. They were written when the Regiment was out
of the line and resting at Marles les Mines. You were with
it, at least, for a part of this time because it was there that
you were sitting in the Mess and suddenly found that the

Overseas Daily Mail, which you were reading, was ablaze in your hands.

It must have been a favourite trick – setting fire to someone's newspaper as they sat quietly, trying to read. Someone should revive the practice. And who would have thought that the cap of a Verey light would have blown out the grate of the fire and almost disembowelled the doctor? Being the Medical Officer, or the Chaplain to the Forces, didn't spare you from the pranks and high jinks. It probably just made you a more tempting target. Monty wouldn't have minded – in fact, he would have relished the set-to. But did it diminish his ability to perform his duties as a chaplain? As we've seen, some members of the Church certainly thought so, but I'm not so sure. I think what mattered to most men at the Front was that their padre was physically and spiritually brave. They wanted them to share the dangers, and they wanted them to embody a resonant, unflinching faith. If at the same time their padre showed that he had a sense of humour, then so much the better. Monty was reading H.G. Wells's *Mr Britling Sees it Through* in November 1916, as were many of the men at the Front, and it is revealing about how the 'English' saw themselves in their struggle against the Germans:

> One remarkable aspect of the English attitude towards the war was the disposition to treat it as a monstrous joke. It is a disposition traceable in a vast proportion of the British literature of the time. In spite of violence, cruelty, injustice, and the vast destruction and still vaster dangers of the struggle, that disposition held. The English mind flatly refused to see anything magnificent or terrible in the German attack, or to regard the German Emperor or the Crown Prince as anything more than figures of fun. From first to last their conception of the enemy was an overstrenuous, foolish man, red with effort, with protruding eyes and a forced frightfulness of demeanour. That he might be tremendously lethal did not in the least obscure the fact that he was essentially ridiculous. And if as the war went on the joke grew grimmer, still

*it remained a joke. The German might make a desert of the world; that could not alter the British conviction that he was making a fool of himself.*[27]

On the night of Sunday, 12 November the officers are making their way up to the front line 'one by one'. It is ominously quiet and there is a heavy mist. Ever since 10 November the British artillery had been subjecting the German lines, communication trenches and wire to an 'intense bombardment', starting at 5 a.m., reaching a peak of violence at 6 a.m. and finishing at 6.15 a.m. for an hour, when the 'usual daily programme' would resume. The idea was to keep the Germans in a state of profound anxiety and guessing as to when the actual assault would start. The objective of the battle, scaled back massively since Haig's earlier, optimistic days, was to advance to 'the Yellow line' (the Frankfort and Munich trenches), taking the 'Violet' and 'Green' lines along the way, but only pressing on to the 'Blue' and 'Brown' lines if progress and the weather were good. The Germans had spent the past few weeks reinforcing this sector, in expectation of just such an attack.

In plain English, the infantry were to advance a few hundred yards across the French countryside and occupy or overrun the heavily defended German trenches that lay in the way. The 5th Infantry Brigade, incorporating the 2nd Ox and Bucks Light Infantry, was on the right. Two small villages, Serre to the north and Beaucourt-sur-Ancre to the south, represented the end points of the 'Yellow' line – the road that linked them was the objective.

The heavy shelling on the 11th had drawn a 'vigorous' response from the Germans. British shells, falling 'in torrents' onto Serre, had reduced it to flames. As night fell on Sunday, the 12th (round about the time that Monty was setting fire to himself), 'zero-hour' was agreed and, as *The History of the Second Division* puts it, this was news which 'gave the troops the greatest satisfaction'. Tanks were drawn up in readiness and there does seem (despite the bitter experience of the past four months) to have been an unlikely surge of optimism. As they waited through the long night in their front-line trenches (the trenches, in case we forget, that were often waist-deep in water), men were served 'hot coffee and cocoa and something to eat'. There had been weeks of meticulous planning leading up to this moment. The 2nd Ox and Bucks Light Infantry was to move up in support of the 24th Royal Fusiliers, who were to be first over the top.

*The History of the Second Division* details what each man was carrying; as I understand it, this weighty load was significantly lighter than the crushing burden that men had carried into the firing zone on 1 July 1916. Some lessons had been learned:

> *Each man of the attacking parties carried 150 rounds of small-arms ammunition, 2 Mills bombs, and 2 sandbags; one iron ration, one day's rations, besides the unexpended portion of his daily ration. His haversack, covered by a piece of red material to facilitate aeroplane observation, was carried on his back . . . About twenty men of each company carried picks and shovels for consolidation purposes.*[28]

The men, then, were well provisioned and prepared. And yet:

> *Patrol reports up to the evening of the 11th had reported No Man's Land in a frightful condition – the mud was inches thick, and made reconnaissance difficult; the constant shelling to which the enemy's front lines had been subjected had ploughed up the ground in and about his trenches, and gaping shell holes and mine craters full of water were everywhere, making the crossing hazardous.*[29]

At 5 a.m. on the morning of the 13th, an artillery bombardment was launched, to reassure the Germans that it was business as usual. A thick autumnal fog cloaked everything and visibility in no-man's-land was down to about 30 yards, which made setting off in the right direction, not to mention maintaining that direction, almost impossible. Officers were told to use compasses, but this was found to be harder under fire than it had been on the practice fields.

The 6th Infantry Brigade, to the left of the 5th, ran into immediate difficulties. The first wave of attackers, the South Staffords, clung too close to the advancing British artillery bombardment, and many were pulverised by their own guns. The majority of the attackers reached the first German trench, though, without too many casualties, and took it. But the fog was making coherent movement almost impossible, and units to the left and right were blundering into each other. Much of the wire remained uncut and impassable, and the British artillery (its effects unable to be seen in the murk) swept onwards ahead of the infantry, giving the Germans time to emerge and set up their machine guns.

The ground ahead:

> had been ploughed up into a fine soil, forming a deep sticky mass into which the men sank, in places up to their waists . . . a galling machine-gun fire was opened by the enemy, who, when the barrage had passed over his position, came up out of his dug-outs, quickly manned his trenches, and from the direction of Serre poured a storm of bullets onto the wire, which he knew to be uncut and holding up the advance of his adversaries.[30]

Along with the machine guns came the heavy artillery, 'causing many casualties'. Mud clogged the men's rifles, making them useless. They fitted bayonets, threw their two bombs into the fog, and clung to the mud in the withering fire. We're told that one subaltern – yes, just one man – made it through to the objective; he flung his bombs, was wounded and crawled back through the wire. The surviving men of the South Staffords fell back to the old British front line, as did the vast bulk of the 6th Infantry Brigade (those that could still move), with just one group of the 13th Essex (about 50 men), who had been attacking to the right of the South Staffords, occupying and holding their halfway objective, the Green Line.

Things went much better for the 5th Brigade, at least at first, with the 24th Royal Fusiliers advancing 20 yards behind the British barrage but not actually *in* it. The wire was demolished.

Germans emerging from their dugouts were captured or killed. The Highland Light Infantry had similar success. The 2nd Ox and Bucks advanced behind the Fusiliers, and the first four lines of German trenches were rolled up and occupied. It was still only 7.15 a.m., but the Highland Light Infantry reported that 'all appears to be going well', and by 9.30 a.m. 430 German prisoners had been passed back 'to the cages'.

With the fog still hanging heavy, though, an attempt to reach the Yellow Line became hopelessly muddled. Once again, the Germans appear to have had time to recover, and 'as the attack progressed . . . artillery fire became intense, and with machine-gun fire, snipers, and bombing parties, the enemy was able to inflict heavy losses on the devoted troops of the 5th Infantry Brigade'.[31] Incredibly, by 11 a.m., only five hours after 'zero-hour', the Highland Light Infantry, who had said that all was going so well, had lost 50 per cent of 'other ranks' and fifteen out of their twenty officers.

The rest of the day was spent consolidating whatever ground had been captured. This is how Monty saw it, initially four miles from the front line, doing what he could for the wounded as they trickled, then flooded, into Casualty Clearing.

Monday, 13 November 1916
Find tent ready at Beaussart and everyone asleep. Shave. Lie down and wait for Barrage of artillery to open. Intense bombardment opens at 5.41. Great noise in spite of heavy blanket of mist and whole earth shakes. Hear that 1700 guns in action on narrow front. About four miles behind Front Line by Railhead. Wait for wounded to come. Breakfast with Croft, Roberts and [illegible] (RAMC) at 6.30. Wounded arrive in twos and threes at 7.30. Soon begin to stream in. Mostly slight wounds. But some very shaken and many shell shocks and burned cases. Bring good news from 5th Brigade front and Beaumont Hamel taken by Highland Division. A good many 52nd and Highland Light Infantry and several Machine Gun Corps. Busy myself getting them comfy whilst they wait to see Medical Officers. Give them cigs etc. Very

busy. Snatch a sandwich for lunch. Order of procedure – on arrival wounded sit in two waiting tents for their turn to be examined by MOs. They then receive a label 'A' or 'R' (Acheux is for the Base and Blighty or 'R' slightest wounds for Rest Camp). Are given a good meal, hot tea and sandwiches etc in Tent and are passed onto 'A' and 'R' tents to await Horse and Motor Ambulances to carry them down. In afternoon see Tanks which had gone up in the morning return without having taken part in the Attack. They are immediately ordered out again. Attend to several wounded officers who come in. Fog still heavy and mud terrible. Hear bombardment had made German trenches unrecognisable. At 5.30 p.m. conduct party of five men along Railway track (broad gauge) to Red House (Advanced Dressing Station) Mailly. Reach Red House at 6.15. Report to Major Robertson C.O. 5th FA. Mean to stay in Barn there and to conduct parties in shifts during night. Go to Officers' Mess where find Father Stewart Duthrie and three MOs. Begin to shell us and Railway. One at corner of house so retire into cellar. See Capt Hill (52nd) wounded slightly in foot by one of our bayonets, also Sergeant Bexford (52nd). Wait till a lull in shelling and then Duthrie and I make back along Railway. Just in time as they begin shelling it again. Arrive Beaussart W station at 8.45. Things have slackened there. Chat with Dr Cassidy who has come from 100 FA to help and now shares my tent. Make myself some supper. Duthrie shares it and leaves for Beaussart for the night. Bed and good all-night sleep.

Here is the strange, contradictory world of a chaplain at the Front. Monty wouldn't have had any medical training, and yet he is at the dressing station, dealing with a 'stream' of wounded men. Some of them are badly burned; there are many 'shell shocks'. Monty dispenses the longed-for 'Blighty' tickets, the blessed label that would get a wounded soldier sent home, and not just to 'Rest Camp' and another dose of fighting. He goes in the dark up the railway track to see if he can help bring more wounded men out but has to retire to the cellar under fire. He, unlike most of the men, is then able to get back to his base and make himself supper. He sleeps well.

If we wanted an apt image of the first day's fighting, then poor Captain Hill, wounded in the foot by a British bayonet, seems grimly appropriate.

The next day the 5th Infantry Brigade was to make another attempt to reach the Yellow Line. The attacking battalions formed up in the captured Green Line, but once again heavy fog deadened and obscured everything. Indeed, many units, moving up overnight, failed to reach the Green Line in time:

> Deep mud, shell-holes mostly full of water, tangled wire, blown-in German trenches waist-deep in holding mud, all tended to loss of direction and touch. The result was something near chaos.[32]

The compasses were once again redundant – although on this occasion they found out (surely they'd known before?) that steel helmets and rifles made them unreliable. Those units that had made it to the Green Line in time moved forwards, but it was mayhem in the fog. Swept by enemy sniper fire, devastated by their own artillery, it is a miracle of tenacity and heroism that some men managed to hold onto small sections of the enemy trenches. Again, losses were running at up to about 50 per cent. By the end of 14 November, the 2nd Division was in control of the old German front line, but impetus had been lost. It sounds much like what had been happening ever since the British Army stepped out so innocently and so bravely on 1 July 1916: much, apparently, had been learned, but so much was still, disastrously, the same.

Monty is still tending casualties, but he is getting the news nonetheless.

Tuesday, 14 November 1916
Repetition of Monday morning only slacker. Learn from 6th Brigade people that they have been held up on our left and a good number captured. In consequence we had to withdraw from yellow line to green line again. 3rd Division

on left also held up. Also 99th Brigade men coming in after having gone through the 6th Brigade to try and make good – not a success. Witness in afternoon a most wonderful bombardment. The flashes and thunder of the guns an unforgettable experience. Old French farmer who is digging turnips is almost in the midst of the batteries, quite unconcerned. Watch the Ak enemy shrapnel bursting right along Mailly Sucrerie Road and in belt of trees behind Sucrerie where our own batteries are. A good many heavy crumps also. Aeroplanes up and many Hun sausage balloons. Chat with Blair. Hear that Grey is missing. Watch all this just by Tanks depot and by Railway line. Tank stuck. Give Tank Officer some tea. Spend evening with Highland Division Ambulance next door as our Ambulance is closed down for night. Chat with Corporal Rolland, D Company, slightly wounded. Bed.

Wednesday, 15 November 1916
Still slacker in morning. Bedfords and 11th Warwicks (37 Div) who had gone over us to take yellow line come in. Gibbs C of E Chaplain to Bedfords comes through wounded in thigh and finger. Wounded whilst reading Burial Service over officer in shell hole right up in Front – two bullets going through his book. Look after him. Comes from Lambeth parish. Cheery soul. Blair comes to say that MGC is being relieved at night. Go over Tanks with Tank officer. One Tank stuck here for 12 hours. Hear without surprise that nine had been stuck up at the Front. Mud fearful and Tank officers fed up at having been sent in to such conditions.

Arrange to go up with Blair to meet MGC at night. Fairly slack day. Ride up with Blair at 7.30 after having despatched my things to Bertrancourt billet. Meet Bell by Windmill, hear that Company has done awfully well especially Oxenden, that losses have not been great, but that Grey is badly wounded in head and was lying out some hours before found. Ride back to Bertrancourt after making enquiries at Red House about Grey. Find we are quartered in same camp with 24th Royal Fusiliers opposite pond at B. Cold and frosty weather. Have dinner. Go round to men who have returned with Bell and give them cigs, news. Bed.

On the 15th, the Division made another attempt to straighten its front line by pushing forward. They tried to use tanks, but they sunk in the mud – as Monty says, this was not popular with the tank crews. Monty also meets a padre who has been wounded while reading burial services at the Front – two bullets passing through his Bible. Perhaps this made Monty wonder whether he should have been closer to the action himself, but there's no sign of it yet.

Over the next two days, the 2nd Division is relieved at the Front by the 32nd Division and will be slowly filtered back for rest and training. They have fought tenaciously. The men who Monty meets seem proud of what they have done. And yet, as *The History of the Second Division* makes clear: 'The Division's losses from 13th to 16th November (inclusive) were, in killed, wounded, and missing – officers 129, other ranks 2,767. The Division captured 11 officers and approximately 1,000 other ranks, during the five days' fighting.'[33]

I've tried to work out how many yards the division advanced over those five days. Was it 500 yards? They reached the Yellow Line, briefly, but ended up falling back to the Green Line. They did, it is true, capture that. All talk of a further advance to the Blue and Brown Lines dissolved in the fog. The Germans were pushed back, inflicting heavy losses – but receiving them, too. They made no attempt to counter-attack.

Things are winding down and a post-mortem is starting. Monty is doing his best to find Grey, a badly wounded officer; in the end, he writes to Grey's fiancée.

Thursday, 16 November 1916
From 2–4 a.m. officers and men return, Oxenden first and Marshall last. Congratulations and then sleep. Rise at 8.30am. Breakfast. Hear all news. Go round sections – 24th distributing cigs and papers, after having gone round to

Senior Chaplain to the Forces to ask him to enquire about Grey. Walk in afternoon with Oxenden and he relates his share in battle – a pretty hot one. 5th Brigade and Highland Division done well but a good deal of their work nullified by failure of 6th Brigade and 3rd Division. Meet Collett. Ride over after tea with Heppel to Corps Operating Station to see if Grey is there. Staffed by Australians. Glorious ride. Frosty. Find Grey is not there but telephone through to Puchevillers and hear that he was put on Danger list night before and had just been moved down to Base. Get back at 9.30. Write to Grey's Fiancee and his former Guardian. Bed.

Friday, 17 November 1916
Go round about 100 52nd who have returned with 24th Royal Fusiliers 52nd and 17 Royal Fusiliers. Go round with Collett to Senior Chaplain to the Forces and find Division have moved. Play football in afternoon with MGC. Shoot two goals. Many aeroplanes up. Frosty. Have tea with Trench Mortar Battery. Many wounded. Go round with Boyd to Highland Light Infantry who have also done very well. Return to Mess. Dinner. Bridge. Bed.

It's easy to say, but perhaps Monty is feeling left out of the action. His role, to boost morale and offer cigarettes and chats, is necessarily a frustrating one. He is a cheerleader on the sidelines for the troops who have 'done very well'. The only shooting Monty does is on a football pitch. But still . . . he visits hundreds of men, spreading warmth and condolence. He never stops chatting. His concern is palpable.

It is strange and distressing, I find, to read of a full-scale divisional attack (and there were other similar battles going on to the north and south of the 2nd Division at the same time, as Haig pushed once again for that elusive breakthrough). It starts with trepidation and hope; the men are launched at their objectives; they founder in the fog, the mud and the enemy fire; many, horribly, are gunned down by their own side; there are humbling instances of heroism and bloody-minded determination; and then, somehow, it drifts into inconclusive anti-climax. The final objectives are not captured, but some of the earlier stages are; the men dig in to consolidate what they have gained; the Germans rain shells on them; and the 2nd Division, after five days, with enormous casualties, is shuffled out of the line to regroup. Monty, at the back, but gauging the mood accurately, picks up the exhilaration and pride, as well as the disappointment.

Saturday, 18 November 1916
Rain and Mud. Write letters in morning to Britten's fiancée and sister (Britten mess waiter killed in action Nov 13th) and to Lieutenant Carter's (C section) mother (died of wounds Nov 14th). Pouring in afternoon. Bridge. Go round to 52nd and have tea in Mess – they came out in morning. Capt Rowson killed – immediately died of wounds etc. About 14 officer casualties and about 300 men. Hear moving at 10 a.m. next morning. Return to Mess. Dinner. Bridge. Write to K. Bed.

After the fog and then two days of glorious weather, the rain and mud have returned. The regiment is counting the cost of the battle and it is grim: 14 officers and 300 men, says Monty. The chaplain's job, a horrible one, is to write to the mothers, sisters, fiancées and fathers of the dead and dying. There's nothing in his diary about what he feels about the battle. Once, before we found everything he had packed away, just about the only thing we knew about my grandfather's war was that he went to serve as a chaplain, but he lost his faith in God. There's nothing about that here, though – not yet. It is only the rain and the mud and wounds and death – and bed. Monty, after a long silence, writes to his wife.

# SEVEN

# 'In the morning and freshness of day'

Monty and Kathleen were married at St Margaret's Church, Westminster on Wednesday, 28 May 1913. No photographs survive of the event. Monty's father had stayed in India with his alarming second wife, but it's safe to assume that Auntie was there, along with Monty's three sisters and his friends from school, Cambridge and the Church. These included Cecil Champion, who had recently married Monty's sister Eva, his great friend 'Tummy' and of course Walter Bigger, school and university friend and brother to the bride.

Kathleen's younger brothers were there too – Bill, Jack and Edgar Bigger – along with her parents and a slew of relatives and well-wishers. The sole bridesmaid was her great friend Ruth Underwood. The society pages of 14 June edition of *Lady's Pictorial*, as well as carrying much excitable and fulsome news about the doings of the likes of the Dowager Countess of Ancaster and Mr Nigel Legge-Bourke, carried portraits of the couple and this simple announcement:

> GUILFORD-BIGGER
> On the 28th ult., at the Church of St. Margaret's, Westminster, by the Right Rev the Lord Bishop of Ely, assisted by the Rev M Linton Smith, MA, and the Rev HFS Adams, MA, the Rev E Montmorency Guilford, son of the Rev E Guilford, of Punjab, India, to Miss Kathleen A Bigger, daughter of Dr and Mrs Bigger, 'Aberfoyle',

*Streatham Common. The wedding cake was supplied by Messrs. Buszard, Oxford Street, W.*

There's no clue as to who was my grandfather's best man. It could have been Cecil Champion, Monty's friend from Cambridge and now also his brother-in-law, who cuts a dash in many of Monty's photos from this time and had accompanied him on a rather wet walking tour to Switzerland two years earlier. Then again, it might have been 'Tummy', later 'Uncle Tummy' to Monty and Kathleen's adoring children, another great Cambridge friend who had also been ordained recently into the Church of England. Clearly 'Tummy' wasn't his real name – it was Thomas Cleworth – and he seems inappropriately slim in the one photo I have of him, taken outside Monty and Kathleen's first home in Blundellsands on the outskirts of Liverpool. He and Monty are standing in their vicar's dog collars and dark suits, smiling at the camera, as is Kathleen, also in a dark suit and slightly stooping underneath the most enormous hat; next to Kathleen is Ruth Underwood, the bridesmaid, in cream, looking away. Tummy remembered the day in a letter to Kathleen written in 1924, consoling her because something terrible had happened to Ruth, and lamenting the fact that his and Ruth's flourishing friendship never developed into something more, but 'what an appalling Parsonic prig I was becoming – and what a dreadful hat you wore'.

Tummy was a priest when war broke out in 1914 and like Monty he became a chaplain and was thrown with no preparation into the Western Front. And there, like Monty, his faith buckled and shattered – although unlike Monty he never found a way back. The loss of faith can't have been that unusual, but perhaps most priests found it easier to stay inside the Church after the war rather than face even more uncertainty from outside its comforting structure. 'The War to End All Wars' left more than just the dead and the maimed; not even those who survived it were left unchanged – for Tummy it ripped away his faith in God and left him battling depression (or as he called it, 'cynicism') for the rest of his life. He was a sweet, kind man, much loved, who my aunt remembers tried his hand as a chicken farmer, and then a fur farmer, and then perhaps in any number of other occupations. He drifted. While Monty, as we know, when he arrived in France in 1916 was 'waging a war of his own against something he [also] called Cynicism'.

But enough of that. We need to get back to the May morning of Monty and Kathleen's wedding. Hymns included 'O God, Our Help in Ages Past', 'Lead Us, Heavenly Father, Lead Us' and 'O Perfect Love, All Human Thought Transcending'. They left the church to the sound of Mendelssohn's 'Wedding March' and proceeded to their reception at the Westminster Palace Hotel and what would seem to most of us in these lily-livered days a life-threatening feast of soups, lobster cutlets, salmon, turkeys, hams, lamb, ducklings, rhubarb tart, raspberry cream, strawberries, ices and, God help them, Messrs Buszard's cake.

Two days later, on 29 May 1913, one of the guests had recovered sufficiently to be able to write to a member of the Biggers' Irish contingent, many of whom had presumably missed the wedding.

Dearest Sessie,

The event is over! and all passed off so well. The day was perfect, the church which of course is a very fine one, was prettily decorated with palms and flowers, and there were people in all the centre pews to the very back, and a large number [illegible] although the wedding party did not I suppose number more than about 50. Kathleen made an ideal bride. She looked perfectly sweet – so elegant and graceful and yet so simple and natural. Her dress suited her beautifully. I felt I should like everyone to see her, and that everyone was missing something who did not. Ruth Underwood was her only bridesmaid, and as charmingly dressed, a flowered chiffon, a pale lavender shade, crinoline hat to match with large soft satin bow hanging, a bouquet of sweet peas to match. It was most uncommon and dainty and she looked her best. The reception was at the Westminster Palace Hotel. The room there too was prettily decorated – the bride and bridegroom went off at 4 o' clock. She looked very stylish in her plain coat and skirt (something between grey and a fawn, a brown hat with two very handsome feathers). They drove back to Aberfoyle, and there she changed again for something suitable for [illegible].

Once the final costume-change was over, Monty and Kathleen left for their honeymoon at the Two Bridges Hotel in Exmoor – and married life.

I never met my grandmother, Kathleen. There's a picture of her sitting in bed, cradling my older brother, Toby, as a baby, but she died before I was born. She didn't leave a great number of letters or diaries and what she did leave is very matter-of-fact. My mother didn't talk about her too often. I don't know why, except it's possible that even 30 years after her death she found it too hard to contemplate her absence. Or maybe we didn't ask.

What I do know is that she and Monty had that rare thing, a wonderful resilient marriage, and that throughout their lives people would turn to them for warmth and strength. Of course they had their fair share of tribulations, but their marriage was strong and it was filled with laughter and nonsense. It didn't even falter when 'The Old Hag' (Edward Senior's second wife, now renamed – by Monty? – and the object of considerable fascination to her terrified step-grandchildren) returned with her husband from India in the 1930s to live in the same small Rutland village. When the older woman wasn't crushing passers-by under the wheels of her primitive electric wheelchair, she was busy spreading rumours that Monty and Kathleen's marriage was on the rocks. My aunt remembers – and the whole village must have heard – her mother yelling at the old woman to leave her house and never to return. The most extraordinary thing about this thrilling occasion was that Kathleen was shouting. Kathleen never shouted; in fact, she was generally a calm, quiet person. She was often tested, though. Years later, when she and Monty moved to Dorset, their new neighbours were amazed to see the recently retired vicar charging through his new house, hooting with laughter and locking all the doors, while his elderly wife shrieked round the outside, trying to get in before she was locked out.

Kathleen was brought up in a household that encouraged this kind of behaviour. The Biggers were Irish Protestants, and her father, William Grimshaw Bigger, had come to London to study and practise medicine, following in a family tradition. He had married Emily Philadelphia Whittard at St Matthew's Church, Brixton, on Wednesday, 16 June 1886. Their breakfast feast, a proper Victorian one and none of this lightweight Edwardian nonsense, had included quails, tongues, capons, ham, lobster any which way, a Perigord Pie, lamb, and *seven* kinds of cake *followed by* dessert. William, though, had cunningly married into a family of tea merchants, so perhaps he just sat there drinking cupfuls of the stuff to keep his liver and brain clear. Five children had followed in fairly quick time. Kathleen, the oldest, was born in 1887, followed by four boys: Walter (who would become Monty's great friend) in 1888, William (or Bill) in 1890, Jack in 1893 and little Edgar in 1899.

Kathleen then was an older sister in a household of boys. They lived in Streatham, a pleasant and green Victorian suburb in the south-west of London, first of all in Queens Park Gardens, near the common and then, presumably as William's practice flourished, in a big red-brick house called 'Aberfoyle' which they'd named after a family home back in Ireland. Not much survives from these days (not even the house) but there are many photos, some formal and staged of mysterious and handsomely bearded Biggers, but also dozens of the family having *fun* – in the gardens of Aberfoyle mostly, but also on holiday in Donegal and Cornwall. We shouldn't read too much into photos, of course, but Kathleen's father's whimsical good humour seems to bubble up through the sepia, while her mother just looks so amused – by him and everything around her. Dogs tumble over the picnics and gangs of young lads sprawl on the seaside rocks. Kathleen giggles with her friends and hugs her brothers. Whole families grin and clutch at one another, looking carefree and unflustered. An air of hilarity hovers over every scene. At some undated point my youthful grandfather begins to appear in some of the photos. He is, there's no denying it, looking handsome – and rather pleased about the turn of events. As we leaf through the albums, more Guilfords appear in the frames, mingling with the Biggers: Auntie's there, and Eva and Edie, and even by 1912 the energetic, older Edward Guilford, bounding over from India for a fleeting visit.

It is mostly photos that survive from those days, but the joy bursts from them. There's also a lovely little letter, written by Kathleen onto the outline of her own hand, which she must have traced and cut out and then posted to her mother from Ireland. Judging by the size of the hand, Kathleen might have been about ten – perhaps her mother was at home in Streatham, nursing another of those boys. The tiny handwriting wends its way around the fingertips before landing in the palm of the hand:

> My dear Mother, Perhaps you will think this is a rather funny one, I do. We have been making Miss Phelp dinner on the shore. We get some red stones and break them into a kind of powder, then we are going to put some sand and water and then I hope Miss Phelp will eat it. I have written to Uncle Walter and told him that I can ride. You would have to scold Miss Phelp if you were here. She has bought us a bucket and some chocolate. Give my love to everybody. With love from K.A.B.

And then, on the back of the hand:

> PS I have just got a letter from Mrs Dashwood. She wants us to go over on Friday and she will meet us at the pier, if fine we are to go. I am going to write a postcard to tell her what time we are going. PS Has your heart cracked yet, dear motherie? I hope you will be able to read this letter!

Did Miss Phelp survive her seaside dinner? We don't know, but the Biggers had a lifelong love of practical jokes and jollity, and they passed it down through the generations. My wonderful cousin, Betty Baskett, the daughter of Kathleen's brother Bill, gave us a flavour of it when I found her sniggering under a bed playing hide and seek with my young children. She was well into her 80s.

They also spent a lot of time in Ireland either on holiday or staying with and visiting relatives. Kathleen's brother Bill ended up living there, once he'd left Palestine, as did brother Walter, after a lengthy stint in Surrey. In 1910, Kathleen made a motor tour of England, Wales and Ireland with her mother (for at least part of the journey) and an unspecified number of others – although we do know from this entry in her diary that she was joined on 23 June by Walter:

*Walter came to us at Waterford, and we packed into the motor, rather a tight squeeze with three inside, and started. It was an unfortunate day all through. Thirteen miles from Dungarvon the car gently stopped, the petrol had run out. We paused for meditation as to what to do, and then Bernard went back a little way to a tiny village we had just passed to make enquiries. By great good luck he actually found a small shop there where they sold it. So we filled up and drove on. Just before Dungarvon we found that one of the tyres was flat and it had to have a new inner tube put in. We had lunch at Dungarvon and drove on some way and then discovered that the tyre was flat again. The wheel then had to be changed. Shortly after this it began to rain and continued to do so steadily for the rest of our drive. Cork looked awful in the rain and some of the country roads we positively had to paddle through, they were so greasy and flooded. We had some difficulty in finding Blarney, as there were a great many different roads and no sign posts, and everyone we asked always said, 'On straight'. We arrived at St Ann's Hill about six.*

It was a happy life, I think, those pre-war days, especially if you were lucky enough to own a 'motor' and just about the most alarming thing that could happen was a deflated inner tube. Kathleen enjoyed herself with her friends and family, although she could thank her lucky stars that her feckless husband-to-be wasn't on hand to pour water into the petrol tank. And surely she'd heard that there are no straight roads in Ireland?

There was also music in Aberfoyle. My grandmother played the piano and tried in later years, painfully, to teach her daughter Biddy the violin. They had concerts every Christmas, organised and performed by the children. In 1901, you could have heard Miss and Masters Bigger sing 'The Three Pigs' or recite 'No Joke to be a Baby', while Mrs and Miss Bigger performed the duet 'Christmas Chimes', Masters W.K., J.A.W. and C.E. Bigger sung 'Creep Mouse' and the patriarch of the house, Mr W.G. Bigger, recited his 'Contradictory Proverbs'. (Question: 'What authorises you to have 16 wives? Answer: The Prayer Book – For [four] better, for worse; for richer, for poorer.') Ah, the days before television.

Monty left Cambridge University in 1911 and must have made up his mind fairly soon that he wanted to marry Kathleen. Perhaps it was long before – he wrote that postcard to her from his school in 1907, signing off with his 'heaps of etceteras'. Then again, there's the reference in Queens' College's *The Dial* magazine saying that he's 'not yet in love'. Also in that year he sent this postcard to his sister Eva from Switzerland:

> Eva, How I hate you! Where is my card or not re. the train next Saturday, O most perfidious of sisters?! It is terrifically hot here and we are rather dreading the journey back. I'm so glad that you and Screwes had such a good time together. You will be interested to hear that I am not yet in love out here. Best love, Monty

I'm not so sure about his protestations about 'not being in love'. Maybe his sisters teased him because he was always falling in love. It's clear enough that Monty was bowled over by Kathleen – he probably was from the moment he met her, thanks to that lucky friendship with her brother Walter. The very last entry in Kathleen's 'Book of Devotional Quotations', which she must have kept and filled in from a fairly young age, which has 102 entries mostly concerned with God and duty, is this poem in Monty's handwriting:

> How wonderful, Dear, the prospect bright
> How sweetly the Vision calls
> For youth is ours, and Love's keen sight
> And God to break our falls.

\* \* \*

All but one of Kathleen's brothers went on to become doctors, presumably much to the delight of their father, William Grimshaw Bigger. Walter, the eldest, who had made such great friends with Monty at school and Cambridge, qualified in 1913, one year before the outbreak of war. He went on to serve in the Royal Navy in the First World War and then worked as a GP in Surrey, before heading, with some relief, to Donegal. Apparently he delivered Julie Andrews into this world while he was working in Walton-on-Thames; almost as pressingly, in 1957 he stood in for Monty in order to 'give my mother away' at her wedding. Monty and Kathleen were in New Zealand and my parents were in a hurry.

William, two years younger, qualified as a doctor in 1915 and by 1917 he was in Palestine with the British Forces, tending to the wounded as the battle to drive back the Ottoman Empire ebbed and flowed. My aunt Biddy remembers him well, although he was usually referred to as 'Mad Uncle Bill' by her and my mother, who adored him but thought he was quite wild. He stayed and worked as a doctor in Palestine after the war and brought up his children there; he loved the Palestinians, and we all thrilled to the story of the bullet hole through the radiator of his car, put there during some roadside ambush – the next day someone brought him a horse by way of an apology for mistakenly ambushing their beloved doctor.

Edgar, too, qualified as a doctor, in 1926. He was much younger than the other children and for some reason features very little in the photos or tales that have been passed down. Perhaps he was too young, and I'm afraid he was rather ignored.

Jack, though – or John Alfred Whittard Bigger, to give him his full name – it is clear that everyone loved Jack. In a family of pranksters and sportsmen, Jack stands out. He has the loveliest, gentlest smile. There are pictures of him flourishing a cricket bat like a young Jack Hobbs (although he should probably work on pushing out that left elbow a bit further). Unlike his brothers (and of course his sister), he wasn't training to be a doctor; instead, aged 20, he is described as a 'Woollen Merchant' working for Messrs Standen and Co in Jermyn Street. And when, on 4 August 1914, Great Britain declared war on Germany, the very next day Jack must have been just about first through the door, enlisting in the Territorial Army. He was one of the thousands of young men buoyed up by patriotism, romance, good fellowship and the knowledge of the righteousness of their cause (not to mention a bellyful of beer), who poured in their thousands into the recruiting offices in those first days and weeks. He was twenty-one years and eight months old – and sadly we shall have to come back later to what Jack did in the war.

Kathleen grew up surrounded by boisterous boys, games and stupid jokes, but also a profound sense of purpose. None of the Biggers went on to serve in the Church, but their religion was important to them. Kathleen would, I think, have been proud to marry a priest; and she and her brothers had a sense of perspective as well as fun. This becomes clear enough when we stumble across Bill in the pages of Siegfried Sassoon's diary, 'grubbing roots' in the hills of Palestine:

*March 26 1918*
*The Medical Officer (Captain Bigger), late of Emmanuel College, Cambridge. Lean, grimy and brown – goes out grubbing roots on the hills – knows every bird a hundred yards off – rather like a bird himself – different species to the other officers anyhow. The sort of man who used to cruise about on rivers and canals and remote streams, looking at the by-ways of English counties and studying wild life. Eyes like brown pools in a Scotch burn – scrubby moustache – foul pipe – voice somehow suggests brown water flowing. Knows tenderness for dumb and piping*

*creatures. O, the coarse stupidity of some of the others. Minds like the front page of the Daily Mirror. Cairo; cocktails; warshop; etc. Suffocating boredom of the forced intimacy of living with them. They see nothing clearly. Minds clogged with mental deadness.*[34]

It's warming – no, it's moving – to think of Siegfried Sassoon roaming the thyme-scented hills of Palestine with my great-uncle Bill, looking for birds. Sassoon had arrived in Palestine in early March, reeling and traumatised from his time in France: a minor celebrity for his very public denunciation of the war ('I believe that the War is being deliberately prolonged by those who have the power to end it'); confused from his experiences at Craiglockhart Mental Hospital (where he had been sent by his friends and the authorities, who seemed to agree that it would be safer to have his sanity examined rather than the truth of what he was saying); and in the end determined to get back to France to fight, to be with his comrades-in-arms, rather than do any more thinking. Instead he was sent to Palestine. He was bitter, angry and empty, but he found himself in the soothing company of Bill Bigger.

> *The Battalion Doctor has made all the difference to me lately (mentally) . . . Am learning about birds from him. Went out yesterday and was shown Critchmar's Bunting, Nubian Shrike, Syrian Jay, Lesser Whitethroat, Redstart, Arabian Wheatear, Goldfinch, and Blackcap. Also a Kestrel and some Egyptian Vultures. Can't think what I should do without the Doctor!*[35]

Sassoon wrote his poem, 'In Palestine', on 30 March 1918, and it evokes an oasis of peace in a troubled time:

IN PALESTINE
On the thyme-scented hills
In the morning and freshness of day
I heard the voices of rills
Quietly going their way.

Warm from the west was the breeze;
There were wandering bees in the clover;
Grey were the olive-trees;
And a flight of finches went over.

On the rock-strewn hills I heard
The anger of guns that shook
Echoes along the glen.
In my heart was the song of a bird,
And the sorrowless tale of the brook,
And scorn for the deeds of men.[36]

Three weeks later, Sassoon notes the departure of Bill Bigger in his diary:

*19 April 1918*
*The little doctor, WK Bigger, goes away to join the 10th Division, who are staying in Palestine. I shall miss him and his bird-lore much; also his cheery, whimsical companionship.*

The Biggers spread humour and good sense, that much is clear. Monty loved Kathleen, and I'm sure he was also thrilled with his new family. Given that his mother was long dead and his father continued to bestride India, this was probably no small consideration. There's no doubt he adored Auntie and his sisters, but from May 1913 he had also found himself two extra parents and a full deck of brothers.

Monty and Kathleen's first home was at 14A Bridge Road, Blundellsands, Liverpool, in which diocese Monty was working as a priest. Their first visitor was Ruth Underwood and third through the door was Jack Bigger, swiftly followed by his parents, who stayed for a week. It must have been quite a squeeze: a postcard of Bridge Road shows it's a wide, handsome street, with tall 'modern' houses, newly planted trees and a long parade of shops; Monty and Kathleen lived above one of them in what an estate agent would now call a well-appointed maisonette.

Monty had become a deacon in March 1912 (the bottom

rung of the priesthood), and there's a mightily impressive scroll to prove it:

> *By the Tenor of these Presents We Francis James BY DIVINE PERMISSION Bishop of Liverpool, DO MAKE IT KNOWN UNTO ALL MEN THAT ON Sunday THE Twentyfourth DAY OF March IN THE YEAR OF OUR LORD ONE THOUSAND NINE HUNDRED AND Twelve AND OF OUR Consecration THE Twelfth We, SOLEMNLY ADMINISTERING HOLY ORDERS UNDER THE PROTECTION OF THE ALMIGHTY IN the Parish Church of St Nicholas Blundellsands within our Diocese and Jurisdiction DID ADMIT OUR BELOVED IN CHRIST Edward Montmorency Guilford BA of Queens' College and Ridley Hall Cambridge (OF WHOSE VIRTUOUS AND PIOUS LIFE, CONVERSATION AND COMPETENT LEARNING AND KNOWLEDGE IN THE HOLY SCRIPTURES, WE WERE WELL ASSURED) INTO THE HOLY ORDER OF Deacons, ACCORDING TO THE MANNER AND FORM PRESCRIBED AND USED IN THE CHURCH OF ENGLAND, AND HIM THE SAID Edward Montmorency Guilford DID THEN AND THERE RIGHTLY AND CANONICALLY ORDAIN Deacon, HE HAVING PREVIOUSLY, IN OUR PRESENCE, MADE AND SUBSCRIBED THE DECLARATION OF ASSENT, AND TAKEN AND SUBSCRIBED THE OATH OF ALLEGIANCE AS SEVERALLY APPOINTED BY THE LAWS OF THIS REALM AND THE CANONS OF THE CHURCH OF ENGLAND. Given UNDER OUR HAND AND EPISCOPAL SEAL THE DAY AND YEAR ABOVE WRITTEN.*

There's a very handsome red imprint at the bottom of the scroll from Francis James, Bishop of Liverpool, to seal the deal. A further, equally portentous scroll informs Monty that as the Bishop is satisfied as to the soundness of his Doctrine and the integrity of his Morals, he'll be paying him the sum of £140 per annum in four quarterly equal portions.

One year later, and just two weeks before his marriage, Monty was promoted to the priesthood. There's no mention of any extra cash in the elaborate phrasing, but I'm happy to say that the Bishop remained convinced that Monty's conversation was 'virtuous' and his life 'pious'.

Monty, then, was training for a life of priesthood. There's no sign that he wants to go and join his evangelising father in India (quite the reverse, if anything), but he is clearly dedicated to the life and progressing as planned up the ecclesiastical ladder. It may interest those who don't know about these things to hear that budding priests are tested on their sermon-giving skills, along with their theological knowledge. Monty's sermons had struck the right chord with the examiners, or so says one of his father's friends in a letter to the elder Rev. Guilford in May 1913:

> He [Grey, the examiner] told me, what I think I must pass on to you, for you will rejoice in earnest thanksgiving, that your son's sermons, which in his capacity of Examining Chaplain Grey had seen, were some of the best he had seen in the many that had come to him during his time. He said they were well worked out, instructive, 'with a particularly helpful and striking application'. I was very glad to hear this, and pass it on to you, as a matter of earnest congratulation, in a promising Clerical son. Why not try and get him out as a Chaplain, if not a Missionary?

Monty's father was keeping an eye on his son from far-off Tarn Taran and harboured hopes that he might join him. Events in Europe would have made that unlikely, even if it was what Monty wanted. I don't think it was, although Monty hadn't yet summoned up the courage to tell his father. Another letter, written to Guilford Senior by Monty's vicar, M. Linton Smith from Blundellsands in January 1913, gives a better indication of the direction in which young Monty is heading:

> Your son is a very great comfort and help in the parish; personally no one could be pleasanter and more ready to help in every way and to learn what must be largely new

work; he is very careful and conscientious and places a far lower value upon his services than I do. He will make a very good preacher, his main fault at present being a certain want of life and variety in his delivery; but that will mend with confidence, and his matter and language are extremely good; he is winning the confidence and affections of the poor, always a good test, and is generally liked by the congregation. His best work, however is done among the young men, who are opening their hearts to him in the frankest fashion: I have learnt more about the real outlook of the place on life during the last 6 months that your son has been here than during any previous period of my ministry in the place; and though the revelations have been somewhat saddening, they are nonetheless valuable for that, which proves their frankness. I am sure that he ought to do good work, especially among students, for his sympathy draws out confidences; in this way he reminds me of no one so much as Dr Chavasse; and much as we shall regret his departure for India, I am sure that on those lines there must be very great openings for him there. He lacks as yet the knowledge and experience needed to meet some of the difficulties raised, but the great gift of drawing confidences is there, and experience will come with time . . .

Monty's lifelong ability to draw out confidences, especially from the young, or otherwise neglected, is already in evidence, even it seems making him the bearer of bad news to the vicar (who is also under the impression that Monty will be heading to India at some point soon). Incidentally, the Dr Chavasse who is mentioned is Francis James Chavasse, Bishop of Liverpool and signatory of the document that ushered Monty into the priesthood. Chavasse was one of the few bishops making an effort to improve the training of priests at this time, having set up a small theological college next to the palace, in 1900. Monty would have spent time there, but he was also it seems attending classes in 'Psychology, Logic, Ethics, Hygiene, History and the Theory of Education' at the University of Liverpool, where he was impressing his teachers with his liberal mind, his good humour and his tact. If any of his various mentors or tutors had a bad word to say about Monty (like, for example, the postcard from Cecil Champion to Auntie that said Monty would have written but he'd decided to 'sleep on until lunch') then I haven't found it.

Monty's training was typical of a Church of England priest at the turn of the twentieth century. He was well schooled in theology, ethics and logic. Good to hear about the 'Hygiene' too. He had also had a fair amount of practical work in the Liverpool parish where he was posted – perhaps more than many. And no doubt he would have been adequately prepared for a life in the peacetime church. But on 4 August 1914 any chance of that disappeared. Monty carried on with his training to the end of the year, as war hysteria grew, and on 11 May 1915 he took a commission in the British Army as a Chaplain to the Forces. He was one of the earlier chaplains to join up – although there were also a number of church ordinands who took another route and chose to bear arms and fight.

Once he had his commission, Monty was posted to Woolwich, and was attached to the 30th Division. In September 1915, he is sending a postcard from Salisbury Plain to Kathleen:

> Arrived here at 5.30 p.m. this morning, after a very comfy night [always the sleep!]. Have just been nosing around and have found a furnished house in this street (one and a half miles from camp) which is going for a fortnight. I am seeing about it tomorrow morning, and will either write or wire you. We would share with another officer and wife. It is a jolly little village and the Camp is quite nice. Heaps of love, Monty.

Kathleen trailed after Monty, from Camp to temporary home, to barracks, seeing him when she could. But it was complicated. Their daughter, Ruth Compigne (named after their friend Ruth Underwood, but with an added Huguenot flourish), had been born on St Swithun's Day, 14 July 1914, just three weeks before

Europe entered meltdown. It is said that Britain's declaration of war on Germany came as a surprise to many of its citizens, but perhaps it was even more shocking to Monty and Kathleen, who must have been completely wrapped up in their new baby. The war intruded almost immediately, though, and Kathleen and Ruth would often stay with her parents rather than at the various lodgings that Monty diligently found – Monty would get to see them when he could. Photos of the proud father pushing Ruthie around in a wheelbarrow and dressed in a rather natty blazer are soon replaced by Monty in his Army uniform.

The family moved to Woking in Surrey in 1915, presumably so Kathleen could be closer to her parents. Monty fell ill, very close to the date when he was first meant to be posted to France with the 30th Division. Then Auntie fell ill and died, again delaying his departure. So it wasn't until September 1916 that Monty was at last able to embark for France. He was trained as a Church of England priest. He'd had a few weeks' basic acclimatisation to Army life. He might have been schooled in 'Hygiene', but he'd probably never had to dress a wound or tend a bleeding man. The war was going badly and the Bishop of London was bellowing that every last Hun must be obliterated, but when Monty 'left The Croft with K at 6.50 for Victoria' he left with a sense of purpose. The shy young sportsman, recently ordained, who enjoyed a joke but was often ill, who spoke quietly, but with certainty, of his faith, hugged his wife in the Charing Cross Hotel and headed for the testing ground of his generation.

# EIGHT

# 'Dragged out by horses but too late for service'

In mid-November 1916, the 2nd Division moved out fast from the front line, with Monty among the throng, and headed several miles to the rear, to recuperate, re-equip and train a fresh delivery of much-needed newcomers. There were after all many gaps to fill in the ranks. *The History of the Second Division* doesn't have much to say about the end of 1916, other than this:

> *Throughout the month of December 1916 the Divisional Diaries have little to record excepting the training and general routine work, relieved by sports and entertainments whenever possible. The Divisional, Lewis Gun, Bombing, and Gas Schools were busily engaged in the training of officers and men for the next offensive.*[37]

It is also noted that Major-General Walker, VC, CB, who had welcomed Monty to France three months earlier, had been replaced by Major-General Pereira, CB, CMG. So there was a shuffle at the top.

Monty's diary reflects this lull in the fighting, although in his ill-defined capacity as Chaplain to the Forces, he might have been expected to come into his own as the genial parson with a screen projector and a troupe of dancing girls (well – young lads in drag, more likely). On a cold, dry Sunday in mid-November, the 52nd Ox and Bucks almost sprint away from the

121

Front, covering 11 miles in four hours. Not bad for a bunch of battle-weary, kit-burdened men whose boots were heavy with the claggy mud.

> Sunday, 19 November 1916
> Move off at 10.30am. Cold and dry. Brigade march to Amplier 18 kilometres. Arrive 2.30 p.m. Good billet with Trench Mortar Battery. Tea. Go up to 52$^{nd}$ Camp. Mud terrible. Evening Prayers at 6 p.m. in Machine Gun Corps' Billet (large barn) behind our billet. Good crowd. Talked on 'Motives' as applied to recent offensive. Undulating country. Dinner. Chat Osbourne. Bed in bed of same room as Hepple and Marshall.

The men may have been exhausted, but a crowd of them gathered to hear Monty talk in a large barn about 'Motives' as applied to the recent offensive. There's no record of this sermon, but Monty was surely trying to make sense of the recent mayhem, both for his audience and himself. Perhaps it's the closest he ever got to preaching what the generals all wanted their chaplains to preach – this war is a Just War, we are on the side of Right, our God sanctions you to fight and to kill.

In the years of his training to become a peacetime priest, or even an evangelist in India, it is unlikely that Monty's teachers would have dwelled very long on the Christian notion of a Just War. And once the war did start, no one (not even the clergy) would have wanted too much open discussion about the rights and wrongs of bearing arms, or (heaven forbid) turning the other cheek. The overwhelming majority of the British people took it for granted that we would fight with God on our side. Article XXXVIII of the Church of England is very clear: 'It is lawful for Christian men, at the commandment of the Magistrate, to wear weapons, and serve in the wars.'

There's no ambiguity about that. 'Christian men' should render unto Caesar the things which are Caesar's – and in this instance what Caesar wanted was to slaughter the Boche until they backed out of Belgium.

Monty loved his Tennyson, so he'd have felt the hot tug of the poet's words in Part III of *Maud* – just as many of his countrymen did:

> Let it flame or fade, and the war roll down like a wind,
> We have proved we have hearts in a cause, we are noble still,
> And myself have awaked, as it seems, to the better mind;
> It is better to fight for the good, than to rail at the ill;
> I have felt with my native land, I am one with my kind,
> I embrace the purpose of God, and the doom assign'd.[38]

Yes, I'm afraid it's true. There was a strain of yearning among the European nations at the turn of the twentieth century to fight a cleansing war. It may have been just a certain class in those nations, I don't know – although sadly if that was the case, it was the class with its hands on the levers of power. But the people of Europe had gorged on centuries of wealth and even as they craved more, they longed for a purging return to a simpler age, where 'no more shall commerce be all in all'. Chivalry. Purity. Comradeship. Young German conscripts went to their deaths in droves believing they were raising Europe up from its materialistic hog-wallow. 'What these young people need is a damned good war!' the clichéd armchair generals bellow and certainly, until it all went obscenely wrong, that's what many in Monty's audience would once have felt. Maybe some of them felt it still. But probably not in November 1916, two years into a war that showed no signs of ending, when so many of their friends were dead in a struggle over a few sordid miles of land. What most soldiers wanted now was for it to stop.

They did not want it to stop at any price, though. By the end of 1916 there seems to have been a grim determination that the British Army would not stop fighting until they'd forced the Germans back into their own lands – and taught them never to come out again. The glory days may have been over, except among new arrivals, who were quickly put straight if they seemed too gung-ho, but that did not mean that Monty's audience would have wanted to give up and go home. Home, yes, but only on their own terms, with the enemy beaten. How we view 'The War to End All Wars', and the people who fought in it, is skewed not just by the agonised memories of disappointed men, writing long after the war was over; no, much more than that, we are colossally misled by the looming, insurmountable barrier of the *Second* World War, which has rendered any sense of the rightness of the British and French cause in the earlier one redundant. The Second War has gone down in popular memory as The Just War – the war against tyranny, fascism and the genocidal slaughter of the Jews. God would have blessed that war, for sure. To most of us, the earlier war has become the epitome of pointless slaughter.

So it is hard to see the First War clearly over the righteous fury of the Second. If people fought and died for freedom from 1939 to 1945, we tend to see the earlier lot as victims, as slaughtered innocents – maybe even as naive dupes, fighting and dying in their millions for a worthless cause. The men who were there have become caricatures: the blustering nincompoop of a general, the gormless upper-class twit of a captain, the cheery, uncomplaining 'Tommy' and his cynical, wisecracking mates – but this is an insult to their memories. Most men in Monty's audience would have seen their cause as just and right. They wouldn't have been bogged down in the niceties of whether Kaiser Wilhelm was provoked into launching a pre-emptive defensive war before he was choked by the Triple Alliance. Their cause was very clear: the Germans had invaded Belgium and France and if they didn't stop them now, then the weak would have no protection from the strong. Sure, there was a lot of extra noise about the Huns bayoneting nuns and machine-gunning Belgian civilians, and everyone knew that the Germans had been the first to introduce poison gas to modern warfare (even if the British had wasted no time in enthusiastically developing their own programme), but at that time most British soldiers felt strongly that they were fighting on the side of Right. And who are we to say that they were wrong?

Whatever Monty had to say about the 'Motives' behind the most recent offensive, there was no time to linger because the next day they are off again, covering another eleven miles in four hours over undulating country.

Monday, 20 November 1916
March as Company to Bonneville 18 kilometres – through Beauval. Arrive at 2.30 p.m. Difficulty in finding Billets. Mess in farm. Take it quietly. Bed in Mess in bed with Bell and Oxenden in another bed. Undulating country.

Oxo and Bell are sharing a bed, but Monty gets his own. We are left in no doubt that the country is 'undulating'.

Tuesday, 21 November 1916
Move off at 9.20am, our Company march to Franqueville 10 kilometres. Walk with Oxenden and Lieutenant Russell and Hardy and Lovelace (Oxenden's groom). Jolly country – wooded and undulating. Arrive 12.30 p.m. More difficulty about billets. Mess in Farm where Mademoiselle does needlework. Lunch. Walk with Oxenden to Domart 2½ kilos away. County town. Pretty. Not many shops. Buy sweets and come back to tea. Find new Transport officer, Christopher, Canadian from 51st RN Division has joined. His Company badly knocked in push south of Ancre. Bridge. Dinner. Bed with Blair in Farm House opposite Mess.

Wednesday, 22 November 1916
Rise at 8 a.m. Breakfast at 8.45 a.m. Write letters and this diary during morning whilst Company is busy. Good billets for men. Glorious day. Go for ride with Marshall and Christopher on the uplands. Have Oxenden's mare Nancy enjoy myself enormously. Hilly country well cultivated. Ride in to Domart. Secure horses and go up to a commanding position above the town to see the Church. Fairly old and quite simple inside. Interested in 'Explication de Catechism' on lectern. Have tea in Officers' tea rooms. Buy papers and ride home before dark. Write to K. Dinner. Bed.

Monty pokes around a Roman Catholic church – this one is undamaged – and seems to be enjoying himself riding in the uplands with his new friends. As well as finding the idea of him playing bridge extraordinary, my aunt was amazed to hear of her father riding horses. He wasn't so keen on the brutes in later years, but here it sounds like he's having a glorious time, cantering around on Oxenden's neat little mare, Nancy. When Colonel Richard Crosse was posted to Ireland after the war, and Monty had moved to Cottesmore in Rutland (with its plentiful stables and pastureland), Crosse lent Monty his horse, a vast charger and war veteran called Brown Bess. This in turn provoked a blizzard of satirical verse from 'Pullthrough' when Monty inadvertently told him about it, several years later:

No wonder you never told me of it at the time of its occurrence because it would have provided me with the means to rend you mercilessly. No wonder Cottesmore rocked with merriment. No wonder the school children sang:

'Ride a cock-horse to old Oakham Cross
To see our gay parson on a great horse,
Reins twixt his fingers, in button hole, rose;
Gee Gee, don't canter, he'll fall on his nose.'

No wonder your choir-boys irreverently hymned:

'Onward Christian soldiers,
Marching as to war
With our parson Guilford
Riding on afore,
Mounted on his charger,
Spoiling for the fray,
Hoping he will conquer
And fight another day.'

No wonder your bishop, who chanced to pass you in his car when you were out riding, on returning to his palace, went direct to his study, took out his Diary for Matters Episcopal and wrote therein:

GUILFORD. E.M. Cottesmore. Too bucolic to be considered for preferment.

Another day passes, and the 52$^{nd}$ Ox and Bucks are on the march again with an early start and the slim chance that they've arrived at their 'winter quarters', as Monty likes to call them. If Monty thinks that he'll be able to settle down in the village of Hanchy until the spring, then he has misjudged the realities of modern warfare, which will not be stopping for winter, nor for him to help bring in the harvest.

Thursday, 23 November 1916
Early start. Rise at 5.30am. Breakfast 6.15am. Start off at 7.30am. Company march to Hanchy 7 kilometres. Arrive at 9.30am. Mess in large Farm. Rumours that this will be our winter quarters. Bedroom with Bell and Oxenden, two beds and nice big room.

Slack morning. Walk with Christopher after lunch to see RFA transport horse attached to us which is nearly dying from colic. Find it much better after dose of whisky. Walk on to Yvrench – a country town two kilometres away, where Brigade and Divisional Headquarters RF and Highland Light Infantry, EF Canteen. Back to tea. Write to K. Dinner. Bridge. Bed at 11 p.m.

The rumour about 'winter quarters' has proved false. I don't suppose any Army rumour ever did prove true – certainly not one that promised rest, peace and freedom from early starts.

Friday, 24 November 1916
Breakfast at 9.15 a.m. Start at 10.30 a.m. to Hiermont. Nice day. Five kilometres march. Arrive at 12 o' clock. Mess in Farm. Not feeling very fit. Sleep after lunch in large double bedroom which I share (in another farm) with Oxenden. Nice stove. Wake at 4.15 p.m. Make our own tea at the stove. Hot bath (bath just arrived in parcel). Dinner at 7.30 p.m. Go to bed at 9.30 p.m.

Saturday, 25 November 1916

Wet day. Rise late. No breakfast except cup of coffee which I make for myself. Lunch at 12. Start at 1.30 p.m. in pouring driving rain. Ride whole distance because I strained tendon in my heel. Slow going. 10 kilometres march to Canchy. Arrive feeling rather dreary in dark in advance of Company. Go round to 52nd Mess in Chateau. Have tea and arrange to join them temporarily on Monday to settle down with them in their winter quarters. Arrange services for next day. Visit Trench Mortar Battery re. services. Dinner at 8 p.m. Bed at 10.15 p.m. with Bell and Oxenden. Sleep with Ox in double bed.

Sunday, 26 November 1916

Rise at 6.30 a.m. Holy Communion, one 52nd officer at 7.40 a.m. in Oxford and Bucks Mess. Breakfast. Service in Barn at 52nd Headquarters at 10.15 a.m. (16 present). Holy Communion four present. Go round to Brigade Headquarters re. mule being attached with me to 52nd. Get their consent. Learn the destinations of Regiments. Arrange with Dr McTurk for inoculation. Visit 52nd. Meet Browne who is going on leave tomorrow for a fortnight. Arrange to take on his work. Am late for inoculation and not done in consequence. Lunch. Ramsey returns for a few hours before going to front to take over Company. Evening Prayers at 6 p.m. 30 present. Holy Communion, 12. Speak on 'Motives'. Dinner. Write. Bed.

There is a sense here of a regiment (including Monty) shaking itself down and sorting itself out. The logistics involved are mind-boggling – the Division straggles back from the Front, and immediately needs food, shelter, training, transport, re-arming, tending, entertaining and re-populating. Monty needs an inoculation and (perhaps in the light of his most recent escapade with a horse) a mule. Browne appears (there is no mention of their argument) and Monty takes on his work. It is Sunday, and he returns to the theme of 'Motives'.

The Guilford family in Reading. From left: Edward Snr, Monty, Edie, Lily, Louisa (their mother) and Eva.

The young Monty, ready for school in Ramsgate.

The Bigger children. Clockwise from top left: Walter, Kathleen, Edgar, Bill (holding Spot the dog) and Jack.

The Bigger children's concert, held at Aberfoyle, Streatham, Christmas 1901.

Edward Guilford Snr, missionary:
Bible studies in the Punjab.

Monty and his brother-in-law
Cecil, the Edwardian dandies.

Monty and Kathleen on their
honeymoon in Dartmoor, June
1913.

The beloved Auntie, seated, with,
from left, Lily, Monty, Edie and Eva.

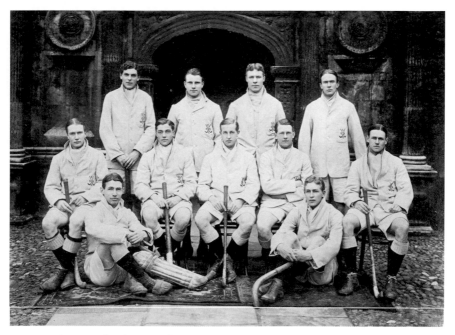

The Cambridge Hockey Blues: young men on the eve of war.
Monty is seated on the ground, front right.

Monty (right), the muscular Christian,
back from a pre-war boxing match. *Inset*: Monty,
in uniform, holds his baby Ruthie aloft.

*Top*: One of Monty's alarming postcards home: a chaplain holds a burial service at the Front. *Middle*: The Bapaume–Albert Road, February 1917. *Bottom*: A soldier rests on a captured German gun near the Sugar Factory.

*Top*: A splintered and pulverised forest, winter 1916. *Middle*: A derelict tank, with the graves of its crew, late 1916. *Bottom*: The long road to the Front, January 1917.

The grave that Monty dug for his friend Captain Nick Hill, MC, January 1917.

'*Kamerad!*' Monty's friend 'Eagle' dresses up as a surrendering German.

Life in the trenches. From left: Colonel Crosse, Vernon, Fullbrook-Leggatt.

Monty (right) and Oxenden ('Oxo') try to look
nonchalant. *Inset*: Jack Bigger of the East Surreys.

The war is over and the remaining troops of the 52nd Ox
and Bucks parade in Zons. *Inset*: The Rev. Dick Sheppard,
smoking on the steps of St Martin-in-the-Fields, 1922.

Monty, warden of the YMCA in Bedford Place, in the
second row with Kathleen. Ruthie beams at the front.

My grandfather in his 50s.

'Brad' and his grandson Toby settle
in for a long chat in his garden.

Monday, 27 November 1916

Breakfast 9 a.m. Take Wright to Doctor. Arrange for my transfer to 52nd and for baggage to be taken by their transport. Lend 'Cathedral' to take Kinsey and Oxenden to Abbeville. Company moves off at 11 a.m. Stay with Wright till arrival of Ambulance. Leave by self at 12 and walk seven kilometres to Fontaine-Sur-Maye where find 52nd just arrived. Go round some of the billets. Lunch in Mess. Find my own billet 'The Rectory' – sitting room and bedroom leading into one another. Very nice. Ride over with Dr McTurk and Lieutenant Slade Baker to Brailly Divisional Headquarters and see Bate. Get back to tea. Read. Dinner. Chat. Bed. Two new officers.

Here then are the 52nd winter quarters, in a village called Fontaine-Sur-Maye, a few miles north of Abbeville, fairly near the English Channel – and a comfortingly long distance from the Front. Monty has been allocated rooms (dubbed 'The Rectory' by some wag) with his own sitting room and bedroom. It sounds almost cosy.

And now follows a number of days where the war does indeed seem to recede and, as *The History of the Second Division* has it, the general routine work is relieved by sports and entertainments. Monty is preoccupied by trying to turn the local school room into a 'Rec Room' – a space for fun and games – and is seeking permission from the local French mayor, who does not fall in immediately with the plan, despite the *entente cordiale*. Monty takes Captain Hill with him on the first occasion and, when that doesn't work, turns up later with Colonel Crosse, who is also rebuffed. Anyone who has ever dealt with a French *Mairie* will sympathise. Monty is also going to take over the running of the canteen, which is what most chaplains ended up doing – at least until the later stages of the war, when it was realised that there were probably better qualified and better trained people who should be doing the catering. Some chaplains thought they should only be doing God's business while in the Army, but

I'm sure Monty would have enjoyed the chats – and the cigarettes.

Tuesday, 28 November 1916
Breakfast 9.15am. Go round with Captain Hill to see Mairie re. School room for Recreation room and piano. No luck. Unpack in my billet. Lunch. Play football. Tea. Go round to my billet with Colonel Crosse and to Mairie for Rec Room. No luck. Dinner. Read. Write. Bed.

Wednesday, 29 November 1916
Breakfast 9 a.m. Start for Estrees Crecy station on Cathedral at 9.30 a.m. with Lyle. Train at 10.20 a.m. through Crecy Forest. Arrive 11.30 a.m. at Abbeville. Shop. Lunch at Hotel de France. Buy paraffin stove 12 francs. Go to Church. Field Cashier (100 francs). Tea. Train 5.50 p.m. Arrive Estrees Crecy at 7.20 p.m. Cathedral back. Dinner. Read. Bed.

Thursday, 30 November 1916
Chaplains meeting at Brailly at 10.30 a.m. Get back to lunch. Go round billets with Whitfield in afternoon to look for Rec Room. Tea [crossed out!]. Distribute papers. Tea. Read. Go round to billet to see Harris re. taking on Canteen. Dinner. Read. Bed.

Friday, 1 December 1916
Go over on Cathedral to Noyelles-en-Chausée. Arrange service for Sunday at 11.15 a.m. Go in to Yvrench and buy stock for Canteen with Harris. Walk on alone to Maison-Ponthieu and see 17 RF re. service and Brigade Headquarters. Arrange for Voluntary service and Holy Communion at 5.30 p.m. in the school. Lunch with Machine Gun Company. Rubber. Watch footer match. Ride over on 'Molly' to S. Lot and tea with Trench Mortar Battery and arrange service at Maison. Ride home with groom Kennedy and arrive at 6 p.m. Interview Marshall re. Confirmation. Find Stores has nearly sold out. Dinner. Bed.

It is not easy for Monty to add store-keeping to all his other duties. He returns from a day of visiting his flock, bridge-playing and tea-drinking to discover that the cupboards in his store are practically bare. The next day he audits the accounts and dispatches Harris to buy more stuff urgently. He is also chatting to some French refugees, in English I expect – although he now knows enough of the lingo to be brandishing the word 'frere' in his diary.

> Saturday, 2 December 1916
> Breakfast 8.45am. Audit accounts with Harris and send him to buy more stuff. Write and talk to French Refugees from Armentieres who are the housekeepers for Madame here. Monsieur invalided home from Salonika with Frere. Footer with A Company. Prepare.

The next day, Monty embarks on a long, cold drive in 'Cathedral', ministering to several different outfits, before sleeping in a bed in the Mess. It is December – and it is shaping up to be the coldest winter on record. Monty succumbs to one of his fevers.

> Sunday, 3 December 1916
> Holy Communion Officers' Mess 7.30am. No one. Morning Prayers in Barn at Rectory at 9.30 a.m. (52nd). Between 20 and 30 ('Influence'). PS in school Noyelle-en-Chausée for 2nd Highland Light Infantry, 50 present. Drive back in Cathedral to lunch. Start 2.20 p.m. in Cathedral. Arrive Maison-Ponthieu at 3.30 p.m. Place Altar etc in School (very cold drive). Tea with Machine Gun Company. Service in School 5.30 p.m. for 17th RF, 5 Machine Gun Company and 5 Trench Mortar Brigade, 40 or 50 present, 17 to Holy Communion. Walk back with Osborne and Stables. Dinner and stay the night, sleeping in Mess on bed.

> Monday, 4 December 1916
> Wake up with bad cold. Send Cathedral on and have lunch with Osborne. Walk back in afternoon – part of way with

RFA column who are trekking to Froyelles. Tea and bed.

Tuesday, 5 December 1916
In bed with flu. Temp 103 degrees.

Wednesday, 5 December 1916
Still in bed but normal and now escape Hospital. Read.

Thursday, 6 December 1916
Still normal. Visit from Ellis and Coffin. Get up to lunch in
Mess. Stay in and write all afternoon and evening.

Friday, 7 December 1916
Regiment goes to Noyelle for General Inspection. Breakfast
at 10 a.m. with Doctor. Read and write. Go round in
afternoon with Colonel Crosse to find suitable Rec Room.

Monty is up and out of bed – he was spared a trip to the hospital
– and is now back with Colonel Crosse trying to find a suitable
place for the wretched Rec Room.

Saturday, 8 December 1916
Breakfast 9.30 a.m. Write and prepare in Billet. Bate (Senior
Chaplain to the Forces) comes round at 12 re. services. Chat
and he arranges to take Highland Light Infantry and Maison
Ponthieu services. Have lunch in Mess. Go round in
afternoon and help Ellis with footer ground. Dinner. Bed.
Prep.

The Sundays are rolling round thick and fast, and the war might
as well have ended for all that Monty mentions it. In his morning
service, he talks about the '1st stage on the Road to God' – we
must acknowledge the reality of 'sin', that it is here, and it is
real. Later that evening, Monty talks about 'the Centurion', the
Roman soldier who had many men under his command but
who pleaded with Jesus to cure his servant. It wouldn't hurt to
remind the military that there is an Authority beyond their own.

Monty has also been shopping, and without Kathleen there to restrain him picks up lace, knick-knacks, a harmonium, a paraffin lamp and a great bundle of postcards. Even so, perhaps she won't mind, because Monty sends the first of many postcards from northern France to her on 8 December. It shows the village of Domart-en-Ponthieu (Somme), which Monty has visited on his recent travels, and a bunch of men and children are standing on the careworn streets, staring somewhat belligerently at the camera. The postcard is stamped on the back as 'Passed Field Censor 226'. Monty tiptoes past the censor with this noncommittal comment: 'As I have a good many picture postcards to get off my hands, I have had the brilliant notion of sending you one every other day between each of my letters.'

The rest, written in pockmarked pencil, is illegible, but we do now know quite how often Monty was writing home.

More importantly, the Rec Room (which is now a temporary hut and not housed in a village hall or school room, thanks to the obduracy of the French mayor) has turned up.

> Sunday, 9 December 1916
> Holy Communion Service in Rectory at 8 a.m. No one. Morning Prayers in Barn at Rectory at 11 o'clock, 30 present ('1st stage on Road to God'). Holy Communion eight present.
>
> Chat with Madame and Suzanne. Afternoon – hut turns up. Try to find site. Put up notices re. Evening Service. Tea. Service at 19 Piccadilly. 25 present. 'The Centurion'. Dinner. Jellicoe with Ellis. Bed.

The Army routine settles on Monty. Now that the temporary Rec Hut is here, he has to agree with the French where it can be sited. It's possible that they may have rather forcefully suggested that he shove it up his English Channel, but something must have been decided in the end – meaning that his next preoccupation now rolls into view: the dismantling and re-building of a harmonium for his church services and the choir he is putting together for some Christmas entertainment.

Monday, 11 December 1916

Go round with Interpreter (Monsieur Flamard) and find site for Rec Hut. Breakfast canteen. Accounts with Harris. Write. Go on with Giles after lunch to Noyelles Chaussée to watch footer match 52$^{nd}$ v Highland Light Infantry (52$^{nd}$ 4–0). Tea. Unpack harmonium in billet and also Fortnum and Mason's Xmas parcel (no.2). Chat with Gunter. Go round with him to his billet. Chat Lance Corporal Butler and co. Dinner. Jellicoe. Write K. Bed 10.30 p.m.

Tuesday, 12 December 1916

Snowing. Write letters. Pull harmonium to pieces with Jones. Confirmation class at 5.15 p.m. Four present. Dinner. Bed.

Monty loved DIY. He was quite hopeless at it, but it was an addiction that he had to feed. The long-suffering Kathleen would call him for lunch from whatever corner of the house or garden in which he was lurking and he'd drift in for a couple of minutes, before muttering, 'Hang on, but I've just got to . . .' and then he'd be gone, turning up two hours later covered in glue and with a badly damaged thumb. There are dozens of his plates and ornaments scattered around his descendants' homes, all of them chipped, cracked and clumsily mended with slatherings of inappropriately coloured glue. There are some (once) invaluable Crown Derby plates he has popped together with brass staples. He lashed priceless first editions back together with Sellotape. But most of all he loved his glue. He probably just wanted to put things back together again, although it's surely too neat to think that the impulse dated from the war.

He must have been in clover, pulling that harmonium to pieces with Jones. We can only hope that Jones knew what he was doing – and in fact, in Monty's postcard of 13 December, it is revealed that he does:

No letter today worse luck! We have had a fall of snow, and everything is unspeakably slushy. I spent this afternoon taking the harmonium down and hope with the assistance of a professional organist to mend it up. Heaps of love to all Monty.

The front of this postcard shows a scene of unbearable bleakness, of blasted tree stumps, shell holes and shattered buildings; of a small convoy of ambulances pulled up in a pile of rubble; of men milling round stretchers and slumped in ditches. 'RAMC Picking Up Wounded in a Captured Village' it says – and yet the village no longer exists. It has been pounded back into nothingness. I suppose you could say that the village – or what is left of it – is 'captured', but it has to be one of the least heartening pictures that anyone could receive from a husband who is away at war. Perhaps this never occurred to Monty – more likely he wanted to share something of what he was seeing with his wife.

Wednesday, 13 December 1916
Go in with mule by train to Abbeville. Lunch with William Fox at Hotel. Tête de Boeufs. Shop with him getting hinges as new etc for harmonium (and also before lunch at Canteen). Buy lace and hankies for K in morning. Tea with William (Lieutenant) Fox in his rooms which are delightful. Meet Captain Rawlinson there. Catch 5.50 p.m. train back meeting Fielding back from leave. Dinner. Jellicoe. Bed.

Thursday, 14 December 1916
Chaplains' meeting at Brailly. Football for D Company v C Company in afternoon. Receive a black eye. Bath. Chat Gunter. Put (faulty) harmonium together with Jones. Dinner. Bed.

Friday, 15 December 1916
Ride over in rain on Colonel's chestnut to Highland Light Infantry and Machine Gun Company. See Brown and fix up for services and confirmation candidates. Bridge and lunch with Machine Gun Company. Oxo back from leave. Walk

with him. Meet Osbourne. Chat with Newark and Lance Corporal Russell. Ride back to tea with Highland Light Infantry. Get back for confirmation class at 5.40 p.m. Four present. Find harmonium nearly mended by Jones. Dinner. Bed.

Thanks to Jones – who was no doubt happy that Monty's duties had taken him elsewhere – the harmonium is nearly ready.

Saturday, 16 December 1916
Go round with CO re. Rec (Nissen) Hut. Watch footer ground being prepared. Write and lunch. Go over in Lorrie with CO and two other officers to National Mission meeting (Talbot Assistant Chaplain General of 5th Army giving address) at Yvrench in theatre. About 100 officers from 2nd Division present. Discussion. Tea. Ride back. Go round to billet and finish harmonium for the morrow's service. Dinner. Prepare. Bed.

As well as finishing the harmonium on Saturday (there's no mention of Jones now . . .) Monty had been with Crosse and others to an address by Neville Talbot on the 'National Mission', more fully known as 'The National Mission of Repentance and Hope'. There is no word from Monty that this might have been an especially inspirational moment, but the National Mission was intended to be just that – launched in the autumn of 1916, it was a belated attempt by the Church of England to use the war to fire up the nation, to repent for its sins and bring it back to God. Anyone wanting the detail on the Mission's predictable, report-choked outcome should read Alan Wilkinson's excellent *The Church of England and the First World War* – what is most remarkable about the five major reports that it spawned, he says, is that there is almost no discussion about the ethics or morality of the war.

Perhaps this is not surprising. For every Sassoon or Graves raving against the iniquities of the war and the absurdity of the Church's position, there were many more calling for a Holy War against the German Antichrist. The Church of England, not for the last time, found itself somewhere in the awkward middle. There were pacifists among their number, but there were far more followers of our old friend the Bishop of London, Winnington-Ingram. He is named by Wilkinson as being the man who did 'much to popularise the belief that the nation was engaged in a Holy War'. Here he is in a sermon preached in September 1914 (he hadn't dithered or delayed, weighing up the issues):

> *But when we have said all that, this is an Holy War. We are on the side of Christianity against anti-Christ. We are on the side of the New Testament which respects the weak, and honours treaties, and dies for its friends, and looks upon war as a regrettable necessity . . . It is a Holy War, and to fight in a Holy War is an honour . . . Already I have seen a light in men's eyes which I have never seen before.*[39]

He was at it again in June 1915, writing:

> *I think the Church can best help the nation first of all by making it realise that it is engaged in a Holy War, and not be afraid of saying so . . . Having once realised that everything worth having in the world is at stake, the nation will not hesitate to allow itself to be mobilised. You ask for my advice in a sentence as to what the Church is to do. I answer MOBILISE THE NATION FOR A HOLY WAR.*[40]

Other clergy tried to get Winnington-Ingram to withdraw the term 'Holy War'. 'We are not Mad Mullahs preaching a Jihad' wrote Scott Holland, Dean of St Paul's, in *The Guardian* later that month. Archbishop Davidson no doubt wrung his hands and continued to push for no reprisals and the most civilised approach possible to the bloodshed ('I'm terribly sorry, but do you mind if I just press this bayonet in here?'). But, as Yeats wrote in 1919 in 'The Second Coming', 'The best lack all conviction, while the worst are full of passionate intensity' and the roaring supporters of Holy War beat their drums ever louder and kept themselves on the front pages.

In April 1915, in *The Church in Time of War*, Winnington-Ingram had written:

> *I believe that not only will CHRIST welcome them as comrades in arms, but over every one who dies in this war with his face towards the foe, if he dies in CHRIST, will be said those words: 'This is My beloved son, This is My beloved son, This is My beloved son, in whom I am well pleased'.*[41]

In a Holy War, if you die with your 'face towards the foe' (but only that way, it seems), then you will enter paradise. Siegfried Sassoon walked past the Bishop of London after excoriating him in his poem 'They' and 'he turned a mild shining gaze on me and my MC'. The Holy War mongers did not carry the nation with them, but an approval of sacrifice – of the ultimate sacrifice – lingered in the atmosphere. On the other side, Kaiser Wilhelm had been whipping up a similar frenzy, not just among his German forces, but in an attempt to get the Muslim inhabitants of Britain's empire to rise up and overthrow their colonists. One month before the outbreak of war, he wrote:

> *Now this entire structure must be ruthlessly exposed and the mask of Christian peacefulness be publicly torn away . . . Our consuls in Turkey and India, our agents, etc, must rouse the whole Muslim world into wild rebellion against this hateful, mendacious, unprincipled nation of shopkeepers; if we are going to shed our blood, England must at least lose India.*[42]

He had his wish in November 1914 when Sheik-ul-Islam, speaking for the Caliphate of the Ottoman Empire, declared a Holy War against Britain, France, Russia, Serbia and Montenegro:

> *Of those who go to the Jihad for the sake of happiness and salvation of the believers in God's victory, the lot of those who remain alive is felicity, while the rank of those who depart to the*

*next world is martyrdom. In accordance with God's beautiful promise, those who sacrifice their lives to give life to the truth will have honour in this world, and their latter end is paradise.*[43]

In Germany in 1917, a popular song was this, 'A Hymn of Hate Against England', by Ernst Lissauer:

French and Russian they matter not,
A blow for a blow, a shot for a shot,
We fight the battle with bronze and steel,
And the time that is coming Peace will seal,
You will we hate with a lasting hate,
We will never forgo our hate,
Hate by water and hate by land,
Hate of the hammer and hate of the crown,
Hate of seventy millions, choking down,
We love as one, we hate as one,
We have one foe and one alone – England![44]

Mr Britling's friend quotes part of that poem with bemusement in the H.G. Wells book that Monty was reading. Mr Britling found it 'incomprehensible'. 'What have we done?' he wanted to know, to deserve the vitriol. But the hatred swelled on both sides. And the 'best' were squeezed. Except despite all this rage and fury, the bombast and the bloodlust, at the Front in his winter quarters, Monty preached about 'Healing' and 'Joy', and the vast bulk of the British Army – and the German, French, Austrian, Russian and Italian Armies – felt no hatred at all.

It is Sunday again, and Monty talks about 'The Kingdom' and 'Healing'. On Monday, he does his accounts, and on the next two days he lapses into silence.

Sunday, 17 December 1916
Holy Communion at 7.20 a.m. at 'The Rectory' (3 present).
Morning Prayers at 9.30 a.m. at the Nissen Hut (33 present, 'The Kingdom'). Holy Communion following, 8 present. PS at Noyelle School for Highland Light Infantry 11.15 a.m.

139

(50). Holy Communion following (1). Lunch. Sleep 2.45–
5.15 p.m. Evening Prayers in Nissen Hut at 6 p.m., 65
present ('Healing'). Get 12 Volunteers for choir. Chat with
Sergeant Pilcher. Dinner. Write. Bed.

Thursday, 21 December 1916
Chaplains' meeting. Get picked up by Senior Chaplain to
the Forces of 2nd Corps in car on way home. Arrange with
him for Casino at Crécy for Concert. Walk over with Sergeant
Price and Private Shenton (A Company) to Crécy. See
Casino. Tea in 'B' Mess. Fix up Boxing night and following
night for Concerts. Walk back and ride in lorry.

Friday, 22 December 1916
Try to arrange the concert party and ring up Division re.
troupe. Ride over with cavalcade of officers to see Brigade
sports. Wretched day. Look in at Highland Light Infantry on
way home. Confirmation class, eight present.

Saturday, 23 December 1916
Write and prepare. Hockey game for 52nd v 2nd Division;
train at Brailly in quagmire. Lose 2–1. Choir practice 5.30–
7.45 p.m. 15 present.

Sunday, 24 December 1916
7.30 Holy Communion (3 present). 9.45 a.m. Voluntary
service (50) (The Attractiveness of Christ). Highland Light
Infantry 11.15 a.m. PS (70) ('Joy'). Go round with concert
party to CO in afternoon. Arrange to include 39 Division
troupe in party. Tea. Voluntary service (70) (Joy).

Monty's choir has been practising, he has a black eye from a
game of football – and he gives his audiences a double-dose of
'Joy' on Christmas Eve. He has also turned into the Entertainments Officer – Sundays find him talking about 'The
Attractiveness of Christ' in the Barn, and on other days he's
sprinting around the hockey pitch in a quagmire, or setting up

a boxing bout. Quite often he can be found in the canteen handing out fags or the latest papers from home.

On Christmas Day, once the services are over, Monty and a number of officers head to the site of the Battle of Crecy. His friend Neville writes about it to his sister on 2 January:

> *You were rather a scholar in history as far as I can remember, so you would know all about the battle of 1346. We walked over the ground on Christmas Day and it was very interesting to think of the great battle that was fought on it 500 years ago. There is a little stream running alongside the road with water cress (Crecy) in it.*
>
> *Yesterday I played football for 'B' against 'C' Company. We were rather badly beaten, and I am afraid I was not in any way an asset. One part of the ground was half under water, and I happened to be on the right wing and spent most of the afternoon wallowing in the mud and water. Luckily I was able to borrow the Padre's bath after the game.*[45]

There is no mention of the football game in Monty's diary, but it's good to see that his bath proved popular.

> Xmas Day December 1916
> 7.30 a.m. Holy Communion 12 present. 9.30 a.m. Voluntary Carol and Holy Communion service. Singing went well (60). 21 at Holy Communion 10.45 a.m. Highland Light Infantry. Holy Communion 6 present. 11.45 a.m. 5th F.A. at Gueschart (travel with harmonium and organist in FA car). Holy Communion 6 present. Lunch. Walk over to Crecy with 10 officers and handbook on battle of Crecy. Sit on mound where Edward III viewed battle. Tea. Play solitaire with Suzanne and [illegible]. Chat in billets. Write. Dinner. Bed.

From Christmas to early January, Monty and the rest of the 2nd Division are engaged in keeping themselves busy and warm. Snow arrives, then sleet and sludge. It is bitterly cold, and Monty scurries about, trying to keep himself and others entertained. He plays plenty of sport – or wallows in mud – and puts on concerts; he fulfils his role as a chaplain and a preacher; but the fighting, which has been a lingering presence, has now disappeared altogether. It will be back with renewed ferocity, but however cold, or bored, the men became, they know where they'd rather be. Or so you'd think. C.E. Barnes, one of the 52nd's army of poets, wrote a little ditty called 'At Rest', of which these verses are a flavour:

> A private at drill who was frying
> At Saulty one hot summer's day,
> While his comrades around him stood sighing,
> Took a pace to the front and did say.
> Chorus:-  Oh I want to go back to the front, sir,
>     And rest in the line one more spell,
>     For although it's not nice in the trenches,
>     I'd much rather choose my own hell.
>
> There we don't have to trail arms by numbers,
> We are not a bit keen on 'right dress'
> We don't shine our boots or our buttons,
> But live in a nice sloppy mess.
> Chorus.
>
> It isn't all jam in the trenches,
> I may stop a bullet or shell,
> But in spite of the muck and the stenches,
> I carry on there fairly well.
> Chorus.

There is more, but it's hard to believe that it is true.

Monty spent Boxing Day morning writing, before playing hockey in the 'slough of the footer ground'. There is a concert at Crecy that afternoon, and Monty strolls over to it with Colonel Crosse. And then he strolls back again. The Senior Chaplain to the Forces has asked Monty to take his services while he's away

– a sure sign that Monty is starting to settle into his role. The next day there are more sports, and Monty rides over this time to Noyelle, where he watches the Brigade mounted sports. Todd wins on 'Scarry', with the Colonel's second horse (presumably not the mighty Brown Bess) lumbering in second.

The days are quiet. Monty reads a lot and holds the occasional confirmation class. He is still puzzling over those canteen accounts. His postcard to Kathleen on 27 December thanks her for her 'two topping letters'. He is 'so glad Ruthie is better and hope Jack was all right for Christmas in spite of the CS tablets'. The picture on the front shows a company of grinning soldiers, waving their tin helmets (and an immense mallet) aloft, striding towards the Front. They could not look happier. It is 'The Worcesters Going into Action'.

On Saturday, 30 December, Monty gets a ride in a lorry with the confirmation candidates (about thirty of them) into Abbeville for lunch (or in Monty's case, two lunches; he tucks into one with the men at the Soldiers' Rest Rooms, before meeting up with Hornby and some other chaplains for his second meal at the Officers' Club). Weighed down with food, Monty shepherds his flock in front of Bishop Gwynne, the Deputy Chaplain General, for their confirmation into the Church of England. There are about a hundred candidates in all from three divisions, although Monty doesn't say where the service took place. Perhaps the Catholic Church had relented and allowed Bishop Gwynne to use one of its churches.

The next day, a Sunday, Monty is given a car to take him to the Parade Service at Crecy. There are about 200 people, 'including several staff officers', to hear him talk, so Monty whips out his trusty old favourite, 'Joy', which he must have had off pat by now. Monty's car breaks down on the way back, but he's there in time to greet Bishop Gwynne, give him some tea and treat him to another service, with music by the Divisional Band, at 6 p.m. There is a large congregation and the Bishop 'goes off immediately after'. It is New Year's Eve, but Monty (and most of the others) are in bed straight after dinner. Even James Neville's letters contain no mentions of any riots or revels on the last day of 1916. Monty's last postcard of the year is a picture of 'The Cathedral of Malines after the bombardment' – another tableau of devastation – and in capital letters it says: 'GUERRE 1914–1916'. Hang on, I thought, that's not right – the war lasted until November 1918. But of course for all the postcard-makers knew, it might last for ever.

That is probably how it seemed to Monty. On the first day of 1917, he is poring over the accounts with Harris – these accountants sure do know how to make work for themselves – and goes for a long walk with Captain Hill, on which they discuss 'Religion – organised v. individualistic'. His concert party is held the next day – there's a marching bugle band, a torchlight tattoo down 'Piccadilly' and many flares are loosed off into the night. The 2nd Company of B Signals Party gives a concert in the Hut until 9.30 p.m.

On Thursday, 4 January, Monty takes a trap to Crecy, before taking a train to Abbeville, where he lunches in the Officers Club, has tea with Fox, takes dinner in the Club with the vicar of Abergavenny and then rolls back to Fox's rooms, where they stay up till 11.45 p.m. talking about the 'position of the Church and our unsettlement as to the future'. Fox, another chaplain, shares the general unease about the Church's ability to inspire or even interest the nation. G.A. Studdert Kennedy, aka 'Woodbine Willie', summed it up with this heartfelt outburst:

> *What the bloody hell is the Church doing here? An amateur stretcher bearer or an amateur undertaker? Was that all a Christian priest could be in this ruin of a rotten civilisation? I have pondered as I sat down after singing a comic song to the men at rest. An amateur comedian struggling to make men forget for one short hour the horrors in the midst of which they live and are called upon to die; always an amateur, always more or less inefficient and untrained, I was typical it seemed to me of the Church I loved and served.*[46]

By the end of the war, Studdert Kennedy had answered his own anguished questions. He knew, in the end, why he was at the

Front and his faith in his God and his Church had been tested but remained strong. Every priest who found themselves hovering around the edges of this cataclysmic war would have had to answer the same questions about themselves, their faith and their Church, and it seemed as though the more they saw, the less easy those questions would become.

Monty may have been enjoying a holiday from the fighting, but doubts and uncertainties were crowding in. On Friday, 5 January 1917, he is in Abbeville, having spent the night in Fox's rooms. He prays in the Soldiers' Room Chapel the next morning, has a final tea with Fox and then heads back to the 52nd billets. There is a steeplechase near Crecy battlefield the next day, which perhaps inspires his Sunday Sermon: 'The Race of Life'. He and Captain Hill engage in yet another discussion about religion, this time chewing over the institution of marriage. Monty would have been enthusiastic.

Saturday, 6 January 1917
Write in Mess and prepare for Sunday. After lunch went to 2nd Corps' steeplechase near Froyelles. Quite close to battlefield of Crécy. Band and great crowd. Five horses. Course 1½ miles. Tea. Choir practice (12). Dinner. Preparation. Bed.

Sunday, 7 January 1917
7.20 a.m. Holy Communion (5). Corps Car to Crécy at 9.30 a.m. Service 9.45 a.m. ('Friendship of King'). Back to Fontaine for Service at 10.50 a.m. (40). Holy Communion (15). No address. On to Noyelle. On way car runs into ditch and gets stuck for ½ hour. Dragged out by horses but too late for service. See Sergeant Fairclough. Lunch. Chat with Hill in his billet on Religion and Marriage tie. Tea. Service at 6 p.m. (70). 'The Race of Life'. Dinner. Stock taking at Canteen. Write till 1 a.m. Bed.

Ever since the 2nd Division left the line, there has been an air of unreality hovering over events, and indeed over my grandfather's diary. The entries have been brief; it feels at times as though his mind is elsewhere. I am sure that is true. He has only been in France for a little over three months (which is longer than most infantry subalterns lasted), but has already confronted horrors and dilemmas he would never have expected. Perhaps he tried to put any uncomfortable questions to one side. He seems determined to do a good job. Erich Maria Remarque, writing in *All Quiet on the Western Front*, was grimly aware that nothing could remain suppressed for long:

> *In fact we don't really forget anything. All the time we are out here the days at the front sink into us like stones the moment they are over, because they are too much for us to think about right away. If we even tried, they would kill us. Because one thing has become clear to me: you can cope with all the horror as long as you simply duck thinking about it – but it will kill you if you try to come to terms with it.*[47]

What did my grandfather try to do? Did he try and suppress his doubts? Or did he try and make sense of the killing, and try to reconcile his faith in a loving God, a God of joy and wonder, with the random, industrial-scale butchery?

# NINE

# 'This is no time for tears'

My grandfather's postcard to his wife sent on 6 January 1917 shows a freshly dug grave. 'The Burial of Two British Soldiers on the Battlefield' reads the caption. There are 11 men standing round the gaping hole, bareheaded, leaning on their spades; a 12th man, the padre, clutches his prayerbook and appears to be saying a few words.

'Not a very cheery card, I'm afraid, to send you,' writes Monty, in an excess of understatement.

> The SCF [Senior Chaplain to the Forces] goes on leave today, so that with luck I expect to get my leave in about a fortnight's time. It seems too good to be true but perhaps . . . I wrote to Jack today. The CO is applying for him. Love Monty.

For the rest of the month, Monty will be preoccupied with trying to get leave to go home – and trying to get Kathleen's brother, Jack, transferred from the East Surreys to the 52nd Ox and Bucks. He has asked Colonel Crosse, who is happy to help (with Jack, that is; I shouldn't think Monty dared mention his leave), and the whole family is hopeful that the brothers-in-law will be able to see out the war in the same regiment. Jack is not yet in France, but his great friend, Gordon Fuller, is already in the Ox and Bucks, so there's even more reason for Jack to put pressure on his own colonel in the East Surreys to see if he can get transferred.

When I went through Monty's papers, I found a tattered magazine cutting, dated 3 August 1918:

*THE SPORTSMAN'S ROLL OF HONOUR*

*Capt (T) Gordon Howard Fuller, Ox and Bucks Light Infantry, who was killed by a German shell on July 7th 1918, whilst assisting one of his men who was wounded, was the only son of Mr Ernest Arthur Fuller, solicitor, and was a nephew of the late H.G. Fuller, the well-known Cambridge and England Rugby football player. Born in 1890, Capt Fuller was educated at St Clare, near Walmer, and Monkton Combe, Bath. He was articled to his father. He played cricket regularly for the Streatham Club, and in the winter of 1913 was in the Surrey hockey eleven, playing regularly; he was also reserve man for the South of England. He was deeply interested in the Church Lads Brigade.*

Gordon and Jack were cricketing friends from Streatham and great enthusiasts for the Church Lads Brigade. Would it have made a difference if Jack had managed to get transferred to the Ox and Bucks – to Jack, or Gordon, or Monty? It might, just possibly, have changed something. But in January 1917 that is all ahead of them – and in the meantime the Ox and Bucks are on the move and heading back to the Front.

Monday, 8 January 1917
Rise at 7.30 a.m. March at 9.45 a.m. after tearful farewell with Mme Hélen and Suzanne. March to Prouville through Brailly, Yvrench. Arrive at 3 p.m. Nice billet. Tea in Mess. Read by fire in billet. Mme's husband at war, wounded. Clean large bedroom. Dinner. Bed 9.50 p.m.

Tuesday, 9 January 1917
Start at 11 a.m. March to Gézaincourt – 1½ miles from Doullens – and arrive at 3.45 p.m. (12 miles march). Meet Oxenden. Promise to go in to dinner with Machine Gun Company who are stationed there too – also Highland Light

Infantry and Brigade Headquarters. Find a Divisional Canteen and take possession for 52nd Canteen. Tea in Mess. Crowded. Bedroom with two beds in next room – share with Major Baines. Go off to Machine Gun Company. Dinner. Bridge. Oxenden has the MC. Bed at 10 p.m.

Wednesday, 10 January 1917
Rest for day and night at Prouville. Spend morning in Canteen chatting with men. Stock is nearly sold out. Walk to Doullens with Oxo at 12.30 p.m. Meet Colonel Crosse, Disney and Slade Baker. Crosse gives us lunch at Hotel de 4 Fils. Oxo gets hair cut. Shop. Oxo buys silver spoon for Ootie. Doullens not much of a town after Abbeville. Tea. See some of the 89th KLR Brigade. Walk home with Oxo. Chat about Future life and loss of individuality. Distant Bombardment on Ancre front. Bridge and dinner with Machine Gun Company. Get back to Mess and find that bedroom has been transformed into cloak room and Ping Pong Salon. Play game with Nick Hill. Bed and read. Hot rum and water and aspirin to scotch beginning of cold.

There's a change of pace in Monty's diary. He may have been preoccupied by getting home, but he also appears to be energised by the sudden movement, even if it is towards the Front. He mentions the war for the first time in weeks (the distant bombardment on the Ancre front) and appears to becoming proficient at keeping a canteen well stocked, even on the move. Oxenden has the Military Cross – and celebrates by getting his hair cut and buying a silver spoon for 'Ootie', who is most likely his wife or fiancée and not his dog. Monty seems to accept the fact that his bedroom has been transformed into a cloakroom and 'ping-pong salon' with equanimity, challenging Captain Nick Hill to a game. They probably teased out a few more ethical dilemmas in between rallies. Monty, like his maternal grandfather, is a firm believer in sloshing down the grog when facing any of life's little difficulties and stops this latest cold in its tracks.

Monty's famous fevers may keep recurring, but that's not the experience of James Neville (who sounds like an overpoweringly healthy young bullock of an 18 year old). Neville's letter to his father, written on 23 March 1917, has this to say on the subject of illness:

> This sort of life keeps me fit, if it does nothing else. I am always having letters from home telling of heavy colds, while here none of us ever feel ill, and I am sure the weather is not any less inclement here than in England. [Too right: they had just endured the worst winter on record, many of them wading around in half-melted ice in the trenches.] I really think I have chosen the right profession. I love an open air life, and although we have rotten times, these are all compensated for by the marvellous fun we have out of the line. That is due to the Regiment and I am sure that many are not nearly so lucky as I.
>
> And if I can survive this war, I am absolutely free of myself and all men.[48]

Years later, Monty had drawn a pencil line against this last sentence. There's no comment, so I have no idea if Monty is agreeing, or if he agrees with Remarque, and the memorable opening statement in *All Quiet on the Western Front*:

> This book is intended neither as an accusation nor as a confession, but simply as an attempt to give an account of a generation that was destroyed by the war – even those of it who survived the shelling.[49]

But back to Monty's cold . . .

*Thursday, 11 January 1917*
Cold no worse. Start at 10am. March of nine miles to Talmas. Arrive at 1.30 p.m. Billet in room next ['Bingo'] Baines. Billiard table in Café. Read '[Mr] Britling Sees It Through'. Good book. Tea. Read and write. Dinner. Bed at 10 p.m.

Monty thinks H.G. Wells's *Mr Britling Sees it Through* is a 'good book' – so I wonder what he made of this passage, when Britling realises that the war, the great chivalrous crusade of Right against Wrong, Good against Evil, is in truth just like any other nasty, unjustifiable, squalid and monstrous squabble.

> *It was all a dream, the dream of a prosperous comfortable man who had never come to the cutting edge of life. Everywhere cunning, everywhere small feuds and hatreds, distrusts, dishonesties, timidities, feebleness of purpose, dwarfish imaginations, swarm over the great and simple issues . . . It is a war now like any other of the mobbing, many-aimed cataclysms that have shattered empires and devastated the world; it is a war without point, a war that has lost its soul, it has become mere incoherent fighting and destruction, a demonstration in vast and tragic forms of the stupidity and ineffectiveness of our species . . .*
>
> *I tell myself that though the way is long and hard the spirit of hope, the spirit of creation, the generosities and gallantries in the heart of man, must end in victory. But I say that over as one repeats a worn-out prayer. The light is out of the sky for me. Sometimes I doubt if it will ever come back.*[50]

Does Monty now find himself repeating a 'worn-out prayer'? Not yet, I don't think. His faith is being challenged – but the real test is still ahead of him.

Friday, 12 January 1917
Read and write in Mess. Lunch. Move on three mile march to Rubempre after lunch. Find Mess at R in Café. Long talk with Hill, Whitehead, Fielding and Lyle in Mess about the origin of the church, its authority and Religion in general. Dinner. Bed at Billet down road.

The regiment is slogging back towards the Front, but on Saturday they get a lift in some London buses – which must have been a treat, although there must have been some who didn't appreciate the reduction in their journey time to the Front.

Saturday, 13 January 1917

Long ride starting at 11 a.m. for the whole Regiment in London Motor 'buses through Albert where see the havoc shells have made and the leaning image of the Virgin on the Cathedral. Had lunch two miles before get to Albert in the Headquarters bus. Quite good fun and like a picnic although very cold. After Albert pass through the most amazing scene of desolation caused by the July 1$^{st}$ advance. Ground everywhere pitted raked by shells and cut up as by an earthquake. Dinner back at Wolff Hut between La Boiselle and Ovillers. These two villages are only recognisable as villages by desolate stumps of trees and a few scattered bricks. Ovillers church is simply a spike of bricks about 8ft high. All round the Huts (Nissen 30 x 16) and oval in shape the ground is scoriated with trenches and shell holes. Scattered everywhere are 'dud' shells, bombs and all the wreckage of war. Scattered here and there are pitiful little crosses and occasional bits of leg and boots show above the ground. Opposite the huts are 9in howitzers, and all round various batteries. About five miles from German Line. Our section of the Line is just in front of Pys – in front of Courcelette and Pozieres. The Line is held by detached posts – very crude and scattered.

Dinner. Bed in Hut with other officers.

The bitterly cold weather had made it impossible to dig deeply in the frozen ground and improve the trench systems, so the 'Line' was indeed very crude and scattered. *The History of the Second Division* states that:

*Communications were as yet far from perfect. So bad were the latter when the Division took over the line that (and it may seem strange to write it) no one possessed an accurate knowledge of the actual positions of the front-line posts. 'It was not,' said the General Officer Commanding on the 29$^{th}$ January, 'until we got these photographs [air photographs of the Divisional area] that we had an accurate knowledge of where our front posts really were.' Reliefs* *often failed to find the posts they were sent out to relieve. And heavy snowstorms frequently added to the difficulties.*[51]

The front-line men on both sides are lost and huddled against the winter, sheltering in shallow scratches on the ice-bound surface, waiting for spring. The only significant military activity is in the air. That, and the daily dose of shellfire. It is Sunday, and Monty prepares for another sermon.

Sunday, 14 January 1917
All available space being taken up impossible to arrange service for the morning. Canteen carried on by Harris in his own Platoon Hut. Go for a walk with CO and Company Commanders to Divisional Headquarters to see a specimen of a post. On the way by side of Albert Road we see a <u>huge</u> mine crater fired by British. We see post which is very small hut neat and covered in section of trench. Afterwards walk on to Cromwell Huts to see Machine Gun Company quarters – Christopher and Beck – others are up the Line. Get back to lunch. Arrange Evening Service in Hut 49 at 6 p.m. Spend afternoon reading home mail and preparing. Hut full. 36 at Holy Communion (speak on 'In Quietness in Confidence shall be your strength').
Dinner. Bed. Bath rather cold as other people.

Monday, 15 January 1917
Busy during morning shifting Canteen to another Hut and checking Accounts. Walk over in afternoon to Machine Gun Company. Have tea with Blair and Heppell and stay to dinner. Arrive back at 10 p.m. Walk on with Blair to Aveluy to 6th Brigade to see Hornby re. Leave.

Monty's efforts to get leave are persistent, but fruitless. Chaplains to the Forces were technically volunteers, so perhaps that meant that he could hop on a ferry home any time he wanted, but the reality is very different.

Tuesday, 16 January 1917

Holy Communion at 7.45 a.m. in Mess. Lyle and Grant present.

After breakfast inspect Canteen and walk over with Lyle and Whitehead to Aveluy to see Hornby if possible S John? re. Leave. See skull on way. Hornby out again. Aveluy shelled the day and night previously. Get back to lunch. Inspect Canteen and leave instructions. Read and chat in Mess. Tea early. Regiment leaves for Line 4–5 p.m. Write up this. Proceed with CO and Whitehead walking to Aveluy. Find Quartermaster's stores after much searching. See Hornby re. Leave. No use. Dinner in cellar of Quartermaster's stores. A good deal of shelling, heavy in village. Sleep on stretcher. Good night.

The regiment is moving up to the Line, in one of its endless shuffles. The sight of a skull is still of sufficient novelty to be worth mentioning – after a month away from the Front Monty has probably forgotten all about its little treats and treasures.

Wednesday, 17 January 1917

Get up at 8.45 a.m. News comes in that Hill was killed last night going up the Line. Go with C.O. to Brigade Rear Headquarters Cromwell Huts after breakfast to verify report of Hill's death. Get on to Regiment and find it is true. Walk on to Divisional Advanced Headquarters to see Mackenzie.

Meet Bell to arrange to go up with him to-night at 7 p.m.

Back to lunch. Five new officers turn up, Hayman, Barnes
. . .

Arrange for Canteen to come down here from Wolff Huts.

Talk and write. Have tea. Go to Cromwell Huts for Bell. Find Bell is not going up after all because of sore throat. And so he details Corporal Kemp to guide me up and we start at about 6.30 p.m. We go at a good pace over the frozen ground. I find my pack etc pretty heavy. Go through Pozieres along Albert–Bapaume Road and round to left past Courcelette and so to Machine Gun Company Headquarters

154

near Brigade Headquarters. Arrive at about 8 p.m. in time
for dinner and find a warm welcome from Oxo and Todd.
Headquarters is a nice little oval shelter in the midst of
similar ones and of dug-outs. We have as furniture chairs ??
tables and stove found by Oxo and Bell in Courcelette. Oxo
shows me Marriage Register which he picked up in
Courcelette and various bombs. After dinner we retire to
bed in Heavy dug-out opposite. We sleep in wired bunks
ranged along the side two deep. I sleep in Bell's valise and
am quite comfy.

Perhaps my grandfather sounds callous, on the day he learns of
Nick Hill's death, the way he moves on so smoothly to write
about Oxo and Todd and their scrounging for furniture in the
ruined French village of Courcelette. He is 'quite comfy' snuggled
down in Bell's 'valise' – a somewhat startling image. Nick Hill
was his ping-pong opponent and partner in long, discursive
chats about religion; they had spent many hours together in the
few short months they'd known each other, opening their hearts
on marriage, individuality and the Church. Did my grandfather
have nothing more to say than that Hill was 'killed'?

To think that is to misunderstand the nature of my grandfather's diary, which he uses to record events – and rarely his
innermost thoughts. But we also need to consider that after four
months on the Western Front Monty may already have been
changing to become accustomed to the random removal of
friends and comrades. Maybe people tried to learn as quickly as
they could not to become too attached to anyone at the Front.
Perhaps being enrolled in one of the famous 'Mates' regiments,
where everyone signed up together and fought and died together,
just compounded the agony. I don't think that is necessarily so.
In fact, Neville is very clear that the reverse is true, in a letter to
his father on 29 January 1917:

*The longer I am with this Regiment, the more I love it. I've got a
sort of feeling that I never want to be parted from it. I never felt
like that with the 3rd Battalion, but out here we are all such good*

*friends. Brothers we are and brothers we will remain. You can't really know anyone until you come out here.*[52]

And, just two days before Nick Hill's death, Neville had written: 'No one is allowed to be depressed. We are a band of brothers.'[53]

And that's the thing, I think: 'no one is *allowed* to be depressed'. Remarque was right: 'You can cope with all the horror as long as you simply duck thinking about it.' He said more:

> *One thing I do know: everything that is sinking into us like a stone now, while we are in the war, will rise up again when the war is over, and that's when the real life-and-death struggle will start.*[54]

For chaplains, that 'life-and-death struggle' would often start long before the war ended. They were the ones at the Front whose job it was to try and make sense of the senseless; to try and explain, to the men and to themselves, what in God's name was going on. Either that or they fell in with the generals and Winningon-Ingram, and preached Holy War and righteous slaughter. Monty couldn't do that. He may have coasted over Nick Hill's death, but he knew he would have to come back to it – and the millions of other, seemingly random killings – at some point. Monty believed in the love of God; and he wanted to believe that behind this screaming apocalypse, in which the life or death of his friends could seem no more explicable than a lottery win or loss, there was a benign creator at work, whose purpose and point would be revealed if we only had faith. As Monty had put it in his sermon 'Hearsay', he had faith in the teachings of Jesus Christ. 'But it is one thing to hear about and a very different thing to experience. It is the difference between head knowledge and heart knowledge.' What Monty was seeing and hearing and experiencing at the Front, the 'heart knowledge' that was pouring in on him, could not necessarily be reconciled with a benign and loving God.

At just about the same time, in a hospital bed in Rouen,

Siegfried Sassoon was making his own journey away from his Christian faith:

*For the soldier is no longer a noble figure; he is merely a writhing insect among this ghastly folly of destruction . . . I want to find someone who has some faith in the war and its purposes. But they see nothing but their own tiny destinies . . . So much for God. He is a cruel buffoon, who skulks somewhere at the Base with tipsy priests to serve him, and lead the chorus of Hymns Ancient and Modern.*

*I can see God among the pine-trees where birds are flitting and chirping. And spring will rush across the country in April with tidings of beauty. But spring in this cursed 'year of victory' will be but a green flag waving a signal for devilish slaughter to begin. The agonies of armies will be on every breeze; their blood will stain the flowers. The foulness of battle will cut off all kindliness from the hearts of men.* [55]

Before her husband left for the war, Kathleen had found an article in *The Disciple* and copied it into the front of his diary. The story is a strong statement of belief in guardian angels – that a man's faith will protect him from harm, even in the most terrible circumstances. It is also, by implication, a statement that those who do not have faith will find themselves in mortal danger. At some later point, someone – Monty? – tore this story out of his diary and hid it away. Of course, we cannot blame Kathleen for writing it down, or for wanting to believe in something, anything, that would keep her husband safe, but I wonder how long it was before Monty found it absurd to think that a true believer would somehow be safer than anyone else. Or that there was any kind of pattern to the likelihood of a man being torn apart by a shell. All I do know is that someone didn't want the story or the idea anywhere near Monty's diary.

That said, the British soldier at the Front may not have been especially religious, but he was famously superstitious. He'd try anything, even a prayer, if it heightened his chances of survival.

'Angels of Jesus'

In ultra-Catholic circles the popular idea of the Holy Angels has given rise to many mis-conceptions, especially with regard to their presence and appearance to the troops at the Front, and having in view the recent controversies and diversities of opinion on 'The Angels at Mons', I will endeavour to lay before the readers of 'The Disciple' my own views and impressions whilst serving with the British Expeditionary Force.

I have personally never been in the state of blessedness as vouched to the troops in 'The Bowmen', and it never has fallen to my lot to look upon the faces and behold the forms of the Holy Ones, but I have been very near to this state of Supreme Joy and have FELT the sacred presence of Jesus and his company of blessed ones.

On one occasion during a fierce attack on the German position, in the first Battle for Calais, I was leading my section across a ploughed field when a fierce exultation seized me and in a moment I felt and knew the presence of our Blessed Lord beside me, and His dear words 'Lo, I am with thee even unto the end of the world' came to my lips, and for a brief sweet moment during the heat of the battle I imagined myself back at the altar of my home church in England – so near and yet so far.

Pressing forward, we came within easy reach of the German rifles and a bullet chipped a stone at my feet, and a second later another hit the ground to my right, then another to the left, until there remained no longer a doubt that I was the unwelcome attention of a vigilant sniper.

Breathing a silent prayer for Grace as we proceeded, I continued to lead my section until the order came to extend further apart. Repeating the order to my men I moved a few paces to my left and the man who took my place was shot through the heart the next instant, by the sniper's bullet that was undoubtedly meant for me.

Never before or since have I felt the closer proximity of my Guardian Angel as at that moment, and my heart re-echoed the words 'Not my wise, but thine O Lord'.

Further on I took the remnants of my section across a grass-field and made for the security of a deep river fronting the enemy's trenches.

*My men then numbered 10, myself in the middle and five men on either flank.*

*We had not proceeded half way across the field, when a machine gun rattled out and every one of my 10 men were cut down like corn, killed outright, and I with my Guardian Angel traversed the remaining sixty yards or so to safety, and reached my refuge without hurt or scratch.*

*This is only one of the numberless instances of the presence of The Angels, which I have known and felt, and nothing can shake my firm conviction that Jesus and his Holy Angels walked and fought with me on several occasions.*

On the back of the final page, Monty has scrawled: 'Vestment being a stole and the only incense the smoke of battle.'

In mid-January 1917, Monty has very little time to dwell on any of this:

Thursday, 18 January 1917

Roused at 5.30 a.m. and start off with Todd and Oxo at 6.15 a.m. to go round the machine guns' position. A weird tramp over the frozen snow first along duck board walks with a light only and then along tracks guided by wires. The track zig zags round shell holes with which the ground is absolutely pitted. The snow covers all sorts of horrible realities and relics of the Push. We visit Heppel and Blair in their positions. These positions are just bits of trenches with shelters and the beginnings of dug outs. As it gets lighter we see Pys, Amantiers, Le Sars – most wonderful of all we see our men in the front line walking about on the top and the Boches in the distance beyond but not far away walk about in full view. Evidently except for shelling this is mutually a free front although a very uncomfortable one – uncomfortable because Infantry positions are practically without shelter and exposed to all the elements. We return home past place where Hill was killed by shrapnel and past Regimental Headquarters. Opposite this we find a dump of Hun Rifle Grenades and take two. Back to breakfast at 8.20am.

159

Shave and wash after breakfast. Visit Brigade Headquarters and chat with Farquharson and Disney. Arrange to be at disposal of Brigade whilst in the Line. Chat with Lyle and Blackwell whose Headquarters in support are next door and then go along with Oxo to see Baines re. Hill's burial at Regimental Headquarters. Find Colonel of Kings' (Knocker) there and have to wait till first he and then the Brigadier and Boyd are disposed of. Regimental Headquarters dug out very small. Get back to lunch to find Bell has turned up. After lunch walk with Oxo to see derelict Tanks of which we see eight or nine quite close together one with huge rent in its side – also an aeroplane (British). Call on Doctor McTurk at his Aid Post in one of the last standing houses in Courcelette. An unhealthy spot shelled night and day. Have tea with him and 17th RF Dr Winter. Arrange to have Hill's body moved down to Brigade Cemetery during night. Carry plank of wood back and visit Oxo's guns en route. Get back without incident. Dinner. Bridge. Bed. Oxo sleeps in shelter by stove.

Monty is busy arranging for Hill's funeral. He carries a plank of wood up the Line – and no doubt comes back with the bits and pieces of Hill's body laid on top of it. Monty makes sure that he will be 'at the disposal of the Brigade whilst in the Line'. He seems energised to be back at the Front and is rising early. He continues to work on his bridge.

Friday, 19 January 1917

Go round with Oxo at 6.30 a.m. to move two of his gun teams to a new position. Get back about 8.15 a.m. Todd and Ball return from their rounds soon after. After breakfast shave and wash and supervise digging of grave. Take Hill's funeral at 11 a.m. Several officers present. After service chat with Spurge, Neville (Straith) who have come down from front line. Go over with Warren to see Fielding who has also been relieved. After lunch go with Bell to Mouquet Farm, the scene of bitter fighting and the taking of Thiepval. See Thiepval in distance. Go through huge Hun dug out under the ruins of the Farm – close to which is a derelict Tank. The dug out consists of very narrow passages lined with bunks and is most interesting. See 18th Division Machine Gun Company. Walk home to tea and meet Bennett (Derby's curate) en route. I go on to 17th R.F. Regimental Headquarters to see CO re. my being at their disposal. Have tea with them in one of the best British dug outs ever made. Many huge chambers (to sleep 35 men and far better than any Hun dug out). Regiment are still extending it. It is shelled a good deal. Work done by South African miners (Tunnelling Company RE). Get back. Chat with 52nd next door. Dinner. Bridge. Bed as before.

Saturday, 20 January 1917
Get up at 8.15am. Breakfast. Go round with Oxo to his gun positions where RE are working hard to improve trenches and dug outs. Got back to shelter at 12. Shave and wash. Lunch. Pack up and prepare to move. Watch shelling of track out. Some narrow escapes to relieving Machine Gun Company. Place identity peg on Hill's grave. Still hard frost. Chat Sponge. Tea. Hewitt of 6th Machine Gun Company there to take over. Start off at 5.45 p.m. with Oxo to march down. Great congestion at Fraser's Post on Courcelette Road due to Reliefs coming, troops going out and mules and horses unable to make progress on hard slippery road. Luckily no shelling. Finally get through. Short pause at Gum boots store. Very hard to stand up on frozen road. Men continually falling flat. After long weary march finally arrive with A Company via Aveluy at Bouzincourt at 10.30 p.m. Find 52nd Mess and Ellis, Coffin and Chevalier. Find billet with Doctor and Chevalier – iron bunk. Farmhouse. Get up next morning at 12 noon and find Regiment have arrived during night at various times.

Monty places an identity peg on Hill's grave; just one of the hundreds of thousands that are starting to litter this small patch of northern France. Also on Saturday, 20 January (although he doesn't mention it), Monty spends 5c (or maybe ½d) on a copy of *Sometimes* (*Being the Somme Times and Ancre News*), one of the satirical newspapers that were sprouting up to answer the soldiers' need for light relief. On the front page, under Notes and Comments, is this piece:

> *'Engage the enemy more closely!' by sea and by land, under the water and in the air, says a weekly newspaper. 'Now is the time to push them, and push them hard on every front and in every element.'*
>
> *Of course it is not our business to discuss military matters, which the arm-chair gentlemen in Fleet Street are much more competent to do; but we cannot help wishing that Horatio Bottomley, H.G. Wells and one or two others might be given the opportunity of doing 48 hours in a front line trench in the chalk country, when the weather is 'soft', and 'engaging the enemy more closely.'*

Horatio Bottomley was the editor of *John Bull*, and a rabidly enthusiastic proponent of the idea that the only good German was a dead German. On the back of the newspaper are two columns of spoof advertisements, including a call to 'our male friends at home'. *GOOD NEWS FROM THE SOMME*, it starts . . .

But best of all is the article on page two (there are only four pages to this folded sheet), titled:

> *Putting His Pipe Out*
> *One of our Church Army workers who has just arrived in the war zone relates a little experience he had in crossing the Channel. There were a good many civilians on board, of both sexes. Our colleague noticed an elderly civilian at a few paces' distance smoking a pipe, the fumes of which were blowing in the face of a most charming young lady close by. Our friend is nothing if not polite, with a profound respect for womankind: moreover, he was in khaki. He stepped forward and spoke.*

*'Pardon me, sir,' he said, 'but do you realise that the smoke from your pipe is annoying this young lady?'*

*The elderly man gave no reply save a more violent puff than usual. Mr Montmorency (our worker) waited a minute, then continued:*

*'I suppose, sir, you did not understand me. I said your smoking annoyed this young lady.'*

*The man looked at Montmorency, then looked out to sea, and puffed away vigorously. Monty was moved.*

*'It would pain me deeply, sir' he said, 'to be forced to this course, but unless you put that pipe out immediately, I shall feel compelled to throw you overboard.' Now Monty is 6ft 2in, well developed, and, as before mentioned, he is in khaki.*

*Then the young lady spoke, 'I suppose, father, you had better put your pipe out. I should hate to have you drowned.'*

*There are various morals to this story.*

Can that 'Monty' really be my grandfather? He was in fact just under six feet tall – but how many Church-working Montys can there have been, only recently arrived in France?

It is another Sunday at the Front, but this time there's no need for Monty to give a sermon. In the week that follows, Monty's drive to get home reaches new heights – except, when it comes to it, he allows another man to take his place.

Sunday, 21 January 1917
Find service arranged in CA [Church Army] Hut at 6 p.m. Put up notices. Meet Osborne, Chapelle, Mirth, Ellis and Coffin walk over to Aveluy to tea with remnants of 5 Trench Mortar Brigade. Get back to service. Duthrie takes. Help him with Holy Communion (40). Dinner. Bed.

Monday, 22 January 1917
Walk over to Aveluy. Meet Duthrie and go on to Divisional Headquarters. Find Holden there and Bate just returned from leave. Talk about leave. Arrange to come next day. Walk back to lunch. Do Canteen accounts with Harris. Tea. Write letters in billet after tea by fire till 9.30 p.m. Bath.

Tuesday, 23 January 1917
Walk over to Divisional Headquarters. Very cold. Many Hun aeroplanes up being shelled. Bits of shell come down very close to me. Meet Holden and Bates. Agree to let Holden have leave before me. Get back to lunch. Hockey for 52nd v 5th Brigade on cold frozen snow. Lose 4–2. Tea with Balloon section RFC after. Then tea with Disney, Boyd and Farquharson at Brigade Headquarters. Change. Canteen. CA Hut. Chats. Dinner. Bed.

Wednesday, 24 January 1917
Walk round. Prepare for service in evening. Lunch. Ride over in sidecar to Senlis to find Raven, who has come to 5th Brigade in Brown's place. See Adjutant 24th but cannot find Raven. Try to see 2nd Corps Senior Chaplain to the Forces. Tea with Sponge at Brigade Company Headquarters. Also Ellis, Blackwell and Giles. Walk back to Service in CA Hut at 7. Hut full ('What is Life?'). Dinner with Machine Gun Company. Bed at 10.15 p.m.

As war rages, and another great Spring Offensive looms, Monty reminds his audience that:

> An other-worldliness gives to this world its true significance, giving it an importance which otherwise it cannot have. Far from detracting from the importance of life's detail it rescues from pettiness the small affairs of life and one sees life as a 'great bundle of little things' which fall into place in the Eternal Jig Saw Puzzle.

My grandfather was keen to remind the listener – but mostly himself at that moment – to keep his eyes fixed on the bigger picture, because there will be plenty of petty frustrations along the way. It's just as well he's taking the long view, as his leave is postponed yet again. And then it is cancelled altogether.

Thursday, 25 January 1917

Walk over to 2nd Divison Headquarters for Chaplains' meeting at 10.30 p.m. See Bate re. leave. I may go on Friday. Meeting at 11 a.m. Meet Raven. Arrangements made for Services on Sunday therefore leave postponed again till Sunday. Go to lunch at Quartermaster's stores Aveluy. Meet Raven at Church at 3 p.m. Walk with him to Senlis. Arrange for services. Have tea with 'B' Company, Sponge etc. Walk back to Bouzincourt with Raven. Quite a nice man from St Mary's Brixton. Broadminded. Dinner. Hear rumour that leave is closed. Write K that this may be true.

Friday, 26 January 1917

Nothing much during morning. Lunch at Brigade Headquarters. General gives me leave to go on Sunday. Walk over to Senlis with Coffin. Take services to Highland Light Infantry. Prepare Sergeant Fairclough for Holy Communion in Soldiers' Prayer Room. Go to see Sponge. Walk back to Bouzincourt. Tea. Go round to see Machine Gun Company. Dinner. Bridge. Bed.

Saturday, 27 January 1917

Hear at breakfast that leave is postponed for Division because of congestion on French Railways. Canteen. Chat. Coffin. Write. Prepare. Play Hockey for 52nd v 5th Brigade. Win 4–2. Tea at Brigade Headquarters.

Wouldn't you believe it? The bloody French Railways have caused the postponement of all leave. Nothing changes. It is very, very cold.

Sunday, 28 January 1917

Service in Church Army Hut at 10am. Pretty full. 'The Future Life and Sin'. Holy Communion, 35. Move from Bouzincourt at 3.15 p.m. Walk with Coffin through Aveluy to Ovillers. Here are Officers Headquarters – Regiment further up in

Ovillers Huts. Relieve the Royal Berks who go up the Line. Get into Quarters about 6 p.m. Nissen Huts. Two sleeping Huts for Officers and Mess. Sleep in Headquarters Hut (7). Very very cold and draughty.

Monday, 29 January 1917

Walk with Chevalier to Ovillers Cemetery to try to find Lockhart Shaw's Grave. See Harry London's son's Grave but can't find Lockhart's. A great number of scattered graves. After lunch walk over to Aveluy with Chevalier to see Machine Gun Company and Trench Mortar Brigade. Examine damage done to Quartermaster's Stores which was hit by direct shell, several men narrowly escaping. Small hole to cellar below. Chat and tea with Trench Mortar Brigade. Return at 6 p.m. Chat in Canteen. Bitterly cold.

It is bitterly cold, and Monty is desperately unsettled about his leave. It's worse without a doubt thinking you are going, and then being told you are not. Also, playing hockey against the Highland Light Infantry in a predictably 'violent and scrappy' game cannot have helped his sense of calm – no matter that they won 6–2 and made it up with a cup of tea afterwards.

Tuesday, 30 January 1917

Feel so unsettled about leave, go up to see Bate and mooch round. Walk over with Major Boyd (Staff Major Brigade) and Disney to Bouzincourt to play hockey against Highland Light Infantry. Game in snow is very violent and scrappy. Win 6–2. Tea with Highland Light Infantry. Call in at Quartermaster's stores on way back and find Lieutenant Colonel Crosse and Slade Barker just back from leave. Very glad to see him again. Write.

And then, Hallelujah! Monty gets his leave; he can start 'tomorrow' and will be away from France for one month.

Wednesday, 31 January 1917

Go up to see Bate. Out. Write in Mess. Conference of

Officers. Immediately after lunch good news comes through that leave is open again. Go up with Chevalier to see Bate and get Warrant for Feb 29 – to leave here tomorrow. Go to see Quartermaster. Get things together after tea. Write this. Pay [illegible].

This is the last entry in Monty's wartime diary. It is the last day of January 1917 and Monty has two more long years of war to endure. Perhaps he wrote others that are hidden away in some long-forgotten corner of one of his homes. He may have stopped keeping a diary altogether, or destroyed later volumes. It is possible that he never wrote another word – quite possibly he could not face it, or did not know what to say. Perhaps a simple telling of events was no longer an option, when his faith and beliefs were disintegrating.

This much we do know: my grandfather went to war as a Chaplain to the Forces, and he lost his faith in God. He told his family that much, though almost nothing else. In January 1917, he is heading home to his wife and baby – and maybe he plans to talk about the terrible things he has seen and done since they last met. But I don't think so. Famously, the men of 1914–18 never did like to talk much about what they'd had to endure. If they talked at all, they talked to each other. How could anyone else really understand?

But here's another thought. Maybe their wives, sweethearts, children, families and friends, who hadn't been there and couldn't understand, maybe they didn't want to talk about it either? Maybe they only wanted to talk about it a little. But not enough. Never enough. Not over and over and over again, until all the pain and poison and distress were leached out and their poor wounded men were able to look again at the world and think, 'Yes, this is a rational place, or a God-given place, and not a pit of senseless savagery.' Maybe there never was a moment when the horror that had sunk like a stone into a generation of men was raised up and banished. It just sunk in and stayed there and destroyed them all – even those who survived.

# TEN

# Jack

Monty's journey home would have been just as quick as the journey out (although maybe this time he didn't threaten to toss any obstinate elderly gentlemen overboard, in what was very nearly the world's first outbreak of Passive Smoking Rage). Many men found the speed of return utterly disorientating. One day they were mired in mud and gore, huddled in waterlogged trenches or tramping across fields that were layered with rusting armaments and human remains, the next they were sitting on the deck of a peacetime ferry, making the bracingly short dash across the Channel. On board there might even be a few women – nurses, perhaps, or returning sightseers – and unless the soldiers were going home via one of the military hospitals, these might be the first women they had seen for months. Also on board, of course, would be the wounded. In stark contrast to the hopeful, horse-playing, anxious journey out, the decks of the ferry home are filled with the wounded: men without limbs, eyes or jawbones, whose lungs are frothing and heaving from the effects of gas, and those with healthy bodies but shattered minds. Men without hope. Like Monty, they might only have been in France for four months, maybe they'd only been there a week, but they are none of them the same.

Monty would have sped home to The Croft, his in-laws' house on the fringes of London, to see Kathleen and baby Ruthie. In their four months apart, he and Kathleen have exchanged at least sixty letters and dozens of postcards, all of Monty's waved through by Censor Number 226, but now at last they can talk and hold each other. There are many people to see: the Bigger parents and their clan (although Walter and Bill may well have been away); Monty's sisters, Eva, Edie and Lily; and Tummy and Cecil and any other Cambridge friends who were not off fighting. It is unlikely that Monty's father was there to greet him – he and his wife were almost certainly still in India – but Monty would have been busy, with everyone desperate to hear his news. Siegfried Sassoon, home on leave, describes how he tempered his talk to his audience: the bluff, manly chat with the retired Major; the surly reticence with his aunt; the daring or ghastly deeds hinted at with his friends. But with not one of them did he share the truth. Perhaps Monty was the same. He did love to chat, but what did he tell his hungry audience? There cannot have been one who did not have friends or relations away at one of the Fronts.

There are no surviving photographs from February 1917, leaving us nothing that we can stare at and try to read Monty's features during that cruelly short month at home. There are some pictures of Monty in uniform playing with his young daughter, but Ruthie is too young for them to be from early 1917. I am struck by one in which he appears to be swinging her into a crowded pig sty at feeding time, but she's probably aged only about eighteen months and my grandfather looks carefree. There are photos of Monty's father in a garden with a slightly older Ruthie. He is playing football with an apple and has it trapped under his foot, and Ruthie is charging ecstatically towards him. I only mention this because in the background is his second wife, and she appears to be giggling; although in the next photo Edward Senior has picked up Ruthie, who clutches the apple and is smiling at the camera, and his wife is standing straight-backed and grim-faced beside him. Ruthie, with her floppy blonde curls and impish smile, could have caused a basilisk to crack a smile.

Monty, though, is absent from this and every other photo. Until the end of the war, the only photographs that survive of Monty have all been taken at the Front.

Monty may also have been able to see Jack Bigger in February 1917. Jack had joined the 5th East Surrey Regiment on 5 August 1914, taking the oath and signing the declaration in Streatham, round the corner from his home at 512 Streatham High Road. In his medical inspection report, his 'apparent age' was given as twenty-one years, eight months and his height as 5 ft 9½ in. They could be certain about the height, but perhaps they had to be wary about expressing certainty about a new recruit's age. There were plenty who were so keen to join up that they were prepared to add a year or two to their real age. Jack's chest measurement, when fully expanded, was 37½ in. and his physical development was 'good'. He was a sporting young man and pretty well nourished for the time and place.

The 5th East Surreys had been sent straight to Cawnpore in India in 1914, so Jack had spent the first two years of the war safeguarding Britain's interests in the heart of its empire. This was not a waste of time. The war in Europe was sending shockwaves across the world and the empires of the major powers were crucial in providing the raw materials (including the men) for the worsening conflict. Germany would have loved to foment revolt in India, and the Ottoman Caliph hoped his call for Holy War would resonate among the country's Muslims, so the British Government kept a nervous eye on the jewel in its crown and stationed troops there just in case. But by late 1916 Haig's need for new men was so overwhelming that the Western Front was sucking everyone and everything into its churning maw.

It's quite likely that Jack would have met the senior Edward Guilford in India. If so, I am sure they would have got on. They both had a lively sense of fun. Edward's wartime job was to organise the defence of the Punjab – he was the epitome of the muscular Christian – but he would I'm sure have made time to see his son's brother-in-law in the two years that he was posted to the country. Jack headed back to England in late 1916 and was discharged from the 5th East Surreys on 24 January 1917 – 'in consequence,' his military record states, 'of having been appointed to a commission in the 1st Battalion East Surrey

Regiment'. Jack was eager to get to France because it meant a commission as an officer (which was approved on 7 February) and because it meant he'd finally be involved in the fighting. There was time, though, for him and Monty to meet and perhaps discuss how to get him transferred to the Ox and Bucks Regiment, to be with his friend and brother-in-law.

Jack was sent to the Battalion's training depot on 19 February and arrived with the Battalion in France on 17 March. On that day, the 1st East Surreys were moving out of the Line into temporary billets in the village of Béthune, with Jack part of a new draft of 67 men arriving with Captain Congdon. The next day they were off again, heading to the village of Raimbert. In other words, Jack was being inducted rapidly into the Army life of billets, marching, inspections and more inspections. With him he had the pocket New Testament that he'd been given by the vicar of St Philip's, Norbury, J.E.H. Williams, 'as a pledge of prayerful remembrance from the Members of the Congregation and their affectionate friend and Vicar'. The Rev. Williams had chosen these two verses for Jack to contemplate when on the Western Front: 'Be thou strong and very courageous', Joshua 1:7; and 'Wait on the Lord, Be of good courage, and He shall strengthen thine heart', Psalms 27:14. I have the tiny, stained and beaten book in front of me now: the spine has been broken (by Jack?) so it falls open easily on this passage in Chapter 7 of St Luke's Gospel:

> And the Lord said, Whereunto then shall I liken the men of this generation? and to what are they like? They are like unto children sitting in the marketplace, and calling to one another, and saying, We have piped unto you, and ye have not danced; we have mourned to you, and ye have not wept.

Jack had arrived on the Western Front at the very moment when the Germans were making a planned retreat from their overextended forward lines and back to the Hindenburg Line. This was not really one line at all, but a complex network of wire, trenches, gun emplacements and bunkers, dominating all the best positions, which had been designed with all the bloodily won experience of two years of trench warfare. It was a defensive masterpiece that would allow attacking armies to push relatively easily over the first line, before being cordoned and destroyed by concentrated counter-attacks.

The British generals, who had been gearing up for a major attack in March, now found themselves having to move forward across a dying land that had been systematically obliterated by the retreating Germans. Villages were demolished, crops and orchards were uprooted, wells poisoned, and every rock, broken piece of equipment or doorway hid a possible booby trap. The British dug themselves into this scorched earth under the commanding heights of the German artillery; their generals sat down and planned the next round of attacks. There's a gloriously sour comment by Edward Wyrall in his *History of the Second Division* on this planned German retreat:

> *Strange that troops who fought so bravely, as undoubtedly the Germans did, should be 'delighted' to retire from positions which had been soaked with the blood of their comrades in gallant efforts to maintain them. Queer mentality that could see 'success' in an enforced retreat, the abandonment of much war material, and the loss of thousands of troops – killed, wounded, and missing. But humour was never a part of the German temperament.*[56]

Ah, yes, the Germans and their famous sense-of-humour bypass. The British like to fling that particular missile at the humourless Hun whenever they want to remind themselves that they are the cheeky, slightly anarchic (but essentially disciplined), freedom-loving individualists, facing the Prussian automatons. It served the British well as a rallying cry in two world wars, and even if there's nothing especially amusing about a person or a nation that keeps telling you how funny they are, it's clearly part of an enduring national myth. There's that passage quoted earlier from H.G. Wells's *Mr Britling*: the Germans may be about to reduce the world to ashes, but we just find them absurd. Perhaps there's truth in the cliché, although it's probably good to recall that before the twentieth century, when we felt threatened by the French and thought of the Germans as our natural allies, that the latter were often portrayed as jolly, fat, red-faced men, chuckling good-humouredly over their sausages and beer. You'd want to spend a night on the town with them roaring out their drinking songs; far more fun than those slippery, wine-drinking Frenchies.

That more positive view of the enemy in his rather better-built trenches persisted in the First World War – and good-natured banter would often be flung across no-man's-land. The opposing sides would even, it seems, play practical jokes on each other, although as the war ground through its third year, the jokes were fewer and the snipers more persistent. The football matches of Christmas Day 1914 became a distant memory. Siegfried Sassoon, writing his diary in March 1917, felt nothing but nausea for the English and their endless jokes:

> *There is a sort of unreasoning, inhuman gaiety in the air which is beyond description. The English are supposed to be mad in their way of treating the War as a joke, but I think it is only their inherent stupidity and unwillingness to face things. I sometimes feel that everyone (even the Base-Colonels) will suddenly go stark mad and begin shooting one another instead of the Germans. The whole business is so monstrously implacable to all human tenderness.* [57]

Humour and horror mingled inexplicably at the Front, but is it any wonder that very often the gaiety seemed a little strained? Sassoon, of course, shocked many by writing with compassion of the German dead and their grieving mothers, and he was profoundly right to point to the shared humanity of the warring sides, but even so there were real differences between the Germans and their British enemies. It had nothing to do with humour. Here's James Neville, in a letter to his father dated 26 April 1917, musing on a bloodily repulsed German attack:

*Yet the Huns made two other efforts to reach our front line, and in each case they were caught by our guns and wiped out. I don't suppose I shall ever have another opportunity of watching an attack in complete safety. I felt quite sorry for the Huns, for they hadn't got a ghost of a chance. We could even see their officers who follow behind their men, and don't lead them. It looked as if they were driving their men.*[58]

The British officers led their men over the top – they didn't drive them forward from the rear. Their men got it in the neck either way. But it does explain why so many young British subalterns lost their lives on the Western Front. What was the average time a newly arrived British subaltern could expect to last in France or Flanders before he was killed or invalided out? About ten weeks. Jack lasted seven.

Second Lieutenant Jack Bigger, a tiny cog in a monstrous wheel, is training hard with his new battalion. He has also been drafted into the officers' football team, who appear to be thrilled with their new signing. In fact, it's Jack's prowess at football, more than anything else, that makes his Colonel block the repeated requests from Monty and Colonel Crosse for Jack to be transferred to the Ox and Bucks. Was it sporting rivalry that kept Jack in the 1st East Surreys? Quite possibly, but on 23 March he's in the officers' team that narrowly beats the 'Other Ranks' 4–3, which must have been a more than usually competitive match. Also on that day, he was probably one of the officers who rode over to Lilliers to see the 'landscape model of Vimy Ridge' on display at First Army Headquarters. It was apparently on quite a small scale but 'gives a fair, though rather exaggerated, idea of the slope of the ground, and the commanding position of the Ridge'.[59] Alarmingly, Vimy Ridge is to be the target of the regiment's next assault, and they are training incessantly and enduring many lectures on the subject of the 'New Normal Formation for the Attack'.

The weather was atrocious, and it got worse in April. There were frequent snowstorms during the first two weeks of the month, which only stopped for sleet or rain. By mid-April, the battalion was being moved up into the Line, under wild shellfire, although the 'Battalion was fortunate enough to miss most of it'. The state of the road meant that everything had to be carried up to the line by pack. A conference was held on 19 April to allocate positions. Jack's Company (No. 4) is moved to the 1st Line S6 Central. As the Battalion Diary noted: 'This Line is not yet continuous, neither is it wired. It is to be held at all costs.'[60] Hearing this, Jack may have been relieved to be told that he was to be among the men staying back with the transport, although perhaps by now he was eager to see his first bit of action.

While he was waiting, he'd have been able to watch some of the action in the air. It's no wonder the flying machines and their pilots of the First World War were so celebrated and so envied, despite the casualty rates and the horrifying public deaths: at least they could move, and they had a small amount of independence. If you were an infantryman shivering in a mud-clogged trench, looking up to watch the freewheeling dogfights was often the only thing to help you through the long frostbitten days:

*Our aircraft took advantage of the fine weather and several machines assisted the guns. The enemy's fighting patrols could be seen amongst the clouds behind their lines. One of our aeroplanes was shot down in flames as it flew low between the lines.*

*The Enemy's machines appeared to be very fast, and dived with great speed on any of ours that crossed, unescorted, the German trenches below them.*[61]

The pilots did not have parachutes.

Jack had found himself in a very active sector of the Front. Towards the end of April, an assault on the German lines is launched by the 1st Devons, supported by the 1st East Surreys, with disastrous results. There was insufficient artillery support (the wire was not cut, almost none of the German machine-gun posts were put out of action, their artillery was untouched) and, as ever, the weather conditions were miserable. The Devons made some early gains through the slime, but the Line just bulged, soaked them up, then slaughtered them in their hundreds. By the end of the day they had moved one tiny portion of their front line forwards by about 300 yards, at a cost of 15 officers and 260 other ranks. The writer of the Battalion's diary cannot disguise his disgust: 'The troops engaged did all that could be done, but never had a fair chance from the beginning. They were cut up crossing the long stretch of "open" by shrapnel and MGs.'[62]

That was the first piece of action that Jack witnessed. He wasn't involved in the actual assault, and for that he could be thankful, but he and his Company were in close support as they watched the Devons struggle and die.

The next day, the 1st East Surreys were moved back from the Line again. 'Total casualties since 18th, 1 officer 44 other ranks,' notes the Diary. Jack's footballing duties resume, and the officers are beaten 2–1 by the other ranks. The Diary writer (an officer) suggests tetchily that 'a return match is likely in the near future'. The weather turns fine, services are held and concerts staged, and Jack plays football for the regimental team almost every day.

It is now May and at last the sun is shining. Orders arrive for the 5th Division (of which the 1st East Surreys are one part) to relieve the 2nd Division in the line. This prospect could have been exciting: perhaps Monty and Jack will pass in the night? Or even find time to meet up. Jack will be moving on the night of 4 May, relieving the 1st Canadian Infantry Brigade in the front line. I like the sound of Jack's CO, Lieutenant Colonel E.M. Woulfe-Flanagan, even if he won't let Jack leave him for another regiment: on the night before the move, he goes up the line to check that all is OK. He finds that the defensive positions are weak and cannot be held by one battalion. He announces that headquarters' orders are flawed, and doesn't move until more troops are made available – which they are.

The battalion moves off on 4 May. Bombs and rifle grenades are distributed, and they meet their guides who take them up to the front line through the confusing warren of paths and trenches. No. 4 Company is led by 2nd Lieutenant Sutton

(Captain Congdon is back with the transport), with Jack and two other lieutenants in support. Their guide takes them to the support trench, behind No. 2 Company, where they relieve the Canadians, who make haste back to base. It is the moment Jack has been thinking about ever since he left India: he is at the Front for the first time. It is 2 a.m.

The trench Jack finds himself in is far from ideal. The ground has been captured by the Canadians only one day earlier, and, although they have done what they can, it is shallow and exposed. Several sections are isolated and have yet to be joined up. There are no communication trenches, so it is impossible for the front line to keep contact with battalion headquarters, except by using a runner at night; it is just too dangerous by day. Telephone wires have yet to be laid, and once they are, the next day's shellfire destroys them. One of the companies has some carrier pigeons. It is a nasty, vulnerable place to be, and the men dig strenuously through the night to improve their shelter, spurred on by heavy shellfire from the German side. Ten men are wounded. The British guns respond, but their fire falls dangerously short and frantic messages are sent back to stop the shooting. A little later, Captain Hillier in No. 3 Company shoots dead a German Artillery officer who has accidentally wandered into the front line; he happens to be carrying a number of useful maps and badges.

The next night (6 May), Colonel Woulfe-Flanagan pops up in the still inadequate trenches and discovers that they're nowhere near where he thought they were, which explains why the British shells were falling 'short'. More messages are sent back to the gunners. The German guns, unfortunately, have a better idea of what they're firing at, and shells rain down on the British lines, with most falling on the support trenches, where Jack is doing his best to come to terms with the fact that he is being shot at. The Colonel orders a readjustment of the line, and two platoons of No. 4 Company, possibly with Jack among them, are shuffled up to the first line of defences and put under the command of No. 3 Company. There is much frantic digging of trenches – and indeed orders come in from headquarters for all offensive operations to cease while the lines are secured. Shells continue to fall.

Heavy rain begins to fall on the night of 7 May and continues through the next day. Orders are received that the 1st East Surreys will be moving out on the night of 8 May. The Regimental Diary has this startling message: 'Completion of relief to be notified to this office by word FARCE.' Maybe it's a premonition, because on the day that they are due to move to the rear, the 1st East Surrey Companies, nervously crouching in their shallow trenches with no protective wire, no communication with their headquarters, and quite possibly in the wrong place anyway, are overwhelmed by the enemy, who attacks with devastating force from every side.

At first, it is not clear to battalion headquarters what is going on, although they must have guessed what was coming. The day before, hostile aeroplanes had flown 'very low over our trenches for a considerable length of time' – noting, no doubt, the absence of any wire, the lack of any trenches leading back to base, and above all the isolation of the men, who must have looked up and felt the watching eyes assessing their fate.

On the morning of 8 May, at some point between 3 a.m. and 3.30 a.m., while it was still dark, the Germans attacked – from the front at first, when they seem to have been driven back, but by 6.30 a.m. the attacks were coming from left and right. Runners were sent from HQ to try and find No. 4 Company to see if they needed any more ammunition, but they were already cut off. The decision was taken not to send any men to help them but to consolidate the line, because if the Germans kept coming beyond the front line and its support trenches, everything might be lost.

At 6.45 a.m., this message was received at HQ by a runner from the officer commanding No. 3 Company (and Jack was either there or already cut off with the rest of the men in No. 4 Company). It had been sent at 5.50 a.m.:

*Enemy attacking along whole of front. They have been repulsed*
*for the present except I cannot get information from my Right*

*flank. OC No. 1 Company has cleared his immediate front, but Enemy are Massing in Wood in front. He wants Artillery to fire there. Will send up Red Rocket if Attack continues.*[63]

I don't know if a Red Rocket was ever sent up, but the attack continued and by 8 a.m. it was probably all over. Wounded soldiers straggling back to headquarters reported that men were 'retiring all along the line', although 'owing to the wet and damaged state of the ground the men could not charge and were shot down from nearly every direction as they moved back'. By this stage, No. 2 Company had been 'overwhelmed by hand-to-hand fighting'. No. 3 Company, with its two platoons from No. 4, 'were under heavy fire from Left Rear and were likewise unable to extricate themselves'. As for the other two platoons of No. 4 Company, they 'suffered heavy casualties from Shell fire and were probably overwhelmed by Enemy advancing against their Left Flank. Some of them were last reported to be fighting about 50 yards behind their trenches'.

Bayonet, shell, bullet, grenade – no one can say for sure how the men of 1st East Surreys died, slipping and gasping in the mud, but die they did: 'With the exception of the wounded the number that survived out of the 4 Companies was very small.'[64]

There's a separate, four-page report on these events in the Regimental Diary. It's called 'Report on Operations Resulting in the Loss of Fresnoy, 8 May, 1917'. When that many men are killed, wounded or missing (and the final tally was 14 officers and 498 other ranks), it needs more than just another diary entry. The last sentence of the report is clear: 'All ranks did their best and it was through no fault of theirs that the position was lost.' I wonder if one of the survivors managed to deliver the required message to Headquarters: 'FARCE'.

There is no further mention of Jack in the Regimental Diary, as it becomes preoccupied with the forthcoming assault on Oppy Wood. Jack just vanishes without a word or a backward glance. Dr and Mrs Bigger, Jack's parents, waiting for the next letter or postcard from their third son, instead receive this telegram on 14 May 1917:

Regret to inform you 2<sup>nd</sup> Lte JAW Bigger East Surrey Regiment was reported missing on May eighth. This does not necessarily mean killed or wounded. Will report any further news immediately on receipt.

The agony of uncertainty. Their beloved Jack. Monty, back in France, must have heard almost immediately, and rides over at once to see what he can find out or do. He writes to Jack's parents:

France
18 May 1917
My dear Mummy and Daddy
I think you will know how I feel about Jack. But I know that you will want every scrap of information that I can give you and so I will devote this letter entirely to that. Most fortunately I was able to go off almost immediately on horse to Jack's regiment, which was only about 3 miles away. And not only so, but I found Captain Congdon, and the only other officer, Sutton by name, who could give me the latest and most complete information such as it is. It is only kind to tell you at once that neither of them could give me any more definite news of Jack than you already have. But they could and did give me the fullest particulars of the circumstances, which led up to his being missing. Captain Congdon was not in the Line at all at the time but Sutton was in the same trench as Jack, and was the last officer who saw him. The last he saw of him was on the night of May 7<sup>th</sup> when they had dinner together in Sutton's dug out.

Early the next morning, May 8<sup>th</sup>, an attack was made by the Germans – which you must have read about in the papers – and Jack and the men he was with have not been heard of since. I cannot possibly tell you the full circumstances, but they must have been cut off, and knowing what I do, and after thoroughly going into all the details with Sutton, who showed me an exact map of the position they were in, I think that either Jack was killed or else that he was wounded and taken prisoner, and of these two alternatives I at present incline to the latter. The Germans are notoriously anxious to take our officers prisoners and would take every care of Jack if they captured him after he had been wounded, supposing he was. They would do this because they would hope to get information from him. His Regiment is so completely in the dark about him and he is not the only one – because none of the men who were immediately with him are available. I personally think we are justified in continuing to hope that Jack is alive and in German hands for two months from the date he was missing. But unless one gets news from Germany within that time of men who are missing I always think it better not to go on in suspense. I think Fielding will support me in this view. At any rate I have been told all there is to be told and I don't think there is any likelihood of getting news except from Germany. Lists of prisoners are published in the papers as they come through.

I wish I could tell you more fully the circumstances but it would not help you to come to any other conclusion than I have suggested and this is the conclusion Captain Congdon and his Regiment have come to.

I wish I could reproduce exactly all the things Croft, Congdon and Lieutenant Sutton said about Jack. I didn't see his Colonel but Captain Congdon told me that his Colonel thought especially highly of him and that he looked upon him as his most promising young subaltern. He – and Captain Congdon concurred entirely in this – thought so much of him because of his great general keenness. He looked after his men so well that when a senior officer rejoined the Company, Captain Congdon refused to deprive Jack of his platoon and let him keep his command. Also Jack put all he knew into running the men's football and was the only officer who played for the Regimental XI. The Colonel who is apparently a stern Regular soldier was especially pleased with Jack on this last score. Captain Congdon told me that Jack was consistently full of life and cheerfulness. The reason why the Colonel blocked his application of transfer to us, the 2ⁿᵈ Oxf and Bucks Light Infantry, was because he valued him so highly and because Captain Congdon was so strongly opposed to losing him. Jack was evidently in the nicest Company of the Regiment. His Captain told me with great pride that all his Company officers were gentlemen, and that his Company was known as 'the Gentlemen's Company'.

It was Jack's first experience of the actual trenches, but when they were in another section of the line a short while ago Jack did very good work on some dangerous and unpleasant parties, and won high praise.

Sutton was in charge of the Company in the Line and on the occasion of this attack and during the three days they were up there Jack always joined him at his special request in the evening for dinner. They did not live in the same dug out as Jack was on the left of his Company Headquarters, but he saw him in this way every evening and was evidently fond of him. One little touch appealed to me as it will to you. Whenever Jack came on his evening visit he always assured him with high emphasis that he was 'cushy' and Sutton envied him his high spirits.

The circumstances that led up to his being surrounded were absolutely out of Jack's control and it cannot be in the least due to any mistake on his part. This I shall be able to explain at some future date. So that Jack has nothing but credit and high praise due to him. Sutton is a most gallant officer, and it was only by a miracle that he himself got out of it, – a miracle, and sheer persistent refusal to give in. Captain Congdon and Sutton both asked me to express their very sincere sorrow at the big loss their Company has sustained in losing Jack, and to tell you how much they sympathise with you in your anxiety and suspense. And they begged me to let them know at once if we get any news through. His men loved Jack, and evidently his officers did too.

And so, dear Mummy and Daddy, we can just hope and

pray for a time that our dear Jack is alive and being well cared for in Germany. It is so awfully hard for you at home. It's hard enough for me, God knows, and so I can guess how hard it must be for you. We can only fall back on God in our helplessness and strive to rest in the knowledge we have that He is the perfection of Love. But it is hard. I don't feel I can write more tonight. You will understand why. Colonel Cross is awfully grieved. Gordon is away at present, and so doesn't know. I shall try and get over to see him. Thank you so very much for all you have done for Fielding. Captain Fielding's opinion is worth having, and he will tell you frankly what he thinks of what I have told you.

Your loving,
Monty.

The flame of hope still burns that Jack may still be alive. Indeed, of the 498 officers and men listed as killed, wounded and missing, 433 of them are unaccounted for. They could all be prisoners in Germany for all anyone knew. They pray, Monty and Jack's parents, that one of those prisoners should be Jack, but at what point do they accept, in their hearts, that it is not so. Does Jack's mother know already? Monty is praying to God, 'the perfection of Love', for Jack's safe return. 'But it is hard.' Yes, it is hard, isn't it, to pray to a God of Love who presides over such things? The war has come home to Monty – and does he still believe that these shadows of the passing clouds are hiding a Greater Glory? Why is it hidden so deep and so well?

Dr Bigger launches himself into a frantic search for news about his son. At first there is nothing, other than a letter from Jack's old landlady from his days of training in early 1917:

2 Hurry Road Cottages
Canterbury
5 July 1917
My Dear Madam
I was truly sorry to hear of your very sad loss, but I do

sincerely hope and trust that God will of taken care of your dear boy. We do feel for you in your great sorrow for Mr Bigger seemed to twine round our Heart as no other stranger did before. We have never forgotten him and we missed his bright and happy face for a very long time. I hope that you may very soon hear of him we must leave it all in our Father's hand. It seems very hard to say thy will be done if he is gone from us, what a blessed comfort to know he is safe in the arms of Jesus and that you may soon see him again. I don't know what we should do without hope. My Husband is very much grieved indeed but with you dear Mrs Bigger we hope to hear and see him again, when we cannot say, may our God comfort you and support you all in your sorrow and anxiety. We should be pleased to hear any news trusting it will be good news and I pray that God will give you grace and strength to bear up under your great sorrow. May comfort He give you from above.

I remain yours respectfully,

Mary A Warden.

It is not until September 1917, four agonising months after Jack was first reported missing, that the letters start to arrive from Germany. They are sent via the Red Cross, the first two addressed to someone called Miss Ganz. The Biggers are not the only ones looking for news of Jack. Maybe she was his sweetheart; maybe she was just one of the many women who helped trace missing soldiers:

18 September 1917

Dear Miss Ganz

In answer to your letter re. Lieutenant Bigger, I regret to say I saw him killed at Frez-noi by Vimy Ridge on the 8 May 1917,

J.B. Langley, 1st East Surreys.

30 September 1917

Dear Madame, just a line to inform you that the last I heard and seen of Lieutenant Bigger he was killed on no man's land by Rifle fire.

Yours faithfully,

J.B. Langley.

The Red Cross postcards to Dr and Mrs Bigger took slightly longer to arrive but they bore the same news. Second Lieut. J. Griffiths, 7408, had survived, and wrote:

I am answering your letter with some sad news, for J. Bigger got killed in action when I was taken, which grieved me very much.

Private Evans (30745) wrote to his wife:

Please write Mrs Bigger the only information I can give in respect of Lt. Bigger is that I was with him as he was leading his men and I did not actually see him fall but he was not with us 5 minutes afterwards, so it is only one conclusion to arrive at namely he is killed.

The wife of Private Henserman (30607) also wrote:

I am writing to tell you the news I received from my husband concerning your son Lieutenant Bigger. He was sorry to say he was not lucky enough to be taken a prisoner – he did not see him after he had been wounded himself. He was not with them when he was lined up with the prisoners so he was terribly afraid that he was killed.

Private Waters (32299) wrote to his wife:

I am very sorry to have to tell you the sad news of Lieutenant Bigger, but we are obliged to let the relations know if you are sure of them – He was in a shell hole with two sergeants and his batman. The first shell killed them and the second buried them, so if you have not replied to them, tell them as gently as you can and say he was buried respectfully – of course they will never find his identification disc so he will always be reported missing.

The letters and cards kept coming, next from Lance Corporal Spong (22181):

Last seen in trench about one hour and a half before I was captured at Fresnoy on the morning of the 8th 5 17.

And, finally, more detail arrives:

I, Private C O'Keefe (32508), 1st E Surrey Regt have the honour to report to you of 2nd Lieutenant Bigger as follows: The last I saw of Lt Bigger was in a dug out. The sentry shouted that the Germans were attacking and the Officer shouted 'all men on top at once.' There were three men got out and another was shot as he came to the top of the dug out. I think that man was 2nd Lt Bigger but I cannot say for certain as there was a great hurry to get on top quickly.

Does it matter, *how* Jack died? Whether he was shot coming up out of the dugout, or gunned down in no-man's-land, or killed and then obliterated by shell fire? None of them seemed to agree, but they all knew he was dead. Of the 700,000 British dead in the First World War, a staggering 140,000 were never found or identified: they were just mashed into the earth, or shovelled into hasty graves, to bob up again years later under the farmer's plough. All the soldiers who wrote seemed keen to soften the blow, but especially Private Waters, who thought the Biggers would like to know that Jack was 'buried respectfully' by a second shell. He also thought that Jack would always be reported missing, and that they'd never find his identification tag, and yet I have it in front of me as I write this, a small oval brass disc, chipped and rusted, attached to a short chain designed for a slender wrist. 'JAW BIGGER, EAST SURREYS,' it reads, 'Church of England'. There are other remnants of Jack, hoarded over the years by his grieving sister, my grandmother Kathleen. There's the letter from Buckingham Palace, stamp-signed by a printer in the name of King George (too many dead, too many letters, for George to be personally involved): 'I join with my grateful people in sending you this memorial of a brave life given for others in the Great War.'

The War was already 'Great' it seems. The memorial, weighing heavily on my desk, is a thick slab of brass coin, 10cm across, with a lion and a sorrowing Britannia clutching a wreath in one hand, her trident in the other. Two dolphins leap in the background, ruling the waves. 'John Alfred Whittard Bigger,' it reads: 'HE DIED FOR FREEDOM AND HONOUR'.

There are newspaper cuttings, one from the Borough of Wandsworth's paper, with a brief obituary: 'The sympathy of a wide circle of friends and fellow footballers goes out to his bereaved parents.' The other, probably from a national paper, is a list of officers killed in action. Jack is there, 'aged 24', but so are others – a grim list of only sons and dearly loved husbands. Kathleen has clipped out a poem, 'After-math' – and I think it's useful to remind ourselves that the overwhelming majority of Britons were not reading Sassoon or Owen, but this and others like it, their bulwark against grief:

> After-Math
> Yes – he is gone – there is the message – see!
> Slain by a Prussian bullet as he led
> The men that loved him – dying – cheered them on –
> My son – my eldest son. So be it, God!
> This is no time for tears – no time to mourn,
> No time for sombre draperies of woe.
> Let the aggressors weep! for they have sinned
> The sin of Satan – Lust of power and pride –
> Mean envy of their neighbours' weal – a plot
> Hatched amidst glozing smiles and prate of peace
> Through the false years – until the Day – the Day
> When all this kneeling at the Devil's feet
> Should win the world – Ay, let them weep! But we

With eyes undimmed march on – our mourning robes
Be-jewelled by the deeds of those that die,
Lustre on lustre – till no sable patch
Peeps through their brilliance.
In the years to come,
When we have done our work, and God's own peace,
The Peace of Justice, Mercy, Righteousness,
Like the still radiance of a summer's dawn,
With tranquil glory floods a troubled world –
Why then, perhaps, in the old hall at home,
Where once I dreamed my eldest-born should stand
The master, as I stand the master now,
Our eyes, my wife, shall meet and gleam, and mark
Niched on the walls in sanctity of pride,
Hal's sword, Dick's medal, and the cross He won
Yet never wore – That is the time for tears –
Drawn from a well of love deep down – deep down,
Deep as the mystery of immortal souls –
That is the time for tears – Not now – Not now!

'This is no time for tears' – the men at the Front told each other that; the people at home said the same. Later, they said, they'd come to a reckoning. But not now.

Again, does it matter, *how* Jack died? Does it matter if it was a bullet that got him before he'd even fully woken up, or if it was a desperate struggle 50 yards behind his pathetic trench, slipping and missing the lunge of the German's bayonet? Does it matter if he was atomised and then buried by a shell? Well, yes, it mattered to his parents and to his family. They wanted to know. They would have even wanted to know if he had died like the Jack of Sassoon's 'The Hero', the 'useless swine' who had 'panicked down the trench' and been blown to small bits. They just wanted to know. And so do I, nearly 100 years later, I would like to know how Jack died, because that question about 'how' is really just a question about 'why'. That was the question that was starting to gnaw at Monty's brain, just as it had already bitten into Sassoon's and Owen's and so many others who could not begin to find an answer. 'Why' was Jack dead? 'Why' were they all dead? And, asked Monty, 'why' was the God of Love sanctioning this slaughter?

There's more, though. When I started writing this, I knew there was a chance that I was going to find that Jack had 'panicked down the trench'. I knew he had died, and I also knew that no one knew how. It seems we now know an awful lot more, but in fact I didn't really care if Jack had panicked or if he'd died a 'hero'. No, from the beginning I'd had a dread that Jack might have died in a gas attack, like the drowning man in Wilfred Owen's 'Dulce et Decorum Est':

> Gas! GAS! Quick, boys! – An ecstasy of fumbling,
> Fitting the clumsy helmets just in time;
> But someone still was yelling out and stumbling,
> And flound'ring like a man in fire or lime . . .
> Dim, through the misty panes and thick green light,
> As under a green sea, I saw him drowning.
>
> In all my dreams, before my helpless sight,
> He plunges at me, guttering, choking, drowning.[65]

That memory never left Owen's dreams.

\* \* \*

My mother was named after her uncle, Jack Bigger. She was born in 1922, four years after the war ended and five years after his death. Monty and Kathleen named her, their second daughter, Jacqueline, but from the moment she was born she was always known as 'Jack'. Her older sister had two names – Ruth Compigne (tra la!) Guilford – as did her younger sister, Biddy – christened Elizabeth Anne – but my mother was always just 'Jack'. They were similar, too, from what I can tell. Like her uncle, my mother was radiant with life and joy. People huddled round her for warmth and wit – she made lifelong friends who leant on her for wisdom and laughter. She'd have thought this was nonsense, but it's true.

And so the reason I didn't want to find out that Jack Bigger had died drowning, with the gas choking his lungs, is that 90 years after his death I sat alone in a hospital room and watched the other Jack, my mother – my radiant, laughing mother – heave and gasp and fight for every breath and slowly drown as a cancerous poison clogged her lungs and squeezed the life out of her. I must have had a superstition, or a premonition, about learning that these two Jacks, who were so similar, had shared the same death. And I didn't want to find that or even think about it. I did not want to go again into that neon hospital room, with its lifeless cold curtains, grey scuffed floor and tiers of medical equipment. I didn't want to see my mother lying in that hospital bed, in her nightie, with her back to me, heaving and struggling to get some air into her lungs. I followed her every breath. In. Out. And at each breath her gurgling, wallowing lungs filled with just a little bit more of the poisonous, liquid junk. In. Out. She was full of drugs. She couldn't hear me or see me. She wasn't blind, but she couldn't see. At one point in the long night she tried to get out of the bed. She didn't want to be there – and I had to push her back in. I prayed for the awful choking breathing to stop. And when it did I wept with relief.

And the reason I'm writing about this now is not only that my mother and her uncle – the two Jacks – were somehow indelibly linked at her birth, but it is also because no one's death should be easy or casual or lacking significance. People should not be slaughtered with such ease and in such numbers. When I think of Uncle Jack, blown apart or gunned down so pointlessly in a stupid war, it is impossible not to feel rage with the men who led him there. It's hard not to think ill of the generals who sent all those young men to their deaths, although I am sure many of them were doing the best they could – and doing it efficiently enough, even if they had lost sight of what the hell every 'bite and hold' and 'consolidation' meant to the men who were freezing and dying on their orders. More than them, though, it's hard not to despise the politicians who take us into these wars, who are always more concerned with how they look, or with hanging on to their shitty, narcissistic jobs, than with the men who they so gleefully and portentously send overseas. And yet even worse are the men (always the men) who make and sell arms for money. The inventors of the cluster bombs and land mines; the purveyors of poison gas. What kind of monster would do that? And damn to hell the Holy War Crusaders, who seem to think that killing and maiming other people, or blackmailing and browbeating young men to do it for them, will get them into paradise. But none of these people would matter a damn, they'd have nothing to do, if it weren't for the rest of us. We could stop it now. We could starve these people of their wars, show no interest, give them no money; spend our time patching things up, not making things worse. But we don't. We are addicted to war. Ancient wars. Modern wars. There are millions of us around the world, poring over distant battles in newspapers and on television, following the slaughter of armies, the massacre of civilians, drooling over the hardware and the battle tanks and kill counts and the friendly fire. Slobbering over maps, hunched and grunting over images of fighter jets. Ooh, the sexy language: the Hurricanes and howitzers, Tornados and stealth bombers; the righteous murder of the oil dictators' terrified young conscripts. The collateral damage. The bloody, broken bodies of children. We scour the web for the latest updates from the killing fields. Mainline on rolling reports from the pushers of war filth in the media, with their ecstatic talk of 'heavy fighting' and 'major pushes' and 'spring offensives'. They – we – are the people who make wars possible.

God rot us all.

It's a strange thing. I set out to write a book about my grandfather's life as an Army Chaplain in the First World War and have found myself – if only briefly – writing about my mother's death from lung cancer in a hospital bed in Canterbury. I do not feel easy about this and so I found myself promising that if I did write about my mother's death – and at some point it became clear that I would have to – then I would include everything significant that happened that night, however uncomfortable. I do not want my mother to be memorialised only by her death. I will say it again, she was a beam of light in a dreary world, and she brought joy to many over many years. But this also happened that night. At least I think it did. I was strung out on coffee and suffering from grief and no sleep; I had been alone with my mother for several hours. Listening to her struggle for breath was *horrifying*. I couldn't leave. Of course I couldn't leave. I found myself repeating the Lord's Prayer over and over, muttering it under my breath, but at other times saying it out loud. I thought it might comfort her. It *did* comfort me – and I had lost whatever faith I had long ago. But when she died – no, *as* she died – I saw, or felt, a sort of light at the end of her bed – or maybe at the wall at the foot of her bed. I became aware, strongly, of the presence of my dead father in the light, or on the wall. And more than him. It was an opening to elsewhere. I know – I sound like Auntie. I had not slept. I was pulverised by grief. But. I absolutely could not write about the death of my mother if I did not also say this. I must have told someone about it the next day, I don't remember, because several days later one of my mother's friends came up to me and wanted to know if it was true, that I'd seen my father (and more) at the foot of my mother's bed when she died; they wanted me to give them an answer that would contain some hope; they wanted to hear something that would nourish their faith. And all I can say now is what I said to her then: 'Yes. I don't know. Maybe.'

# ELEVEN

# 'What did he dream about, Private Bateman?'

The war does not pause for just one more death. Did you think that it would? This is no time for tears. Monty has to hurry back to his regiment. By the middle of May 1917, Monty has been in France for almost eight months with, so far as we know, only one leave home. He is very tired – they are all tired – and it is likely that one of his senior officers (perhaps Colonel Crosse, or maybe Hornby, the Senior Chaplain to the 2nd Division) is concerned about him. We know this because at some point in May (most likely some time after Jack's disappearance), with the Ox and Bucks stationed near Dieval for a brief period of retraining and replenishment, Monty found himself enrolled as one of the first recruits to the new Army Chaplains' School at St Omer, about 12 miles south of Dunkerque.

It seems absurd, but until February 1917 there was nowhere in France dedicated to the training of Army Chaplains. They would tag along with their regiment before it left for France, as Monty had done in Salisbury Plain, and they might convene for meetings or pep talks with a more senior chaplain – but no one had given much thought to the specific needs of the chaplains. They would not need to know how to handle a gun or a trench mortar, but they would need to know about military matters, Army protocol, court martials, burials, church services, parades, relations with other denominations, where to stand, when to salute, the content of their sermons, and so on.

One chaplain, H.A.R. May, is quoted by Michael Snape in *The Royal Army Chaplains' Department*. He later went on to set up a 'scheme for training newly-appointed Army Chaplains without military experience', in part, it seems, inspired by this incident:

> *On one occasion, when walking with a 'General' at St Omer, we passed a Chaplain, newly arrived (apparently) from England [and] (apparently) inexperienced in military matters. He gave a most original flourish of his arm as he passed. 'Who the deuce is that?' asked the General, wrathfully, 'And what is he doing? – blowing me a kiss or what?' 'He's a Chaplain, sir, and he's saluting you,' I replied. 'Well why the devil doesn't someone show him how to do it?' responded the General.*[66]

But May's 'scheme' was not inaugurated until April 1918 – too late for Monty and indeed too late for most wartime chaplains, who by then were either going to be adjusted to their gruelling duties or they had already headed home in tatters. St Omer was set up in February 1917 by Llewellyn Henry Gwynne, the Bishop of Khartoum and Deputy Chaplain General – who Monty had met fleetingly (but bracingly) back in September. Monty probably didn't need any lessons in saluting, having been an Army cadet at school, but St Omer was less concerned with protocol and more with making sure that chaplains had all the necessary spiritual and moral support. Richard Holmes describes how it came about in *Tommy*:

> *[Gwynne] approached General Plumer in search of accommodation for 'a bombing school for chaplains'.*
>
> *'A what?' exclaimed Plumer.*
>
> *Gwynne went on to elaborate his idea and said how necessary it was to bring back the chaplains from time to time for a 'gingering up'. 'You have refresher courses for machine gunners and others. Why should I not have one for chaplains?' Plumer thought the idea was a good one and offered to put at his disposal a chateau with extensive grounds and beds for twenty chaplains. [Quoted from HC Jackson 'Pastor on the Nile'; London 1960].*[67]

The warden of St Omer was the Rev. B.K. Cunningham and Monty spent a week in May under his gentle tutelage, strolling in the grounds of the chateau in the spring sunshine and discussing his needs and hopes with 19 other chaplains. It sounds ideal for Monty – one chat after another – except that the war coloured everything and at this point there was still no news of Jack. 'B.K.' was probably better suited to Monty's immediate needs than Gwynne, being less preoccupied with giving him a vigorous 'gingering up' and more concerned with helping him find his bearings.

Despite this, one week with a bunch of frazzled fellow clerics was probably not long enough to restore Monty's equilibrium, but a week was all he had. By the end of May, the Ox and Bucks were back in the Line and Monty was with them, settling into a prolonged period of trench warfare. They were back in their old sector near Oppy Wood not far from Fresnoy, which the British had briefly held then lost again when Jack and the 1st East Surreys were swallowed up by the German counter-attack.

The whole Front bulged and stirred restlessly through 1917, as the Allies launched their attacks, pressed into the Hindenburg Line, perhaps bit and held onto a small part of it, then were driven back again. Sometimes the Germans pressed back too hard and too far, and in turn were isolated, exposed and slaughtered. The Front was a coiling, living thing, slippery with sodden mud and fat with human sacrifice.

Incredibly, morale in the British Army remained at manageable levels. It was elsewhere that there were problems, especially with the French, who had endured one unimaginable bloodbath after another. They had held on heroically and beyond all sanity to Verdun in 1916, when they had borne the brunt of the German assaults, but in spring 1917 their latest Commander, Robert Nivelle, launched his own insane attack on the German lines. Perhaps it wasn't such a crazy idea initially – and who could blame him for wanting the invaders out of his country? – but in April 1917 not only had the Russians announced that they would not be joining any large-scale offensive operations that year (there was trouble brewing at home and in the army), but the Germans had withdrawn snugly into their Hindenburg Line, leaving Nivelle's carefully laid plans in tatters. He attacked anyway, with hideous results: casualty rates in the French Army ran at 20 per cent in most units, far higher in others, and although the French made some gains, the spirit of their army was broken. Mutinies followed, and mass desertions, and although Nivelle was fired and the new man, Pétain, restored order, that was the end of the French for the rest of the year as anything other than a holding or defensive force. The same was true of the Russians in the East, which only left the British – and, in the south, facing the Austro-Hungarian Empire, the Italians, who were making progress until the Germans sent help and all but wiped them out.

The major development in 1917 had been the USA's declaration of war on Germany in April. It didn't mean much initially as they had a small army a whole ocean away, but it did mean that at some point, probably 1918, they would start to arrive in force. The Germans were well aware of this – it's what led to their all-out attack in spring 1918 – and Haig knew it too. He could, like Pétain, have settled in and waited for them to arrive. But he was sorely tempted to try just one more big assault.

The eventual longed-for arrival of the Americans was covered by James Neville in a letter home to his father in August 1918, and if he seems slightly bemused, then he's also clear how very welcome they were. There are undeniable echoes from the past, though:

> We have had quite a quiet time in the line so far. The Americans are fearfully keen, but rather dangerous! They loose off at anything, and never wait to see who it is: even when they are in support behind the front line, they are apt to fire at anyone going along the top between posts!! I'm afraid their discipline is not all that it should be, but they will soon knuckle down and lose that keenness which almost amounts to suicide. They had three men knocked out by their own men. One officer, their Intelligence bird, was shot through the neck by their Colour Serjeant Instructor in Musketry! and two privates were killed by some of their mates

*while cleaning rifles. Casualties from enemy action, NIL!! The*
*Intelligence officer is not expected to live.*[68]

Haig wasn't going to wait for the Americans. He was going to win the war single-handedly. Who is to say he was wrong? There's no doubt that by this stage of the war the British Army possessed awesome destructive power; there was also the chance that the Germans were wavering, both at the Front and at home. And so in June 1917 Haig unleashed his armies on the Germans at Messines, in Flanders, detonating almost a million pounds of explosives under their front lines and raining shells onto their support zones; the infantry poured forward, capturing shell-shocked enemy infantry and killing the rest. If they'd stopped there, it would have been an unqualified, if limited, success. But Haig pressed on. The Germans regrouped and the next assault was less successful; the one after that even less so. The rains began in August (in August!) and didn't stop. Was there a curse hanging over these British soldiers? Someone should have stopped Haig; he seems to have been demented in his delusion that just one final push would break the German armies. Surely to God it was clear enough by September that it wouldn't. Hindsight (and in my case ignorant hindsight) is easy. But what is undeniably true is that by November 1917 we had another name to add to The Somme with its associations of futile butchery: Passchendaele – no one who was there could forget or forgive.

A.J.P. Taylor, whose raging *The First World War*, published in 1963, did so much to shape our attitudes to the conflict, is often criticised by more recent historians for his one-eyed view of Haig and the other military leaders, but there's no denying the righteous power of his anger:

*Third Ypres [Passchendaele] was the blindest slaughter of a blind war. Haig bore the greatest responsibility . . . Passchendaele was the last battle in the old style, though no one knew this at the time. Even the generals at last realised that something had gone wrong. On 8 November Haig's Chief-of-Staff visited the fighting zone for the first time. As his car struggled through the mud, he burst into tears, and cried: 'Good God, did we really send men to fight in that?' His companion replied: 'It's worse further up.'*[69]

The total British casualties by the end of this carnage were 275,000, of which 70,000 were dead.

The 2nd Division was spared this particular merry-go-round because they were stationed further down the Line. This is not to say that things were quiet – and they had their own particular battle coming in November – but it was a time of raids, gas attacks, night time patrols and push-and-shove; not all-out war.

Monty kept himself busy by digging a chapel in the mud – or, more specifically, he supervised the creation by a sapping platoon of a small 'church' in a disused dugout in one of the support trenches. With an ironic flourish he called it 'St Peter's Wimpole Street' and it was opened on 25 July 1917. An Order of the Day was sent out to all the companies:

> Commanding Officer wishes it to be known and brought to the notice of all ranks of the Church (C of E) a Recreation Dugout in Wimpole Street (to be known in future as 'St Peter's Wimpole Street') has been finished and is now open for the use of troops. All men off duty in the Reserve Company will be at liberty to make use of the Recreation afforded – Games, Papers, magazines and writing material are provided, but must on no account to be taken away.
>
> The times of the Services will be sent round to all concerned.
>
> E.H. Whitfeld, Captain and Adjutant, 52nd Lt Infantry.

James Neville describes a trip to St Peter's in a letter to his sister on 23 September 1917:

> *I am now going to have my tea before going down to the support line for Church. I never told you that we are now back in the trenches once again. They seem to be our home.*

> *The short rest went like a dream: all over before it began, and,*
> *my word, we did have fun. I have not enjoyed one of our former*
> *rests nearly so much as this last one. I wonder how anyone*
> *manages to exist in other regiments.*
>
> *Our Church is in a dug-out which the Padre has fitted up very*
> *nicely. The sapping platoon made an altar and painted it white,*
> *and now the dug-out is a Church on Sundays and a reading hole*
> *on week days.*
>
> *Later.*
>
> *The service was very nice, but in a way most weird. 'Archies'*
> *were firing a little way behind.*[70]

In the blurred and fading photograph of the front of St Peter's,
it does indeed look like a typical dugout. The doorframe is
painted white and is pressed into the side of the trench, topped
by a double-layer of sandbags. To one side are a few planks of
wood serving as a notice board, with a neat white sheet of paper
announcing the times of the services. To the other side is space
for the 'Recreation dugout notices' – for non-church-goers.
'PLEASE WATER THE GARDEN!' is painted in large capital
letters. Oh, the English and their jokes.

Monty was rightly proud of this chapel in the trenches. There
weren't many of them and it was one of the very few things he
ever told us about his war: that he'd built this chapel, he was
nearly killed by a shell, the Colonel didn't like him at first but
ended up giving him his horse, he won the MC (but didn't feel
like he deserved it), he sat up all night with a man who was
going to be shot the next morning for desertion, and he lost his
faith. When, though, did he lose his faith? We'd be wrong to
think there was a moment when Monty sank to his knees in the
mud and, shaking his fists at the skies, cursed his God. That is
not how it works. Certainly, some chaplains imploded, and
were sent home to recover – or to leave the Church. Michael
Snape describes one Roman Catholic priest screaming and
cursing at generals and colonels at an advanced dressing station,
surrounded by the bloody detritus of war. But for most people,
when they 'lose their faith', what this means is that they can no

longer feel or connect with something that was once alive and is no longer there – leaving instead an absence, or a hole in their being that once was a sustaining joy. Sometimes they are too numb to notice it is gone. For others, the absence is excruciating and, like Faustus, they find themselves in hell.

Trapped on the Western Front in a war without end, Monty would not have needed any sermons on what hell might look like. Even if his faith was slipping away, or gone, it is sobering to think that by July 1917 he had served only ten of the twenty-six months that he would end up spending on the Western Front – let alone the months that he would then have to spend with the Army of Occupation in Germany. My grandfather was a courageous man who must have known that he was desperately needed at the Front. Perhaps he played the fool or allowed himself to be the butt of jokes, but more often Monty's calming presence, his sermons and his 'chats' with distraught and desperate men must have helped them through their hell. And how much more courageous it makes him if at some point he lost his faith yet ploughed on nonetheless, assisting and soothing where he could, burying the dead and consoling the living. Surely faith is a volatile thing that can flare up spontaneously or disappear seemingly for ever. Monty's faith may have been crushed and numbed, but he kept going out of duty and for the sake of his friends. And because, with or without faith, he felt he had a war to wage on 'Cynicism', even his own. My grandfather had a love of life that could not be extinguished.

I have Monty's trench map of the La Bassée area where he was stationed in July 1917. The 'Trenches are corrected to 4 May 1917' it reads, which I suppose shows how static the war had become in that sector. Taking up two-thirds of the map on the right are the enemy lines and trenches, drawn in spectacular detail in red. On the left are the British lines, drawn in blue. Cutting through the middle, from left to right, is the Canal d'Aire à la Bassée, represented by a thick light blue line, hinting at happier days. The British map makers have named some of the German lines: there's the Hindenburg Trench, of course, but also Slag Alley, Mad Alley, Brickbat Alley, Mad Point and Spotted

Dog Alley. The map covers the German lines to a depth of about three miles and shows clearly the Hindenburg defences, with its rows of trenches, wire and communication lines. The British aeroplanes must have been busy to garner this intelligence. German 'entanglements' (i.e. wire) and 'other obstacles' are marked, as are their regular tracks and – to be avoided if possible in the next assault – 'ground cut up by artillery fire'.

The blue British lines pressed up against the German are drawn in more detail but not to such depth, the reason being, I'm sure, that the British were the ones attacking (or thought they would be) so would need maps of the German lines if it went well. The names of the trenches are more homely: Orchard Road, Baker Street, Old Kent Road, Banbury Cross (for the Ox and Bucks to feel at home), Kingsway and Mad Alley (which would lead, if the German lines could be taken, to Mad Point). There must have been a London regiment (or a Londoner) doing the naming, because there's also Cheyne Walk, King's Road, Piccadilly and an Edgware Road, although to the north the names take on a Scottish tinge (Fife Road, Caledonian Road), perhaps thanks to the presence of the Highland Light Infantry. In case anyone got too cosy, there's also a Deadman's Trench. The map looks well used, but then again my grandfather had the ability to get lost in his own home – and try as I might I cannot find Wimpole Street.

Monty had kept three trench maps, as well as a copy of one drawn by Captain C.T. Chevallier (or 'Shoveller') on 23 October 1917, just before the Battle of Cambrai. It's a beautiful, hand-drawn pastiche of a pirate's chart, showing the trench lines, but with caricatures of the officers of the 52nd Light Infantry. On the left, hunched over an oar, 'is that darke horse Leggatt which of old time rowed in a boat on a Fullbrook – ye Isis to wit – but now he ferryeth the younge across ye straits of Iniquity'. Next to him is marked: 'Here ye men eat, when ye moustached man gives them food'. Sitting astride a horse, in full armour, is 'ye ghoste of Neville ye Kingmaker' and in a small hut 'here live sergeantes with cushy jobbes'. At the junction of the two main roads 'dwelles a Padré so blacke that no FULLER on earthe can whitewash him. Also a hoyden lives here'. Monty was the sinful padre, of course; Gordon Fuller was his great friend who was killed in July 1918. On the right of the map there is also a 'Lunatique Asylumme butt that is closed nowe for want of an inmate at yis presente juncture'. It is true. They did, at times, have fun at the Front, despite everything.

'Everything' included a gas attack on 12 July, and on 10 August *The History of the Second Division* relates how:

> *Mustard-gas shells were used by the enemy – 'a little of which', stated one Battalion Diary, 'eventually drifted over part of the front line, making every one sneeze.' [Sneeze?!] But just as every sin brings its own punishment, so the use of mustard gas by the enemy brought swift retribution. Ten tons of lethal gas were successfully projected on the enemy's trenches, along the 99th Infantry Brigade front, on the night of the 15th, the enemy retaliating with trench mortars. Another projection on the same area took place on the night of the 23rd, the gas floating in a huge cloud over the enemy's position. It was followed by yet a third projection on the 31st. During the latter projection No. 10 Squadron of the Air Force dropped phosphorous bombs into the enemy's trenches.*[71]

And so the summer and autumn months passed, while their compatriots struggled and died in Flanders, in a series of raids and retaliations, with gas and phosphorous joining the more conventional weapons. I wonder if it was then that Fullbrook-Leggatt picked up the 'whiff of gas' that constricted his lungs and movement in later life. Religious language like 'retribution' and 'sin' was often used at this time to promote and justify the struggle against the Germans, and not just by the chaplains. But not, as far as I know, by Monty.

There's a letter from Fullbrook-Leggatt to Monty, written on 'the 27th day of the month of the Birth of Pullthrough [September], anno 1945', that includes this vivid, poetic and, I'm afraid, mocking description of Monty's earnest efforts to do the right thing by his 'flock' at the Front. The letter implies that the poem was written some time in 1917:

> Lines on a Padre prating of his Battle Flock.
> Shepherd was I of a Battle Flock that cropped the Flanders fields,
> And I looked for golden fleeces as my spiritual yields,
> But my excellent intentions and the sermons that I penned
> Were heeded by a very few and paid scant dividend.
> For the black sheep far out-numbered the white sheep in my flock,
> And the arrant rams among them were prone to butt and mock.
> They chased me round the sheep folds and robbed me of my crook
> Wherewith (to speak in symbols) I dearly hoped to hook among the Colonel's wicked 'Lambs'* some sad, remorseful soul,
> To dip it clean, to shear it, to make it sweet and whole.
> Ah me! Ah me! In those far days I was a simple one
> And by the Powers of Darkness I was always being done.
> To kick against the pricks is hard: the great apostle said,
> But I have been all black and blue, all scratched and very red
> From the chargings and the buttings of the rams of evil stock
> That ruled the ewes, despite me, in my one time Battle Flock.
>     Yours ever
>     The unchanging Pullthrough
> *In case your senility has caused to forget, the Buglers of HM 52nd Foot were known as the Colonel's 'lambs'.

Monty's friend (and they really were the best of friends) loved to tease him and here it is again, the references to 'buttings' and bruisings. Monty's clerical collar didn't save him from the wilder horseplay. My grandfather seems to have ignored the letter and its gleeful poem, but that only served to provoke this further blast from 'Pullthrough' on 6 November 1945:

Hedge Priest!

(Note the preremptory abruptness of the introduction). You _____

I torture my brain to honour you with immortal verse and you just ignore it, and you proudly term yourself Padre of a Battle Flock – gadzooks.

St Matthew XIII: 57*. Yes, look it up, and once more have reason to honour and respect me. On St Andrew's Day, which perhaps you know falls on 30th November, the Bishop of La Bazeque is to be consecrated in York Minster Bishop Suffragan of Hulme.

The news once more brings back to me that sunlit wintry morning in Zons when he and you came to me and announced that on demobilisation you were going to take up bee-keeping, and barbed words came from my tongue the sting of which was worse than the sting of bees. You have always professed to have forgotten the incident, but both of you took the advice of that lump of human clay for which you asked. And now see what has happened! To you I say the see of Gloucester is at present vacant. Secure it. Go to it and say that you come inspired by Pullthrough, man of the world, archaeologist, philanthropist and poet, and they will welcome you, but if you let me down, remember how Edward II died.

Pullthrough

*And they were offended in him. But Jesus said unto them, A prophet is not without honour, save in his own country, and in his own house.

We shall come back to that 'sunlit wintry morning in Zons' in 1919, when Monty's desire to remain in his Church seems to have evaporated entirely. Fullbrook-Leggatt liked to take the credit for keeping Monty in the Church of England: it amused him that, despite his reputation for ferrying 'the younge across the straits of Iniquity', he had rescued Monty's clerical career. That moment was ahead of them – more likely in late 1917, with the war still raging my grandfather couldn't have cared less whether he had a future career in the Church or not. But he did care enough about the men of the regiment to have carved out his chapel in the trenches and he was there every godforsaken day to minister to his traumatised flock, even if Pullthrough does like to joke that the 'rams of evil stock' had kept the spiritually needy away.

\* \* \*

By the time Passchendaele ground to a halt in early November 1917, it might have been thought that Haig was finished for the year, but there was still one last trick up his sleeve. He planned to launch a tank assault, closely followed by infantry and cavalry, in the area around Cambrai – chosen because the German units there were resting from fighting the British in Flanders, but also because the ground in the area was unusually firm (despite the rain) and would support the weight of the tanks. Cambrai was in that part of the Front where the 2nd Division was spending its days, fending off gas attacks and 'hoydens'.

The planning that went into this attack, even though it does seem to have been decided on rather late in the day, is awe-inspiring. The key was to keep the Germans from guessing what was about to hit them. As there had never been a tank attack on this scale it was vital that no hint of what was coming should reach the enemy. Tanks were brought up to the Line at night by train and hidden in the ruined villages and woods; when they moved, every trace of their tracks was brushed away before daylight. The cavalry were hidden under vast nets; the infantry were squeezed into existing billets rather than building more. Everything happened during the long November nights – by day, all the patrolling German planes could see was the usual British units, hunkered down in their trenches. And yet, hidden in the landscape, were 378 tanks, thousands of horses and over 100,000 men.

It is probable that the Germans got wind of this attack just before it went ahead, but it didn't matter. On the morning of 20 November, there was a savagely short artillery barrage, and then the tanks lurched forward, with the infantry close behind. They rolled over the Hindenburg Line in hours, and by the time the attack ran out of momentum they had pushed forward by over six thousand yards across a front of about six miles. It was the longed-for victory that made church bells ring in England for the first time since the start of the war. And yet, of the 378 tanks taking part, almost 180 of them were out of action, either destroyed by the Germans or broken down. The British could have dug in – and they tried to, although far later than they should – but instead Haig pressed for more and exposed his armies to the inevitable counter-attack. It came on 30 November, ten days after the start of the battle, and it blew the British almost back to where they'd started from, in some parts even further. If the Germans had felt so inclined, they could have rung their own church bells, except that losses on both sides were so shockingly high. There was nothing for anyone to celebrate.

The 2nd Division, in reserve, was called into action on 30 November to help avert what could have become a total disaster. James Neville, lolling triumphantly in a captured German trench in the Hindenburg Line on 29 November, reported feeling 'fearfully bucked at the whole affair, because we are now beating the Boche, and this is the first outward and visible sign of it'. The spires of Cambrai were within sight. One week later, he is back in the old British trenches, lucky to be alive, although happy to report that the 2nd Division had inflicted 'such severe casualties [on] six German Divisions [that they] are now out of the line recuperating'.

'Don't be anxious about me,' he writes to his father, 'I have done a year and there is no reason why I should not carry on for another.'

There was especially savage fighting in the areas around Bourlon Wood and the Sugar Factory. *The History of the Second Division* has praise for the field ambulances:

> *The heaviest work fell upon the right section, evacuation from the aid post in the Sugar Factory being both hazardous and heavy. During the day the shelling of Demicourt, and the sunken road*

*leading to it, became so severe as to render that route unsafe.*[72]

Monty kept a booklet, published in early 1918, telling the story of the 2nd Division at Cambrai. It is of course extremely partial, not to say bloodcurdling, but it does give an idea of the intensity of the fighting – as well as showing that there's nothing the British enjoy more than a heroic, backs-to-the-wall defence against impossible odds:

> *Repeatedly the German 'Group' Commander sowed the fields in front of the Second Division with fresh troops, and as promptly our men harvested each crop with their machine guns. Their arms ached from the sheer physical effort of killing Huns. 'Rifles, machine guns, and mortars have seldom, if ever, had such an opportunity of proving their killing power,' said a distinguished officer afterwards, and every man fortunate enough to have been there endorses his opinion. You may judge of the spirit of the soldiers by the fact that even when wounded they kept on fighting rather than miss such a Heaven-sent opportunity of firing at live targets which they could not miss.*[73]

As a non-combatant, Monty could happily forego the 'Heaven-sent' opportunity to kill Huns – yet it was here, in a battle that started with such promise and ended in the usual chaotic stalemate, that Monty won his Military Cross. The citation, signed by Colonels Herrick and Crosse, Major 'Bingo' Baines, Major Brett, Dr McTurk and the Rev. Hornby, had this to say:

> *Since he first joined the Division, in September 1916, to the present time, he has shown continuous gallantry, self-sacrifice, and devotion to duty. He has completely identified himself with the units in his charge, and shares, to the utmost of his power, in all the conditions of their life.*
>
> *The O.C., 2nd Oxford & Bucks Light Infantry, writes:-*
>
> *'His presence has been and is of the very greatest value to Officers*

*and other ranks alike. He comes up always to the trenches. He*
*magnificently fulfils the duties of his calling.'*

The A.D.M.S., 2*nd* Division, writes:-

'On 28 November, 1917, near Moeuvres, Mr. Guilford volunteered
to go with the D.A.D.M.S., 2*nd* Division, to the Sugar Factory on
the BAPAUME-CAMBRAI Road to ascertain the number of
casualties and whether more Bearers were required. The Sugar
Factory was being very heavily shelled at the time, and the whole
area was swept with shell & machine gun fire. The Rev. E.M.
GUILFORD's action was most gallant and much valuable
information was gained.' He has done specially fine work between
22 Sept. 1917 & 24 Feb., 1918.

There were 205 Military Crosses won by Anglican chaplains in
the First World War, and although Monty liked to say that he
didn't deserve his, he must have been pleased. He didn't receive
the thing until the King's Birthday Honours in June 1918, but it
was the way he went forward along the heavily shelled road to
the Sugar Factory to help the wounded and dying at the tail end
of the Battle of Cambrai that brought particular praise. It must
have taken special courage to put himself deliberately in harm's
way, when he could so easily have hung back. That said, Monty
was a vigorous sporting man (despite the illnesses), and it can't
have been easy for him to have watched his friends head up to
the Front, leaving him behind with the staff officers and the
infirm.

Somewhat typically, there was a minor confusion and
hullaballoo surrounding the granting of my grandfather's MC.
It seems that almost everyone was recommending him for an
award of some kind, but the brigade thought that they had to
propose him for an OBE and not an MC. So he almost ended
up with neither, and then both, before a series of fussy letters
from the Reverend Hornby sorted things out. Fullbrook-Leggatt
got his MC on 7 January 1918, as did James Neville, who wanted
to know what all the fuss was about: 'Nowadays it signifies

nothing, considering that bakers in Rouen get it.'

But Bishop Gwynne was pleased, writing to Monty on 18 June 1918:

> My dear Guildford [sic],
> I am delighted to hear that your gallantry, self-sacrifice, and devotion to duty have won for you the award of the Military Cross. If you had had your due you would I know have received this long ago. It is always gratifying to me to hear of our chaplains identifying themselves with their men, and sharing all the conditions of their life, and at the same time winning their respect and affection as you have done.
>
> I warmly congratulate you. God bless you day by day as you go about your work with this new encouragement. I hope you will soon be fit and well again.
> Yours sincerely,
> Llewellyn Gwynne

In early December 1917, that was all ahead of Monty. The Germans were still pressing hard to recover their lost ground, and the 2nd Division had its back to the wall, harvesting Huns. Monty, though, was pulled out of the Line to attend to something the Army hierarchy considered of vital importance: the execution of Private Joseph Bateman, of the 2nd South Staffordshire Regiment, for desertion. The following orders arrived for him on 2 December 1917:

> CONFIDENTIAL
> [Stamped 'Urgent']
> A.D.M.S.
> A.P.M.
> Senior Chaplain, C-of-E.
> Officer i/c Firing Party.
> 6th Infy. Brigade. (for information.)
> No. 200945 Pte. J. BATEMAN, 2ND S. Staffs. R. having been sentenced to death by F.G.C.M. will be executed about 6.30am to-morrow, 3rd instant, at YTRES.

A.D.M.S. will please detail a Medical Officer to report to the A.P.M. 2nd Division at some time to-day. This Medical Officer will certify as to the death to-morrow.

A motor ambulance will be detailed to be on the road at the entrance to D.H.Q. at 6.20am 3rd instant.

The Senior Chaplain C-of-E will arrange for a grave at either G.C.S. No. 21 or 48.

A firing party of 1 Officer and 12 N.C.O's. and men of 2nd S. Staffs. R. will report to A.P.M. to-day. The Officer Commanding the party will ensure that all ranks are thoroughly instructed in their duties to-day in accordance with attached instructions and will promulgate the sentence.

The A.P.M. will make all arrangements re. accommodation of those concerned.

H.Qrs., 2nd Division.

2nd December, 1917.

Signed GH Birkett

Captain, D.A.A.G., 2nd Division.

Ytres was a small village about 12 miles south east of Cambrai (and a little closer than that to the fluctuating front line). As the officiating chaplain, Monty was expected to find a suitable spot for a grave and to make sure it was dug and ready for its occupant. The execution was expected to go ahead at 'about' 6.30 a.m. – the Army, so efficient and precise in so many things, could not bring itself to state with absolute certainty when the deed would be done. Monty was also expected to spend the night before the execution with Private Bateman, who might want to make his peace with God, ask the chaplain to write a letter home, confess his sins, or just have someone on hand to make the hours pass more easily.

There were 346 soldiers executed by the Army in the First World War, with the vast majority – some 266 – executed for desertion. Richard Holmes has pointed out that the incidence of executions tended to rise at times of great peril or anxiety, so Joseph Bateman may have found himself fulfilling a sacrificial role to keep his comrades dedicated to the fight. Most chaplains never had to witness an execution that was actually carried out. In 90 per cent of cases where the court martial had pronounced the death sentence, the man was given a suspended sentence and let off at a later date. Perhaps it was Joseph Bateman's bad luck to be sentenced to death at a time when the British line was in danger of being broken near Cambrai; then again, he was a serial offender whose execution the Army may have decided should set an example.

It is hardly surprising that executions weren't very popular in the conscript British Army. By this stage of the war, the overwhelming majority of soldiers were civilian recruits, fulfilling their duty as citizens. But by December 1917, many were no longer clear *what* they were fighting for, other than that they were damned if they were going to let the Boche push them around. It meant that executions were seen by many as a clumsy and intransigent way to deal with a problem – and although there seems to have been a long list of offences that could draw down the death penalty, it was very rarely imposed.

Joseph Bateman had joined the Army in November 1914, one of the hundreds of thousands of volunteers who'd rushed forward when Kitchener had made his impassioned plea for help. It was his first wedding anniversary and – who knows? – maybe he'd been out celebrating and called in at the recruiting office on the way home. He doesn't seem to have taken to Army life and just four weeks later went absent without leave for the first time, something he proceeded to do many times over the next three years. The punishments became increasingly severe and by the time Joseph was in France (after a period serving in Ireland when he'd again gone AWOL), the Army resorted to Field Punishment Number One. Short of shooting a man, this was the Army's ultimate sanction once they'd exhausted fines, confinement to barracks, detention and scrubbing out the latrines. As flogging had been abolished at the end of the nineteenth century, this was its alternative: offenders were handcuffed to the wheel of a field gun or to another fixed object for hours at a time, often by both arms, which were then raised, crucifixion-style, above the level of the shoulders. Men would hang there in the heat of the sun, or the biting cold, unable to swipe away flies or move out of the wind. It could be repeated day after day. Joseph Bateman endured this, and many other punishments, but it didn't discourage him from deserting. He never did say why – even at his final trial, at the Field General Court Martial (FGCM) when he could have been pleading for his life, he was almost entirely silent. 'I have nothing to say, and do not wish to give evidence on oath or otherwise' were his only words. He had deserted for the final time just before his regiment was due to go up to the trenches. It's possible that he didn't understand what was happening to him. Like Monty, he had a young child at home and perhaps he just wanted to go and see her and his wife. In the absence of any defence, and given Joseph Bateman's record of serial desertion, the court handed down the death penalty.

Monty kept the instructions for the day. They are torn and smudged and at some point he has mended them (badly) with Sellotape, but they paint an extraordinarily vivid picture of what must have happened at dawn on the morning of 3 December 1917. He joined Private Joseph Bateman for the 'promulgation' of the sentence – and stayed with him for the next twelve hours until he was led out, blindfolded, had a white patch fixed over his heart, and was shot dead from a distance of five paces by eleven men of his unit. Monty read the burial service over his grave, which had been hidden from the view of the prisoner. Some men went to their death blind drunk; others were either wailing or silent; we don't know much about Joseph Bateman's last hours, other than that he slept a little and, at one point, dictated a letter for Monty to send to his wife.

*CONFIDENTIAL*

*EXECUTION OF SENTENCE OF DEATH BY SHOOTING.*
*These notes are issued as a guide to all concerned when*

arrangements have to be made for carrying out a death sentence.

The main object to be effected is to carry out the sentence as rapidly and as humanely as possible.

From the time a death sentence has been passed on a man, he will be in the custody of the A.P.M. [Assistant Provost Marshal] of the Division.

As soon as notice is received from Divisional Headquarters that the sentence is to be carried out, the A.P.M. will communicate with the prisoner's C.O., and make the following arrangements, where necessary, in conjunction with him.

Death Warrant

Obtain a death warrant from Divisional Headquarters in the following form:-

No. _____ Rank _____

of _____ (unit) having been tried by F.G.C.M., and sentenced to death by shooting, the sentence will be carried out between _____ a.m. (or p.m.) and _____ a.m. (or p.m.) at _____ (place) on _____ (date).

(sd) _____

Commanding and Division

Site

Select a site for the execution, with a place of confinement alongside. The site should afford privacy and there must be some form of stop butt.

Time

Settle day and hour of execution. A.P.M. to inform Divisional Headquarters. The best time for execution is just after daylight, but if this is not feasible, it can be carried out just before dusk.

Prisoner to be handed over to a guard of his own unit the evening before the day fixed for the execution, if this is to be carried out in the morning, and to be transferred to a place of confinement vide (ii) above. If the execution is to take place at dusk, the prisoner will be handed over about 12 hours before the time fixed for it. The N.C.O. in command of the guard to be of full rank and to be specially selected. He will receive instructions from the A.P.M.

### Promulgation to prisoner

The proceedings will be sent by Divisional Headquarters to the unit and the sentence will be promulgated by an officer of the unit to the prisoner about 12 hours previous to the execution. This should be done on arrival at the place of confinement. The proceedings of the F.G.C.M. will then be handed over to the A.P.M.

### Chaplain

Ascertain the prisoner's denomination and arrange for services of a Chaplain. The Chaplain will attend the promulgation of the sentence to the prisoner and will inform the latter when it will be carried out. He may remain with the prisoner up to the time the latter is prepared for execution (ie when the A.P.M. enters the place of confinement and demands the prisoner from the guard) and will not be allowed further intercourse with him after that time. He may attend the execution and he will afterwards read the burial service. It is undesirable that he should wear vestments.

### Medical Officer

Arrange with A.D.M.S. Division [Assistant Director Medical Services] for the presence of a Medical Officer at the execution.

### Grave & Digging Party

To be arranged by unit and will normally be in a recognised Burial Ground, but if this is impossible it will be chosen near the site for execution and in this case must be concealed from view of the prisoner as he approaches the spot. Digging party to be provided by the unit. The men will not be allowed to loiter near during the execution.

## Post & Rope

A wooden or iron post firmly fixed in the ground or a staple in a wall should be provided and a rope for tying the prisoner thereto.

## Military Police

Military Police will be employed to prevent Traffic from passing by the place of execution for half an hour before the hour fixed for execution and until all traces of its having taken place have been removed.

## Firing Party

To consist of an Officer, 1 Sergeant and 10 men of the prisoner's unit. The Sergeant will not fire. The Officer will be present at the promulgation of sentence to the prisoner and will on that occasion receive from the A.P.M. any instructions necessary. He will previously instruct the firing party as to their duties, impressing on them that the most merciful action to the prisoner is to shoot straight.

## Procedure

The A.P.M. is responsible for all arrangements and for seeing the sentence carried out.

After promulgation, the prisoner should be allowed anything he wishes to eat, drink or smoke, within reason. He will also be provided with writing materials if desired.

When being prepared for execution the prisoner will be identified by the N.C.O. in charge of the guard in the presence of the A.P.M. and Medical Officer. The A.P.M. will collect pay book and identification disc and make them over to the N.C.O. in charge of the guard, for delivery at the unit's Orderly Room.

The prisoner will be handcuffed or have his wrists bound before being taken to the place of execution.

The Medical Officer will provide a three-cornered bandage for blindfolding and a small paper disc for fixing over the heart. He will adjust these when requested by the A.P.M.

He will also arrange for a stretcher in case the prisoner is unable to walk.

_Firing Party_

_Rifles will be loaded by the Officer i/c Firing Party and will be placed ready on the ground. One rifle will be loaded with blank. Safety catches will be placed at safety. Distance from post, 5 paces. The Officer will bring with him a loaded revolver._

_The firing party will be marched into its position by the A.P.M. whilst the prisoner is being tied to the post. The A.P.M. will so time this that the firing party will be ready for action simultaneously with the completion of the tying up._

_The firing party will march in two ranks, halt on the rifles, turn to the right or left, pick up rifles and come to the ready position, front rank kneeling, rear rank standing. They will press forward safety catch and come to the 'present' on a signal from the A.P.M. The Officer, when he sees all the men are steady, will give the word 'fire'. This is to be the only word of command given after the prisoner leaves the place of confinement._

_When the firing party has fired, it will be turned about and marched away at once by the Sergeant, the Officer remaining behind._

_The Medical Officer will go forward and examine the body. If he considers life is not extinct he will summon the Officer in charge of the firing party, who will complete the sentence with his revolver._

_The Medical Officer will certify death and sign the following death certificate which he will hand to the A.P.M._

_I certify that No. _____ (Rank) _____ of the _____ (unit) was executed by shooting at _____ a.m. on the _____ (date) at _____ (place) and that death was instantaneous (or otherwise)_

   _(sd) _____
Rank etc._

_Removal of body_
_When death has been certified, the body will be unbound and_

*removed to the grave under arrangement previously made by the unit.*

*The A.P.M. will enter on the proceedings of the F.G.C.M. under the minute of confirmation the following certificate:-*

*Sentence duly carried out at _____ (place) at _____ a.m. on the _____ (date)*

*(sd) _____ A.P.M. and Division.*

*He will then attach the death warrant and death certificate to the proceedings of the F.G.C.M. and hand them in to Divisional Headquarters when reporting completion of sentence.*

*Promulgation to Unit*

*The sentence will usually be promulgated to the unit later in the day if the execution takes place in the morning and on the following morning if the execution is carried out in the evening.*

There are many striking aspects to these instructions. We abolished the death sentence long ago in Britain despite the fact that at the time – and maybe even now – there was widespread support for its use. But its use in time of war is perhaps a different matter – Monty seems to have thought so – and, through the official language, you can see an attempt to make things as easy as possible for the condemned man. It is stated quite clearly: 'the main object to be effected is to carry out the sentence as rapidly and as humanely as possible'. I have no idea what Private Bateman chose to eat ('within reason'), or why he or anyone else would have cared if Monty was wearing vestments at the firing ground (did no one want to be reminded of God at that moment?), but most harrowing is the thought of that lonely, silent, handcuffed walk to the prepared ground, with his mates shuffling nervously up to their rifles while Joseph was being tied to his post. The only word he would hear from the moment he and Monty left his cell to the time the bullets thudded into his heart, all he would hear in that final split second, would be the word 'fire'.

The execution of Joseph Bateman had a profound effect on my grandfather. Many years later when he was in his late seventies, he told my older brother Toby about it – who can't have been more than eight at the time. Fortunately my brother has an exasperating memory for facts, dates and conversations.

*Monty: I once spent a night with a man who was going to be shot the next morning.*

*Toby: Why was he going to be shot?*

*Monty: Because he had run away from the army. [Pause] And they couldn't let soldiers do that, they had to make sure the soldiers stayed with the army.*

*Toby: Did he go to sleep?*

*Monty: He slept a little, yes. I didn't – I was so worried, I stayed awake all night.*

*Toby: What did he dream about?*

*Monty: I don't know. He didn't sleep for very long at a time and he was very worried.*

The only word in that conversation that Toby is not quite sure about is the very last one – 'worried'. But then what possibly could have been the right word?

Monty stayed awake all night while Joseph dozed fitfully. At one point Joseph asked Monty to write a letter for him. Perhaps they talked for the rest of the time. Monty, as we know, was good at helping people talk. He was kind, tolerant, open-minded and interested in people and he believed in the power of love; I think and hope he would have been a comfort to Joseph.

But later, when Monty stood and shivered on the firing ground in the grey dawn of that bleak December morning, did he stop to wonder where the 'Joy' was now? Joseph Bateman was just one more victim of the war – killed by his own side, but killed all the same. He was pardoned posthumously in 2006, along with almost all of the men executed by firing squad in the First World War. Just one more death, but it was hard to explain, and chaplains, if they had any kind of definable role at all, were surely being asked to explain to their men and to themselves what in heaven's name was the *point* of all this death.

Wilfred Owen had a theory:

Then Abram bound the youth with belts and straps,
And builded parapets and trenches there,
And stretched forth the knife to slay his son.
When lo! an Angel called him out of heaven,
Saying, Lay not thy hand upon the lad,
Neither do anything to him, thy son.
Behold! Caught in a thicket by its horns,
A Ram. Offer the Ram of Pride instead.

But the old man would not so, but slew his son,
And half the seed of Europe, one by one.[74]

# TWELVE

# The Incident at Zons

From late 1917 to March 1918, the British Army dug itself deep into the French soil and made no more efforts to push the Germans anywhere. This was not just because of the debacle of Passchendaele, or the bitter disappointment of Cambrai, but because they knew that the next major assault would not be coming from them but from the Germans. The Bolshevik Revolution had taken the Russians out of the war and closed down the Eastern Front; the Italians were on the defensive; the French, like the British, were wounded and battered and digging in; and the Americans, on their way at last, had still not arrived in sufficient numbers. German divisions were streaming towards the Western Front, released from their duties elsewhere, and there was no doubt that in the spring of 1918, probably as early as March, the Germans would make an all-out effort to win the war before enough Americans arrived to tip the balance irreversibly in favour of the Allies.

It is likely that Monty had a brief period of leave in January. There's a postcard from his brother-in-law, Cecil Champion, sent on 2 January, which says 'I hear you are going on leave shortly – lucky man'. The front shows the devastated Cathedral of Arras, just in case Monty needed any more encouragement to get the hell out. If we are looking for a time when Monty's faith wavered and was 'lost', then this is it, I think. Or most likely it was the time between September 1917 and the summer of 1918, when the death of Jack was confirmed and it was clear to almost everyone that this war could go on until 1919 or 1920 at the very least. A wet summer was followed by the gloom of winter, and Monty found himself supervising the judicial killing of a bewildered young man and burying not just him but hundreds of others. How many burial services did he carry out in the 26 months he was in France? It's impossible to say – it could have been well over a thousand – and yet ever since he buried his first man, the 'fine, tall' Canadian, he let the subject drop. If I had to choose a time when Pullthrough's letter arrived, urging Monty not to be so low and reminding him of his 'War on Cynicism', then the most obvious choice is that it was during the awful, grinding winter of 1917–18. Who knows, though? It could just as easily have been after the final German assault, when they briefly and almost permanently overwhelmed the Allied defences but were held and everyone knew then that the war was almost won; it could have been then that reaction set in and, with the spirits of the regiment 'so high', Monty felt able to give in to despair.

The 2nd Division was just recently out of the Line when the final, frantic German attack was unleashed on 21 March. The Germans had spent most of the previous week pouring mustard-gas shells onto them, which had led to over 3,000 casualties and 'played havoc' with the men. When the infantry assault came, it was overwhelming and irresistible – and all along the Western Front. The 2nd Division was called back to the Line, hurriedly, and on 23 March, with 'tactical withdrawal' an absolute necessity, they were ordered to stand and fight come what may. There was chaos all around them, with much of the Army in retreat and close to panic, and countless others fighting and dying with heartbreaking heroism, to prevent what would otherwise have been a certain German victory. James Neville's diary of 23 March has one such instance:

*'A' Company had a forward post in our wire, which was well placed to snipe the enemy as he worked forward. However, this post was spotted by the light machine gun team, and its position rendered untenable. 'Bunjie' Littledale, commanding 'A'*

*Company, went forward to withdraw this post, and was killed, hit through the heart and neck. Next, Colvill ran the gauntlet of a hail of bullets and managed to get the men back and Littledale's body as well.*[75]

On 24 March, despite the earlier command to fight to the death (and many had done just that), the Ox and Bucks were retreating again, surrounded by the streaming remnants of a dozen other regiments. James Neville, with his company, was separated from the others (and here his diary includes an image that I am not sure I will ever be able to shake off):

*It was not till 5 p.m., when the enemy were in the outskirts of Le Transloy, that we met the 52nd again. It was a pitiful sight. A small column of men, led by Crosse and Brett, about 80 men all told, marched wearily up the slope. 'D' Company had been cut off in Villers-au-Flos, and only 12 men under Eagle had managed to escape. David Barnes and Bailey were wounded and missing, and Vernon wounded. Ben Slocock had been killed.*

*Just before the 52nd came up with 'B' Company, what remained of the tanks waddled through our line of posts. The enemy field guns, supporting the front line troops, had done them considerable damage, and completely incapacitated not a few. I noticed one tank crew, through my glasses, coming towards us. They all looked very strange and I could not distinguish their faces from their uniform. As they approached I could see the cause of this. The officer's face was completely raw, all the skin off his forehead and face hung like an icicle from the tip of his nose, while the skin of his jaw and chin encircled his neck in a grey fold, like an Elizabethan ruff. His hands were raw too, and he gave me the impression of having been lathered in blood. Actually, he and his crew had been flayed in a burning tank, and he was the most badly burnt of all, as he was last to leave. He asked for some water. I handed him my waterbottle, but he held up his hands and said he could not touch anything. So I poured as much as I could down his open mouth; then he went on back towards Albert. Wounded men came crawling up to our posts, too, beseeching us to carry*

*them back to the main Albert Road on our stretchers; these pitiful*
*requests had to be refused, because our stretcher bearers were*
*already doing the work of four times their number.*[76]

At one point, relates *The History of the Second Division*, the 'Germans got within 50 yards of the Oxford and Bucks, but there their line was broken and decimated, and they could get no further'. It was a desperate, frenzied time, with the trenches overrun and men fighting in the open for the first time since the end of 1914.

Monty was on his way back from a one-week course at Blendecques, a few miles behind the front line. He had no doubt been having the chaplain's usual top-up talks and backbone-stiffening discussions. By then he was a reasonably long-serving padre and might have been expected to share his own experiences for the benefit of newcomers. He probably arrived back with the regiment just as the Germans were overrunning the British first line of defences and may have been thrown into helping the stretcher bearers, as the situation was too fluid for anything else. One 2nd Division padre is singled out in *The History of the Second Division*:

*Three times Padre Murray of the 1st King's rushes back over 400*
*yards of evacuated ground, over which the bullets are falling like*
*rain, to rescue wounded men who had, from sheer inability to*
*carry them, been left behind to the tender mercies of hostile troops,*
*many of whom were maddened by drink looted from abandoned*
*canteens, or smarting under a score of costly rebuffs.*[77]

Monty's canteen looted! It is true, I believe, that one of the reasons the German assault faltered and failed when it had seemed unstoppable was that the German infantry were practically blinded by the sudden freedom of being on the move after years of being shelled and tormented in their trenches by the British. They went mad in the canteens and cafes. The main reason, though, is that the Allies were simply not going to allow themselves to be beaten. Not now, not after all they had fought and died for. Haig captured the moment in his famous dispatch of 11 April:

> There is no other course open to us but to fight it out. Every position must be held to the last man. There must be no retirement. With our backs to the wall and believing in the justness of our cause, each one of us must fight on to the end.

Of course, there are plenty who have suggested that if Haig was so keen for the British to fight it out 'to the last man', then he ought to have moved himself just a little closer to the front line. It's an easy jibe though not a practical one, however gratifying it might have been to see Haig grabbing a rifle and heading for the Front.

When the Germans' first attack wavered, they launched another, but by mid-April it was clear the main danger was over. The lines stabilised (even though the Germans continued to push and the Allies dug and pushed back) and the 2nd Division, the Ox and Bucks and Monty among them, were drawn out of the front line. By 12 April, Monty has found time to write a postcard to his daughter, Ruthie, who is nearly four years old. It shows a picture of the town of Doullens, which is probably where he was based. The town was being used as a hospital and was swamped with the wounded and dying, with doctors, sisters and padres working round the clock. James Neville rolled up there at the end of March, having scoffed down an incalculably old, 'half-opened tin of bully beef' he'd found in an abandoned rat-infested dugout. He hadn't eaten for days, but 'never shall I forget the taste in my mouth after it! For four days I had a dry stickiness in my mouth, incessant heartburn, and a feeling of overwhelming depression, which almost blotted out the instinct of life'.[78] He had fought on for four days, unable to eat or drink, ravaged by diarrhoea, until ordered back to Doullens by Colonel Crosse.

As for Monty's postcard, there is a new censor allocated to decipher his crushed and creeping scrawl. I imagine the previous one has been led away, gibbering.

Another letter for Ruthie from Daddy! Please Ruthie will you make a lovely choccy pudding for Daddy and ask Mummy to send it to him. No! I know what Ruthie might do with it when she has made it she can meet Daddy in France when she wakes up and watch him eat it and he will give Ruthie a lovely slice all for herself and another for Mummy. A great big kiss from Daddy.

There is so much longing in this postcard: a longing to be away from the world of fighting men for a saner world of children and women and chocolate puddings. He writes to his daughter again on 16 May. In a fit of pique, the new censor has tried to obliterate the name of the bridge on the front – but 'Doullens' reads quite clearly through the crazed pen marks. Then on 23 May, Monty is in Le Touquet, sending Ruthie a postcard with a lovely picture of mothers and children with spades on the beach. It's a picture of a world at peace, and Monty is yearning to be out of the war:

> This is where Daddy had such a lovely bathe in the sea. If Ruthie could have looked right across the sea where she was bathing with Mummy she would have seen Daddy swimming and splashing about having such fun. He tried very hard to swim across the sea to Ruthie but it was too far. But one day he will come across in a big ship, and then we can have a lovely bathe together, can't we? Daddy.

Even though the Germans launched one last attack against the French on the Aisne at the end of May, and even though they pushed forward 15 miles, it was a last futile effort. The Americans were arriving at the rate of a quarter of a million men a month, the British were strong and growing in confidence, and their Navy's blockade of Germany was leading to serious unrest in the German cities.

Monty's body, however, has had enough. On 11 June, he is admitted to No. 2 Red Cross Hospital, Rouen (from where, the previous year, Sassoon had written about his loss of faith).

Monty will stay here until 5 July. I have no idea what was wrong with him. He wasn't wounded. I presume it was another of those illnesses that struck him down so incessantly at school and university. But he was incapacitated, and we now know that Bishop Gwynne, congratulating him on his MC, was writing to him in hospital and hoping that he will be 'fit and well again'. Perhaps Pullthrough's letter reached him here, urging him not to give in to gloomy and despairing thoughts. I have a strong image of my young grandfather racked with fever lying in a hospital bed surrounded by the wounded and the mutilated, longing to be home, and allowing himself to wonder, at long last, what was the point . . . What was the point of the war and the lunatic destruction of cities, towns, villages, of churches and cathedrals, of women, children and young men? So many, many young men. It is no wonder he didn't have an answer.

Then again, we talk glibly about a chaplain losing their faith as though it were the same as a man who likes building things deciding that they no longer want to be an architect. This is not what Monty was enduring. It was not his career that was in question, nor even a set of beliefs that he now thought he might quite like to exchange for something else. From his earliest years, Monty had been immersed in the Christian faith and had dedicated his life to it. His 'faith' was the core and essence of his being, and although it was bludgeoned and traumatised, and even if he could no longer see or feel it, even if he felt that it was gone for ever, I don't think that my grandfather's faith was lost that easily. Monty was sick, ill and harrowed and numbed by the war, and it is certain that for many months he just went through the motions of his work, but a fundamental belief in the power of love must have lingered, dormant, within him.

Monty was released back to his regiment in early July but in mid-August he is called away to the 2nd Division Headquarters. I did think that perhaps Colonel Crosse had taken one look at him and decided he was only fit for the base, but this letter shows otherwise. Once again, Richard Crosse is very reluctant to let anyone leave his regiment, with his coy reference to Monty's 'altered circumstances' as though Monty were pregnant or leaving him for another woman. The first words are Monty's, scrawled later onto the top of the letter:

On my being posted as Senior Chaplain to the Forces to the 2nd Division Headquarters where I stayed for only two months before rejoining the 52nd.

16th August 1918
My dear Padre
It is beyond me to make a speech and rather less difficult to write what I feel about your altered circumstances which involve your seeing less of the Regiment – I still refuse to regard it in the light of a departure or leave taking – but I wish to thank you with as much sincerity as I have ever put into anything for all that you have done, in innumerable ways for the Regiment, and for the help you have given me personally, during the past 2 years. One of the chief factors in making them live and, when required, fight, as well as they do has been the prevailing atmosphere of straightforwardness and sincerity of religion for which you have been so largely responsible – where a less broad-minded man would have failed. A Regiment is what its officers make of it: you have been one of those officers and you have helped to make the others.

I cannot but grieve to think of you in the atmosphere of that 'B' Mess, or whatever they call it, but surely there will be a turnover soon. Battle by battle can't last much longer, nor can that shameless vet [sic?] – I only wish there was some alternative but at the moment I see none. Nevertheless I implore you to retain your right to come and go and use and do exactly what and when you like with us – You have been a Rifle Brigade officer and the Rifle Brigade and ourselves are permanent members of each others' messes so it is very right.

After two years together, Monty and Richard Crosse have become firm friends. In the Regimental Diary for 15 August, the writer not only laments Monty's departure (he was 'greatly beloved by the troops and his work very deeply appreciated by all ranks') but adds: 'To Rev. Guilford the Regiment owes its very prosperous Field Canteen'. Monty had done his duty as a chaplain, but he also ran a mean canteen.

His duties as a Senior Chaplain to the Forces (Temporary) involved supervising the various brigade and regimental chaplains, and he possibly spent a satisfactory two months doing just that, but I suspect he wanted to be back with the 52nd Ox and Bucks. That's where his heart lay. They were fighting their way towards Germany by now; the German tide had reached its zenith and was on the wane. One week after Monty left for headquarters, James Neville writes this in his diary:

> Had breakfast at 3.30 a.m. on bacon and bread mixed with sugar!! Damned good. No attack on our front, though there is a terrific barrage on our right. God knows what will happen to us to-day. Just wait and see. Casualties to officers are pretty heavy. Heard that the Colonel has been hit. Damnable! Fulbrook-Leggatt, Wilsdon, Pearson and Brown. Brown has since died of his wounds. He was hit while we were waiting out in the open after crossing the railway cutting yesterday. It was his first time in the line too.[79]

How miserably often that was the case. First time in the line – and never lived another day. Richard Crosse remembers the moment he was hit by a shell in his brief memoirs:

> Almost four years to the minute from when I first saw a shell burst, I was hit by one, 'gunshot wounds, neck and back' according to the label they attached to my person. At the Regimental Aid Post was our faithful padre, the Reverend EM Guilford, whom I was so glad to see.

Monty had drifted up from the base and was able to look after his Colonel. He probably saw Fulbrook-Leggatt there, too –

Crosse was now out of the war, Pullthrough he would meet up with again at Zons. Just one day later, James Neville was also hit – in the right elbow when leading an attack on the village of Sapignies – and after a few days in hospital was also sent home. He has this characteristically mock-heroic sign-off in his diary:

> There was quite a hubbub at the Field Ambulance, near Courcelles. Somebody asked me where I had been hit, and when I said 'in the elbow', he waxed rather wroth and wanted to know what part of the line. The one word, 'Sapignies', seemed to have a magical effect, for the brass-hatted somebody popped off and came back with a still more brazen hat in tow, who, I believe, was our revered Corps Commander. Their faces were wreathed in smiles, like the cats', when I told them that the 52nd – with the accent on the 52nd – had captured the village at 4.30am. It appeared that this infernal little village of ruins played a big part in their scheme of things.[80]

No front-line soldier cared much for the 'brass hats' (the staff officers from the base) by this stage of the war. Indeed most could barely conceal their loathing, so Monty probably returned to his regiment with some relief, even if it brought him closer to the danger. The officers' Mess now had some significant absences. The Germans were in retreat all along the line, although as we know there were still many opportunities for men to be killed, even right up to the last minute of the last day. The General Officer Commanding the 2nd Division, while extolling the spirit of his men, pays a visit to Cambrai, captured at last, and noted this in his private diary:

> The town is much knocked about, and the houses appear to be denuded of furniture, except the humbler ones. There has been a certain amount of damage from shell fire. The main square is a typical piece of German 'frightfulness'; all the houses have been burnt and levelled to the ground, and were still smouldering. The Town Hall . . . is still standing, but burnt out and roofless. The Mark of the Beast is upon the town. There are many senseless and

*groundless accusations against the German, but there cannot be*
*any justification for his criminal and spiteful destruction.*[81]

Monty was never part of the Holy War against the Germans. The
religious imagery used to fan that war ('The Mark of the Beast')
never entered his sermons or chats, so far as we know. But there's
also a reminder of what the Allies had been fighting for, what
drove their determination to win and not just make a conciliatory
peace – although, alas, the peace that followed helped no one.

The Ox and Bucks took part in one final battle of the war, at
Selle, and with German resolve slipping it passed off with only
'slight' casualties. However 'slight', I don't suppose that mattered
to those affected, but men's spirits were lifting and Monty's too.
Everyone could feel that the end of the war was close, and they
prayed to be spared the final bullet – and not press on to Berlin,
as the belligerents at home were urging. Monty had kept the
final communication of the war, sent at 8.30 a.m. by the Officer
Commanding the 2nd Division:

> Hostilities will cease at 1100 to-day 11th Nov. Troops
> will stand fast on line reached at that hour which will be
> reported by wire to Corps HQ. Defensive precautions will be
> maintained. There is to be no intercourse of any description
> with the enemy. No Germans are to be allowed to enter our
> lines any doing so will be taken prisoner. All moves for 3rd
> Division for to-day Nov 11th are cancelled . . .

Was that a final, blundering typo, that reference to the 3rd and
not the 2nd Division? No one would have cared, although many
reports from the Front on that day say that news of the ceasefire
was greeted wearily and with low-key celebrations; it was only
at home that a bacchanalian party was unleashed. Monty seems
to have spent part of the day taking photographs. Groups of
officers sit and smile – no, grin unrestrainedly – at the camera;
even Fullbrook-Leggatt manages a jovial but knowing leer. 'Alf'
Baines, a large man leaning for support on the nearest wall, in
overwhelming boots and a shameless moustache, looks like

someone has just handed him the winning lottery ticket.

Much to the conscript army's distress, many found that the military still needed them and that they wouldn't be hurrying home on the next ferry. This was true of Monty. I don't know when he was told, but by the end of November he is writing from Charleroi in Belgium and then, in early December, inching eastwards towards Germany, he is writing to Ruthie from Bois de Villers near Namur. The postcard, printed with impressive speed, shows the British cavalry being greeted ecstatically in the liberated Belgian town.

> Tell Mummy to keep it. It is a photo of the first English soldiers on horses to ride to this lovely city and all the people are saying how pleased they are to see them. Love and kisses Daddy.

By the next week, Monty is in Germany, first Malmedy and then Cologne. He is with the Army of the Occupation on the Rhine, and he carries with him a mass-printed notice from General Rawlinson, its commander, asking them all to remember to conduct themselves with 'courtesy and consideration for non-combatants'. This is to be a peace march carried out with the usual military precautions, but:

> *every soldier of the British Empire has just reason to be proud. It has maintained the highest standard of discipline both in advance and retreat. It has proved that British discipline, based on mutual confidence between officers and men, can stand the hard test of war far better than Prussian discipline based on fear of punishment.*

So there. And it may be true. But RIP Private Joseph Bateman. Monty was home for Christmas. Before long he had to go back, but he'd be home for good by the end of April 1919. He was kept extremely busy, organising services for a far larger flock than he'd have liked (many padres made it home quicker than he managed), but photos from that time show ice-hockey matches, cross-country races, bands playing – and an undeniable holiday atmosphere. Four years of war were over and these young men had survived. As for those who hadn't, or who waited for them, scarred, at home, well there'd be time enough to think of them later. The couple of photos of Monty from this time show him smiling solidly and gazing directly at the camera.

Monty wrote a postcard to Kathleen on 28 February 1919. It is sent from Zons:

> It is midnight and so only a card tonight. I will answer your letter tomorrow. I do hope Ruthie is better. I quite hope in any case to get to England by the end of March. Have definitely refused to serve in the Army of Occupation except in England. Love Monty.

It's a good thought, isn't it, that the only place Monty would serve in the Army of Occupation would be England, as though it needed occupying? In any case, he put his foot down and it sounds as though the Army listened. He *was* a volunteer after all. But quite what he was going to do once he got back to England was entirely unclear. As the fighting ended, Monty's rejection of his faith seems to become less absolute. He didn't know what this meant and he made the mistake of asking his friend Fullbrook-Leggatt for advice:

> Letter from Fullbrook-Leggatt ('Pullthrough'), dated 18 September 1942:
> I fear me that you must be entered on your dotage if you remember not the occasion of my remarking that you had bees in your bonnet at Zons. Do you remember the main street where, on the north side, was a small dwelling house which housed on the right hand side of its ground floor orderly room and on the left the DEMOBILIZATION OFFICE wherein one Pullthrough held sway? One early spring morning there was a humble knocking or rather tapping at his door and, when he called 'Come in', there crept in the Bishop of La Bazerque and his Hedge Priest.

One Crossley, the Lieutenant to Pullthrough sniggered, and over his senior officer's face there warmed a smile cynical. 'Why do ye priests cross the threshold of one whose name you have preached to be Anathema?'

'Please sir, our work as shepherds to the troops is done and we would go home to _____'

'To what?'

'To keep bees.'

'To keep bees? Why?'

'Because it seems so quiet, restful, and honeyed a life.'

'_____' (language too virulent for print) Have ye not got responsibilities to them? Are there not other flocks that need the care of true shepherds? Get ye hence very quickly, reviling me as ye like, yet remember when later ye regain sanity, that it was in the pagan shrine of the pagan Pullthrough you have ever so maligned that you learnt your duty.

Xxxxx

(And so it was that Pullthrough, though he then knew not them, preserved for two women their husbands not as mere drifting drones, but as men with a call and duty in life.)

Humbly the priests departed to ponder over coffee in the Mess the words to which they had harkened while Pullthrough 'in whom no good is' preached to the young Crossley on the frailty of human beings and of priests in particular.

NOW DO YOU REMEMBER?

The 'Bishop of Bazerque' is H.L. Hornby, Monty's Senior Chaplain. A 'Hedge Priest' is an illiterate, rustic or impoverished priest – one with no learning, who wandered the by-ways, sleeping in hedges, begging and preaching nonsense. What Pullthrough is remembering – and it's entirely possible that Monty may have told him that he wanted to leave the Church and take up bee-keeping – is that Monty and Hornby were by now in full-scale revolt against the institution of the Church of

England. It may be that Monty's faith had been crushed and cauterised by the years of the war, but what he felt in early 1919 was confusion, and even it seems, that 'Christ alone is the way to the reconstruction of the world'. What the world needed now was 'Love'.

Monty's rebellion against his Church took the form of a letter, written by two young Army Chaplains in Germany to the Church newspaper *The Challenge*. It was headlined 'The Younger Generation', his co-author was H.L. Hornby (although the letter was published anonymously) and this is an extract:

> Sir – Your correspondence under the heading of 'The Younger Generation' began with a question as to whether a layman whose views did not coincide with those of traditional Christianity could continue to count himself a member of the Church.
>
> Two chaplains, who feel that they have come to the parting of the ways, now want advice as to whether they can continue to carry on as the Church's accredited ministers; we instinctively shrink from the atmosphere of parish life as we knew it before the war; if we go back to it, we shall do so with reluctance and, at best, a forced interest; and yet we feel, as we have never felt before, that Christ alone is the way to the reconstruction of the world.
>
> To come straight to the point, our trouble is this:
>
> The position of the parish parson at home as compared with that of the padre in the Army seems to be inevitably an artificial one, divorced from the life and interests of the man in the street . . . whilst in the Army the parson has breathed an entirely different air: he has been braced by the sense of his real share in the common interests of his flock, and they have been to him not so much 'his flock' as 'his friends.'
>
> We feel that the activities of parish life in England tend to produce not Christians so much as ecclesiastically minded laymen – a very different thing. Many of those whom we remember as 'pillars of the Church' seem to us less richly

endowed with such virtues as generosity, unselfishness, and humility than the average apparent 'pagan' whom we have met on active service . . .

The public services of the Church do not grip: to attract a man to the Christian life is simple, compared with the difficulty of retaining him, and this difficulty is due largely, we are convinced, to the vagueness and incomprehensibility of the public prayers.

We find it extraordinarily difficult to teach, honestly and convincingly, on the subject of the two great sacraments, as at present administered . . .

We are aware that some will say, 'It is impossible to remain as ministers of the Church while entertaining the view you do as to her life and worship.' Well, that is what we want to know. We have never been so sure that Christianity contains the one hope of salvation for the world; we have never been so dissatisfied with the Church as the instrument of Christianity. We realise that we have come now to a point at which it is necessary to make a decision: what should that decision be? Has the Church any place for us as ministers of the Word and Sacraments? – Yours etc, TWO CHAPLAINS. Germany.

To which Pullthrough's answer was: pull yourselves together and get back to your duty and your wives, you bleating clerics. Bee-keeping! Bah!

It is impossible to know how much of this long letter was written by Hornby and how much by my grandfather. Many padres ended up feeling that they had only ever experienced true Christianity among the heroic unbelievers at the Front and the thought of returning to parish life appalled and depressed them. Monty's letter kicked off a significant postbag at *The Challenge* and he would be offered a job by at least one of the correspondents. And yet there is something distressing about the letter's failure to find even the beginning of a solution. There was no 'Plan B' for Monty. He had joined the Army and left the life of a parish priest behind. The war had torn into and then savaged his beliefs; for a while at least it had destroyed his faith. But the war was now over and Monty didn't know where to turn. It would have been so easy for him to follow his friend Tummy out of the Church. Maybe what stopped him was the thought of Kathleen and Ruthie. Should the Church be destroyed? Could Christ rebuild the world? Monty trailed back from France, his thoughts on his family, but deeply scarred by the past two years. His life, it seems to me many years later, could have gone in any direction.

# THIRTEEN

# 'I have love'

Like so many ex-soldiers released back into a changed world, Monty arrived back in Britain in April 1919 bewildered and directionless. Unlike most, though, Monty had a ready-made career if he chose to stick with it, even if a honeyed life as a bee-keeper seemed, at the time, almost as tempting. It is impossible to know what might have happened, because instead of buying up a load of second-hand hives, Monty contacted, or was contacted by, the Vicar of St Martin-in-the-Fields, Dr Dick Sheppard. It is most likely that Monty did the writing. In 1919, Dick Sheppard was 38 years old and already a famous figure in the Church. Monty may have known him through his articles and published sermons. There was, for example, this – written in 1917 as the 'Casual Correspondence of a London Vicar', and chiming to perfection with the thoughts of Monty in *The Challenge* and many other frustrated and disillusioned Army Chaplains.

> *I am convinced, that for more than three years now the leaders of the Church have displayed complete incapacity for effectual and vigorous leadership, and a disastrous inability to realise that heroic days need and welcome heroic action.*
>
> *Does Authority realise that there are thousands who are standing aloof from organised religion not because of what is worst in them but because of what is best, because a Church that is content to referee the game of Civilisation as the world chooses*

*to play it, instead of boldly attempting in the name of Christ to change the rules of the game itself, has no power to excite their loyal enthusiasm.*[82]

Monty didn't know what to do with his life, he was seared by the war and teetering on the brink of leaving the Church, but Dick Sheppard scooped him up and put him in charge of the Boys' Club of St Martin's. He must have known, intuitively, that Monty had a genius for inspiring young people. Dick told him not to worry about preaching, or even serving as a priest – what he wanted him to do was to set up and become the manager of a club where boys and young men could gather to read and play billiards and table tennis in the crypt of St Martin's. Forget the war, said Dick. Don't worry about what happened, or what you might do next. These boys need you. Dick, too, had been an Army Chaplain, and he knew what was troubling Monty. He had seen what the war did to men when he did his own service in 1914:

> *Some of us were foolish enough to believe that this ordeal through which the nations were passing would deepen and intensify spiritual values and arouse us to a new apprehension of the things of God.*
>
> *We learned as the time passed that men who live constantly in the shadow of sudden death are more apt to turn to the Devil than to God.*[83]

Dick Sheppard lasted only three months in France before his health collapsed. It was the theme of his life. He suffered from asthma (and smoked like a loon), but more than that he was incapable of doing anything without throwing his heart, life, soul and every scrap of his being into it. He knelt and prayed with every dying soldier he could find, he joined the infantry charges, waving his arms rather than a gun, he worked all night in the Dressing Stations, he prayed and preached and flogged his gasping lungs through twelve weeks of sleepless insanity – and was hospitalised home in October 1914 suffering from nervous and physical collapse. That was Dick Sheppard: he was an inspiration to everyone he met, and a charlatan and an actor to many who never knew him. My grandfather adored him and it was Dick Sheppard who brought him back to life again.

In 1914, St Martin-in-the-Fields was a decaying, sleepy old church on the edge of Trafalgar Square (at that time a rather sleazy part of town), whose weekly Sunday services attracted a handful of drowsing aunts and the odd person who had an hour to fill before their train departed from nearby Charing Cross Station. By 1919, Dick Sheppard's services were attracting 1,500 people at a time. A contemporary newspaper article, saved by Kathleen, captures the chaos:

*THE SECRET THAT DRAWS ITS THOUSANDS*
  *By F.A. McKenzie.*

*A church where people wait in queues for admission like a theatre, and where, after even standing room is taken, there is still a disappointed throng that cannot get in! It sounds impossible.*

*My first attempt to attend St Martin-in-the-Fields was an absolute failure. There was not even standing room. On the second occasion, in company with a few hundred others, I stood right through the service.*

*I looked around at the congregation. The very pulpit steps were used as seats. The side aisles were full. Every bit of room to the topmost corner of the back gallery was taken. This is what goes on every Sunday afternoon.*

*We were not the usual kind of congregation. Ex-soldiers in doctored khaki, old men, shabby and careworn, business men who might have just come back from a round of golf, hospital nurses in plenty, lines of girls from West End business houses, every type of man and woman except the smug and the conventional was there . . .*

We're not used to this. Dick was maddened by the suffocating dreariness of the contemporary Church. He struggled and thrashed against it all his life. Naturally, some said he could be a ham actor, but he lived life at terrifying speed and he was driven by an unquenchable, urgent need to help people and to connect them to Jesus's message of love. He rarely slept. At times his asthma was so bad that he could barely make it up the pulpit to preach. His health broke down again and again. But he flung himself at life – he flung himself at people – and Monty latched onto his passion and rage and his bubbling laughter and felt the warmth and the life return to him.

St Martin's became a magnet for Army Chaplains disillusioned with the Church, just as it became a meeting ground for ex-soldiers back in Britain and finding that there was no peace dividend for them. Dick Sheppard threw open the doors of his church and welcomed everyone in. Unlike other churches, you could turn up any time and find someone there to talk to (usually Dick), to give you tea and a bench on which to sleep. The crypt filled every night with London's homeless; by day, it was taken over by Monty's Boys' Club. Another newspaper cutting, clipped out by Kathleen, tells of the club, 'which was visited this week by the Duke of York . . . and is organised by the Rev. "Dick" Sheppard and his energetic lieutenant, Rev. E.M. Guilford, a padre who won the MC in the war'. For a vivid picture of what it must have been like, I prefer the interview which Monty gave to the editor of the *Cottesmore Chronicle* in March 1940. The *Chronicle* was the school magazine of Fleet Central School, which had been evacuated from London to Monty's Rutland village because of the bombing in yet another war; the editor was a young boy called H. Bamberg, finding himself in print for the very first time:

*AN INTERVIEW WITH THE RECTOR*
*All Fleetonians will appreciate the following dialogue in which the Rev EM Guilford, the respected rector of Cottesmore, answers some pertinent questions.*

*Some time ago I presented myself with trepidation at the Rectory hoping to secure an interview. I was indeed fortunate. Wishing this first [and last?] edition the best of luck, the Rector answered my laboured rhetoric with commendable sympathy for my first journalistic venture . . .*

*Myself: What about the boys' club that you started in London?*

*Rector: It was a club for page boys and lift boys, and included most of the boys who worked in that part of London. We used an extensive set of rooms under the churchyard; they formerly were vaults but we converted them and finally we had boxing rooms, play rooms, a gymnasium, a library and canteens. We played cricket and football in the churchyard. In all a thousand boys passed through the club in two years. The present King, he was the Duke of York then, visited us and took tea with us. His signed photograph hangs on the wall of the club.*

*Myself: The Rev. Dick Sheppard was a friend of yours, wasn't he?*

*Rector: Yes, he was my greatest friend and the most remarkable man I have ever had the good fortune to meet. He had a positive genius for friendship, which endeared him to all who made his acquaintance.*

*Myself: Would you tell me about your experiences during the last Great War?*

*Rector: I was in the army from 1915–1919 as a chaplain. Two of those four years I spent in France attached to the 2nd Oxfordshire and Buckinghamshire Light Infantry . . .*

*Myself: What about your life at Cambridge?*

You see? That was all anyone ever got out of my grandfather about his 'experiences during the last Great War'. No matter how probing and tenacious a ten-year-old journalist. But it is thanks to Dick Sheppard that my grandfather found himself coming back to life after those two savage years. And it was Dick Sheppard who reminded him that what mattered was not his 'faith' or his 'Church', but love. Towards the end of his life, Dick had this to say:

'Faith? I don't believe I know anything about faith. Jesus is my God. I don't think I have any faith except that. But I have a love for men: somewhere in me I have love. I hang on to that.'[84]

Monty spent two years working for Dick at the Boys' Club in St Martin-in-the-Fields. For part of that time, he and Kathleen and Ruthie were living at the YMCA Hostel in Bedford Place, just off the Tottenham Court Road and a twenty-minute walk from St Martin's. Monty was the hostel's warden, and he relished shepherding and enthusing the young men who sought its shelter. There is a group photo taken at this time of Monty, Kathleen, the warden of the YMCA, dozens of grinning men and little Ruthie in the front row, beaming and basking in the attention. Kathleen is smiling easily. Monty, on the face of it, is more serious, but he is staring straight at the camera and he looks like he knows that he belongs. In fact, he looks *happy*.

Monty and Kathleen didn't stay in London for much longer. They left for their little village in Rutland and brought up their family. Dick Sheppard went on to found the Peace Pledge Union, the Christian Pacifist organisation, for as Dick put it in one of his sermons:

> *The art of killing is the essence of war, and no Christian can uphold war unless he is prepared to kill his brother. If a man believes in the Fatherhood of God and the Brotherhood of man, war is murder and all war is civil war.*

Dick and Monty continued to exchange letters, and as Dick wrote in his wild way: 'I do really believe that God sent us to each other . . .' He wrote a lot more than that, but his handwriting is even worse than Monty's, so most of it is lost to the world. He was lucky to die in 1937, two years before the world descended into another grotesque orgy of killing. Monty, though, lived on, through the next global war, and many local ones. Wherever he lived, he drew people to him, who loved him for his warmth and his humour. He attracted confidences like a flower draws in the bees. He built his gardens. He survived two heart attacks (but not the third). He worked as a country parson in a remote part of England and then retired to another small village where he and Kathleen built another glorious garden. He chatted and smiled and dreamed through life. But he *never* talked about the war. Not to his family. So I do hope he will forgive and understand my doing it for him.

In any case, I'm going to leave the last word to him, Monty, my grandfather, the Army Chaplain who went to war and lost his faith; although he never, I think, lost sight for long of what really matters.

On 10 December 1922, a service 'for the people' was held at St Martin-in-the-Fields. It happened to be 40 days after the birth of my mother, Jack. Monty, the proud new father, gave the sermon that day and when people realised that it was not to be Dick Sheppard addressing them he could see, he said, disappointment sweep over the congregation like the wind passing over a field of wheat. I have no idea what he talked about, but part way through Monty's book of sermons, carefully saved from his days on the Western Front, is this one, where he points out that 'Love' is what matters above all else. Not war. Love.

> Things 'new as well as old.' The 'old old story' may be wrapped up in new clothes, but it is nonetheless the same. Theories may change from one generation to another – new aspects of Truth may emerge – we may not now be able to 'feel' the words and expressions of older generations and must use our own – nevertheless the content of the good news remains. That God is Love, that Jesus revealed God in word and life and death as no one ever has, that love must be the atmosphere of our relationships with others – all this is true – 'new and old' – for every generation and can never grow stale.

# Acknowledgements and thanks

My ignorance about the First World War was near total when I started writing this book. I had thrilled to the poetry and prose of Siegfried Sassoon, and I loved Pat Barker's *Regeneration* trilogy, but other than that I was in the dark. I told myself that that was also true of Monty when he headed for the Front – and maybe it was good that I was learning as he (and I) went along. My confusion certainly mirrored his and that of almost every other junior-ranking soldier and padre who found themselves drawn into the chaos. Participants in the Great War tended to know a lot about what was happening to them and their friends, but the bigger picture eluded them. Just as it did the generals, we'd like to joke. But the First World War takes a grip on most people who pay it more than the most cursory attention, and like many before me I found myself gripped in its grisly jaws.

I would have been lost without the books of Richard Holmes. In particular, the meticulous detail of *Tommy* gave me a vivid insight into what my grandfather must have encountered, as well as steering me towards many other writers. *Tommy* has a wonderful chapter on the life of padres of all denominations at the Front. For an overview of the most notorious sector of the war, you cannot do better than Holmes's *The Western Front*. David Stevenson's *1914–1918* is even more detailed. There's not much on padres, but it illuminates just about everything else.

A.J.P. Taylor's *The First World War* is still an incredible, coruscating read that has coloured everything we think we know about the war today, and I for one am incapable of resisting its blistering prose. But I can also highly recommend a couple of recent correctives: Gary Sheffield's *Forgotten Victory* and Hew Strachan's *The First World War*. It's not for me to go anywhere near the historical debates that still rage around the causes and the conduct of the war, but both these books helped me re-examine the caricatures and prejudices that filled my head. They are also both great reads and will make you think again about the supposed incompetence of the British Army commanders. That is also true of *Following the Tanks at Cambrai* by Jean-Luc Gibot and Phillippe Gorczynski. The authors have devoted themselves to uncovering every last fact about the world's first tank battle – and their illustrated book is a revelation. *Band of Brigands* by Christy Campbell is a lively account of the same battle; *With a Machine Gun to Cambrai* by George Coppard is a personal memoir. If you just want a book of contemporary quotes, with very little annotation, then I greatly enjoyed dipping into *Voices from the Great War* by Peter Vansittart.

There are a number of books about the battlefields, but I don't think anyone has yet done a better job than Major and Mrs Holt, whose *Battlefield Guide to the Somme* takes you right to where you want to be. A trip to the cemeteries remains a profoundly unsettling experience, as I and my family found when we ventured, emotionally unprepared, into the fields of crosses. Geoff Bridger's *The Great War Handbook* is another useful guide to what to expect.

I would never have thought I would have devoted quite so much of my time to reading and learning about padres in the First World War. Of course, the discovery of my grandfather's archive led me there, but I ended up immersed in the subject. Anyone who wants to know more should start with two books. Michael Snape's *The Royal Army Chaplains' Department: Clergy Under Fire* is the definitive work on the subject of Army Chaplains. It covers a longer period than the First World War, but Snape's powerful and detailed chapter covering the years 1914 to 1918 will tell you most of what you need to know. The other work is Alan Wilkinson's *The Church of England and the*

*First World War*, and I grew to love this book. It is deeply informative – but also passionate and opinionated. A collection called *The Sword of the Lord*, edited by Doris L. Bergen, is also worth dipping into – it explores the whole knotty issue of pacifism, war and Christianity, from a pacifist perspective.

I found myself reading a number of other books by and about chaplains at the Front. They're all worth exploring, often because they're contemporary accounts – and of course there's no better way to clear one's prejudices about the war than by reading what they were saying at the time. Who knows – my grandfather may have met some of these people. Titles include: *Plain Tales from Flanders* by P.B. Clayton; *A Padre in France* by George A. Birmingham; *'Happy Days' in France and Flanders* by Benedict Williamson; *The Best of Good Fellows* by the Rev. Charles Edmund Doudney, edited by Jonathan Horne; *A War-Time Chaplaincy* by R.L. Barnes; *The Church in the Fighting Line* by Douglas P. Winnifrith; *On the King's Service: Inward Glimpses of Men at Arms* by Rev. Innes Logan; and *Somewhere in Flanders: The War Letters of the Revd Samuel Frederick Leighton Green MC*, edited by Stuart McLaren. I have a particular affection for this last book – it seems likely that Leighton's experiences were closest to those of my grandfather – and he writes with candour and eager innocence.

There is of course plenty of great fiction set during the First World War. Erich Maria Remarque's *All Quiet on the Western Front* set the standard and remains a powerful read, as does Edmund Blunden's *Undertones of War*. I have quoted a couple of passages from H.G. Wells's *Mr Britling Sees it Through*, not just because my grandfather was reading it at the Front (as were many others) but because it still has an extraordinary amount to say about the war and changing attitudes to the conflict as news from the Front worsened. If you want something more recent, then Pat Barker's *Regeneration* trilogy and Sebastian Faulks' *Birdsong* both had me gripped.

I have also quoted from Siegfried Sassoon's and Wilfred Owen's poetry. Indeed, Owen's 'Dulce et Decorum Est' took on a new and devastating intensity as I dug deeper into one of the most distressing episodes of Monty's war. As for Sassoon, he was one of the bravest men who ever lived. Not just for his acts of reckless courage at the Front but for his principled, unwavering stand against the war, when it would have been so much easier to recant. The poems, memoirs and his diary are all essential reading.

Although I'd heard much about Dick Sheppard when I was growing up, I had no idea what a complex and revolutionary figure he was. The best place to start is Carolyn Scott's zippy *Dick Sheppard: A Biography*. For the views of his friends and colleagues, try *Dick Sheppard: An Apostle of Brotherhood* by William Paxton et al.

The Imperial War Museum has published a number of good books about the war, which blend original archive material with expert commentary. I especially enjoyed *The Imperial War Museum Book of the Western Front* – although there are many to choose from and I spent many happy hours drifting round the collection. The National Archive at Kew is a revelation – millions of original documents held online and in their vaults – and I was able to immerse myself in the diaries of both Monty's and his brother-in-law's regiments. Just as useful for following the progress of the 52$^{nd}$ Ox and Bucks was *The History of the Second Division* by Everard Wyrall, which provided a wealth of material written either during the war or shortly afterwards. I have quoted several times from this devastatingly evocative book.

Finally, I thought James Neville's *The War Letters of a Light Infantryman* was an amazing work. Neville was only 18 when he went to war, fresh out of Eton, but his letters home are full of insight, joy, humour, compassion and anxiety. He was also Monty's friend, serving in the same regiment, meeting the same people – and so, for me, every letter and diary entry written from the Front resonated down the years.

\* \* \*

Although he's called 'Monty' in this book, I always knew my grandfather as 'Brad', and I'd like to thank him for everything other than his horrible handwriting. I owe a huge debt of gratitude to his daughter, my aunt Biddy – the least of which is that she has patiently put up with a load of tiresome questions about her father. I couldn't have done any of this without the peerless support and enthusiasm of my wife Anna and my wonderful children, Natalie, Alex and Esme (without whom, etc, etc!). My brother Toby has been a source of great encouragement, gripping anecdote and hard facts. Anthony, Brad's first grandson and my Kiwi cousin, has been highly supportive. Mike and Michael Bigger set me on the right track (I hope) with the Bigger family. Rachel Anderson told me most of what I now know about my great-grandfather Guilford and helped me trace the 'Pullthrough' family. Graham Hodgson was generous with his time and research concerning Private Joseph Bateman. I'd like to thank Joan Davies and her sister, Fullbrook-Leggatt's daughters, for their efforts to find information about Brad and for allowing me to quote so extensively from their father's colourful writing. I'd also like to thank Simon Gorton, James Neville's grandson, for allowing me to quote from James's letters and diary. Richard Milner has been a great help throughout, in his job at Macmillan but also as my short-lived agent and ongoing critic. I also owe a big thanks to my current agent, David Luxton, of Luxton Harris, for all his support. Thanks also to Cathy Runciman for putting me on the right track. This book would never have been published had it not been for the encouragement of Iain MacGregor, one-time Mainstream editor. Thanks also to Bill Campbell and Ailsa Bathgate at Mainstream Publishing, and Graham Watson. Richard Howard was generous with his books and his time. Penny Boreham and Gill Hunt have both been amazingly helpful with leads and advice. The Imperial War Museum staff (especially Sarah Paterson) have been full of good ideas and practical help; as has everyone at the National Archives in Kew. Finally, I'd like to thank my parents. For all the obvious reasons but also for hanging onto the brown suitcase that led, what with one thing and another, to me writing this book.

# References and notes

1. Alan Wilkinson, *The Church of England and the First World War* (London, SPCK, 1978), p. 127.
2. Robert Graves, *Goodbye to All That* (London, Penguin Books, 2011).
3. Siegfried Sassoon, 'Christ and the Soldier' in *The War Poems* (London, Faber & Faber, 1983), p. 46.
4. Siegfried Sassoon, 'They' in *The War Poems*, p. 57.
5. J.E.H. Neville, *The War Letters of a Light Infantryman* (London, Sifton Praed & Co. Ltd, 1930), p. 70.
6. Field Marshal Sir Douglas Haig, *Dispatches*, 23 December 1916 (London, His Majesty's Stationery Office, 1916) .
7. Cyril Falls, *War Books: An Annotated Bibliography of the Books About the Great War* (London, 1995). Quoted in Richard Holmes, *Tommy* (London, Harper Perennial, 2005), p. xviii.
8. Richard Crosse, *Seventy-five Years 1888–1963* (privately published).
9. Father Benedict Williamson, *'Happy Days' in France & Flanders with the 47th and 49th Divisions* (London, Harding & More Ltd, 1921), p. 54.
10. Reverend Leighton Green, *Somewhere in Flanders: A Norfolk Padre in the Great War*, edited by Stuart McLaren (Dereham, The Larks Press, 2005), p. 46.
11. Neville, *The War Letters of a Light Infantryman*, p. 158.
12. *Ibid.* p. 174.
13. Everard Wyrall, *The History of the Second Division, Volume I*

(Uckfield, Naval & Military Press), p. 302.

14. Michael Snape, *The Royal Army Chaplains' Department: Clergy Under Fire* (Boydell & Brewer Ltd, 2008), p. 11.

15. Wilkinson, *The Church of England and the First World War*, p. 217.

16. Neville, *The War Letters of a Light Infantryman*, p. 57.

17. *Ibid.* p. 12.

18. Siegfried Sassoon, *The Complete Memoirs of George Sherston* (London, Faber & Faber, 1972), p. 631.

19. Wyrall, *The History of the Second Division*, Volume I, p. 304.

20. Wilkinson, *The Church of England and the First World War*, p. 145.

21. R.L. Barnes, *A War-Time Chaplaincy* (London, A.R. Mowbray & Co., 1939) p. 18.

22. Siegfried Sassoon, last line of his poem 'Attack' in *The War Poems*, p. 57.

23. Wyrall, *The History of the Second Division*, Volume I, p. 304.

24. Snape, *The Royal Army Chaplains' Department*, p. 221.

25. Stallworthy (ed.), 'Dulce et Decorum Est' from *The Poems of Wilfred Owen: The War Poems* (London, Chatto & Windus, 1994), p. 29.

26. Neville, *The War Letters of a Light Infantryman*, p. 26.

27. H.G. Wells, *Mr Britling Sees it Through* (Thirsk, House of Stratus, 2002), p.235.

28. Wyrall, *The History of the Second Division*, Volume I, p. 310.

29. *Ibid.* p, 310

30. *Ibid.* p. 311.

31. *Ibid.* p. 317.

32. *Ibid.* p. 319.

33. *Ibid.* p. 324.

34. Hart-Davis (ed.), *Siegfried Sassoon: Diaries 1915–1918* (London, Faber & Faber, 1983), p. 225.

35. *Ibid.* p. 226.

36. *Ibid.* p. 237.

37. Wyrall, *The History of the Second Division*, p. 326.

38. Sir Alfred Lord Tennyson, *Poems 1830–1870* (Oxford, Oxford University Press, 1936), p. 513.

39. Wilkinson, *The Church of England and the First World War*, p. 253.
40. *Ibid.* p. 253.
41. *Ibid.* p. 181.
42. Hew Strachan, *The First World War: A New Illustrated History* (Pocket Books, 2006), p. 98.
43. *Ibid.* p. 98.
44. Quoted in Peter Vansittart, *Voices from The Great War* (London, Penguin Books, 1983), p. 188.
45. Neville, *The War Letters of a Light Infantryman*, p. 5.
46. Richard Holmes, *Tommy* (London, Harper Perennial, 2005), p. 518.
47. Erich Maria Remarque, *All Quiet on the Western Front* (London, Vintage, 2005), p. 100.
48. Neville, *The War Letters of a Light Infantryman*, p. 31.
49. Remarque, *All Quiet on the Western Front*, opening statement
50. Wells, *Mr Britling Sees it Through*, p. 402.
51. Wyrall, *The History of the Second Division*, Volume II, p. 360.
52. Neville, *The War Letters of a Light Infantryman*, p. 14.
53. *Ibid.* p. 9.
54. Remarque, *All Quiet on the Western Front*, p. 101.
55. Hart-Davis (ed.), *Siegfried Sassoon: Diaries 1915–1918*, p. 133.
56. Wyrall, *The History of the Second Division*, Volume II, p. 381.
57. Hart-Davis (ed.), *Siegfried Sassoon: Diaries 1915–1918*, p. 142.
58. Neville. *The War Letters of a Light Infantryman*, p. 39.
59. Battalion Diary, 1st East Surreys (National Archive, ref. WO 95/1579).
60. *Ibid.*
61. *Ibid.*
62. *Ibid.*
63. *Ibid.*
64. *Ibid.*
65. Stallworthy (ed.), 'Dulce et Decorum Est' from *The Poems of Wilfred Owen: The War Poems*, p. 29.
66. Snape, *The Royal Army Chaplains' Department*, p. 206.
67. Holmes, *Tommy*, p. 510.
68. Neville, *The War Letters of a Light Infantryman*, p. 115.

69. A.J.P. Taylor, *The First World War: An Illustrated History* (London, Penguin Books, 1966), p. 194.

70. Neville, *The War Letters of a Light Infantryman*, p. 66.

71. Wyrall, *The History of the Second Division*, Volume II, p. 469.

72. *Ibid*. p. 499.

73. The 2nd Division at Cambrai 1917 (Aldershot, 1918), p. 17.

74. Stallworthy (ed.), 'The Parable of the Old Man and the Young' from *The Poems of Wilfred Owen: The War Poems*, p. 61.

75. Neville, *The War Letters of a Light Infantryman*, p. 100.

76. *Ibid*. p. 103.

77. Wyrall, *The History of the Second Division*, Volume II, p. 571.

78. Neville, *The War Letters of a Light Infantryman*, p. 108.

79. *Ibid*. p. 121.

80. *Ibid*. p. 126.

81. Wyrall, *The History of the Second Division*, Volume II, p. 675.

82. Quoted in Carolyn Scott, *Dick Sheppard: A Biography* (London, Hodder & Stoughton, 1977), p. 90.

83. *Ibid*. p. 63.

84. *Ibid*. p. 14.

# Bibliography

Allingham, Henry, with Goodwin, Dennis, *Kitchener's Last Volunteer* (Mainstream Publishing, Edinburgh, 2009)

Barker, Pat, *The Eye in the Door* (Penguin Books, London, 2008)

Barker, Pat, *The Ghost Road* (Penguin Books, London, 2008)

Barker, Pat, *Regeneration* (Penguin Books, London, 2008)

Barnes, R.L., *A War-Time Chaplaincy* (A.R. Mowbray, London, 1939)

Bergen, Doris L. (ed.), *The Sword of the Lord: Military Chaplains from the First to the Twenty-First Century* (University of Notre Dame, Notre Dame, 2009)

Birmingham, George A., *A Padre in France* (Dodo Press *c.* 1918)

Blunden, Edmund, *Undertones of War* (Penguin Books, London, 1937)

Bridger, Geoff, *The Great War Handbook: A Guide for Family Historians & Students of the Conflict* (Pen & Sword Books, Barnsley, 2009)

Brown, Malcolm, *The Imperial War Museum Book of The Western Front* (BCA, London, 1993)

Campbell, Christy, *Band of Brigands: The Extraordinary Story of the First Men in Tanks* (Harper Perennial, London, 2008)

Churchill, Winston S., *The World Crisis: 1916–1918: Parts I & II* (Thornton Butterworth, London, 1927)

Clayton, P.B., *Plain Tales from Flanders* (Longmans, Green & Co., London, 1929)

Coppard, George, *With a Machine Gun to Cambrai: A Story of

*the First World War* (Cassell, London, 1999)

Faulks, Sebastian, *Birdsong* (Vintage, London, 1994)

Gibot, Jean-Luc and Gorczynski, Phillippe, *Following the Tanks at Cambrai* (Phillippe Gorczynski, France, 1998)

Gosling, Lucinda, *Brushes & Bayonets: Cartoons, Sketches and Paintings of World War I* (Osprey, Oxford, 2008)

Graves, Robert, *Goodbye to All That* (Penguin Books, London, 2011)

Hart-Davis, Rupert (ed.), *Siegfried Sassoon: Diaries 1915–1918* (London, Faber & Faber, 1983)

Holmes, Richard, *The Western Front* (BBC Books, London, 1999)

Holmes, Richard, *Tommy: The British Soldier on the Western Front 1914–1918* (Harper Perennial, London, 2005)

Holt, Major & Mrs, *Battlefield Guide to the Somme* (Pen & Sword Books, Barnsley, 2008)

Horne, Jonathan (ed.), *The Best of Good Fellows: The Diaries and Memoirs of The Rev. Charles Edmund Doudney, M.A., C.F. (1871–1915)* (Jonathan Horne Publications, London, 1995)

Ivelaw-Chapman, John, *The Riddles of Wipers: An Appreciation of 'The Wipers Times', a Journal of the Trenches* (Leo Cooper, London, 1997)

Logan, Innes, *On the King's Service: Inward Glimpses of Men at Arms* (Dodo Press, 2009)

McLaren, Stuart (ed.), *Somewhere in Flanders: A Norfolk Padre in the Great War: The War Letters of The Revd Samuel Frederick Leighton Green MC* (The Larks Press, Norfolk, 2005)

Matthews, C.H.S., *Dick Sheppard: Man of Peace* (James Clarke & Co, London, 1936)

Moynihan, Michael (ed.), *God on Our Side: The British Padre in World War I* (Secker & Warburg, London, 1983)

Neville, J.E.H., *The War Letters of a Light Infantryman* (London, Sifton Praed & Co. Ltd, 1930)

Paxton, William and others, *Dick Sheppard: An Apostle of Brotherhood* (Chapman & Hall, London, 1938)

Remarque, Erich Maria, *All Quiet on the Western Front* (Vintage, London, 2005)

Sassoon, Siegfried, *Collected Poems 1908–1956* (Faber & Faber, London, 1984)

Sassoon, Siegfried, *The War Poems* (Faber & Faber, London, 1983)

Sassoon, Siegfried, *The Complete Memoirs of George Sherston* (Faber & Faber, London, 1972)

Scott, Carolyn, *Dick Sheppard: A Biography* (Hodder & Stoughton, London, 1977)

Sheffield, Gary, *Forgotten Victory: The First World War: Myths and Realities* (Review, London, 2002)

Silkin, John, *The Penguin Book of First World War Poetry* (Penguin Books, London, 1979)

Snape, Michael, *The Royal Army Chaplains' Department: Clergy Under Fire* (Boydell & Brewer Ltd, Woodbridge, 2008)

Stallworthy, J. (ed.), *The Poems of Wilfred Owen: The War Poems* (London, Chatto & Windus, 1994)

Stevenson, David, *1914–1918: The History of the First World War* (Penguin Books, London, 2005)

Strachan, Hew, *The First World War: A New Illustrated History* (Pocket Books, London, 2006)

Taylor, A.J.P., *The First World War: An Illustrated History* (Penguin Books, London, 1966)

Tennyson, Alfred Lord, *Poems of Tennyson* (Oxford University Press, London, 1936)

Vansittart, Peter, *Voices from the Great War* (Penguin Books, London, 1983)

Waters, Fiona, *A Corner of a Foreign Field: The Illustrated Poetry of the First World War* (Transatlantic Press, Herts., 2010)

Wells, H.G., *Mr Britling Sees it Through* (House of Stratus, Thirsk, 2002)

Wilkinson, Alan, *The Church of England and the First World War* (SPCK, London, 1978)

Williamson, Benedict, *'Happy Days' in France & Flanders with the 47th and 49th Divisions* (Harding & More, London, 1921)

Winnifrith, Douglas P., *The church in the fighting line with General Smith-Dorrien at the front: being the experiences of a chaplain in charge of an infantry brigade* (Hodder & Stoughton,

London, 1915)

Winter, Denis, *Death's Men: Soldiers of the Great War* (Penguin Books, London, 1979)

Wyrall, Everard, *The History of the Second Division: 1914–1918, Volumes I & II* (Naval & Military Press, Uckfield)